The Trekking Peaks of Nepal

'Namaste' – a Tamang porter in the Hinku Valley gives the traditional Nepali greeting. Beyond is the stunning East Face of Peak 43.

THE TREKKING PEAKS OF NEPAL

BILL O'CONNOR

The Crowood Press

First published in 1989 by
The Crowood Press
Ramsbury, Marlborough,
Wiltshire SN8 2HE

British Library Cataloguing in Publication Data
O'Connor, Bill
The trekking peaks of Nepal.
1. Nepal. Visitors guides
I. Title
915.49'604

ISBN 1 85223 173 4

For William, my son

All black and white photographs by Bill O'Connor, except pages 12, 20, 31,
47, 51, 73, 115, 123, 168, 171, 174 (bottom) by John Cleare, 48 and 49 by
John Ball, 50, 55, 57, 58, 61 by Paul Harris, 67 and 68 (bottom) by Alison
Jane Hargreaves, 77 (top) and 85 by Alf Gregory, 89 and 91 by Dennis
Davis, 92 by Wes Skerritt, 138-141 by Chris Watts, 146 by Richard Haszko,
150-152 by Nick Douch, 169 and 175 by Rudolph Schietl, 172 by John
Noble, 173 and 174 (top) by Dr Hamish Nichol, 183 by Stan Armington,
and 88, 142, 153 by John Porter.

All colour photographs by Bill O'Connor unless otherwise stated.

Typeset by Jahweh Associates, Stroud
Printed in Great Britain by Redwood Burn Ltd, Trowbridge

Contents

APPENDICES

Maps

'For I have said that the medium of some men is paint or stone or boats or a schoolroom, or engines, or paper and ink; that of a few is rocks and snow and the uphill movement of limbs.'

Wilfrid Noyce

Foreword

I welcome this opportunity to contribute a foreword to Bill O'Connor's book about the 'trekking peaks' of Nepal, as I feel that the full potential of these eighteen mountains has not been realised. As will be explained, the name (which stems from the fact that they may be climbed with little more formality than the possession of a trekking permit) is not an apt one, as even by the easiest of routes they all, unaided, demand some mountaineering experience. Given competent sherpas and suitable equipment the peaks do, however, open a new world to fit parties of mountain walkers without technical experience, and ascents of such mountains as Mera, Island Peak and the Chulus have over the years given much pleasure to many.

But there is far more in these mountains for the experienced alpine climber. Even by their easiest routes the ascents of Hiunchuli, Fluted Peak, Kusum Kanguru, Chulu West and Kwangde are of a high alpine standard and there are many other routes to explore, mostly unattempted, including severe lines on the other basically easier peaks. In my enthusiasm I must restrain any tendency to write Bill's book for him. But my mind turns to the Great South Face of Mera (one line has been climbed) and the South (Chomrong) Face of Hiunchuli, straight up from the mossy wooded slabs of the Modi gorge. Impossible? Maybe, but go and have a look.

Where do these smaller Nepal mountains fit into the overall Himalayan picture of today? There is not quite the same opportunity for wide-ranging exploration as afforded by the 'under 6,000 metre' rule in Pakistan, but these are fine, named individual mountains with more to attract the technical climber, either as preparation for greater heights or for their own sake.

And what indeed, after the bulldozing no expense spared events in Everest in the Spring of 1988, is the overall Himalayan picture going to be? I am reminded of the remark of a former British Ambassador to Nepal who, when asked to back a helicopter landing on Everest because 'there is nothing else left to do on Mount Everest', replied, 'you can always drive a tunnel under the mountain.'

Hopefully we shall soon begin to see a reaction set in in the Himalaya against the prevailing spate of 'records', many of quite questionable value. Meanwhile, this book by Bill O'Connor may permit a quieter and more personal way for some.

Jimmy Roberts

Acknowledgements

The material for this book was collected over a long period; there is a limit to how many expeditions one can fit into a year, so it goes without saying that many people were called upon for help, advice and information.

To begin with I must thank the people at Mountain Travel in Kathmandu for providing the outstanding services that are their hallmark: in particular Jimmy Roberts, Robin Marston, and Depak Lama, whilst in the UK, Nick Van Gruisen and Rowan Patterson provided information and a telex link with Kathmandu.

My thanks to John Cleare for inviting me on my first Himalayan expedition and for the years of friendship and the midnight oil spent talking mountains, studying his superb photographs and sharing knowledge of Paldor and Naya Kanga. To Dr Hamish Nicol for letting me use his interim guide to Paldor. To Mike Westmacott for his notes on Chulu Far East and Naya Kanga. To Alf Gregory and Dennis Davis for letting me look at maps and pictures of their Merseyside Himalayan Expedition. To John Ball for use of his diary and pictures. To Nick Douch for sending me rare information on Fluted Peak. To David Cox for the generous loan of his Machhapuchare diary with its valuable pages on the first ascent of Fluters. To John Fowler for his Tent Peak Expedition report.

Thanks also go to Dr David Hopkins, Alison Jane Hargreaves, Richard Haszko, Ray Delane, Nick Kekus, Chris Watts, John Porter, Stan Armington, Wes Skerritt, Lindsay Griffin, John Noble, Paul Harris and Rick Allen for their time, information and photographs. To all the people that reported their climbs, and to climbing journals and magazines.

A special thank you to Martin Robertson for all the dark-room work in producing black and white photographs from colour trannies, and to Kathy Foley for her German translations.

My thanks to the Sherpas and porters that carried, climbed and shared the adventure.

Finally, to Sallie O'Connor for her advice, proof reading, encouragement and the birth of a son as the last lines were written.

Introduction

The tiny kingdom of Nepal forms a rectangle of land seemingly crushed between the giants of Chinese Tibet to the north, with which it shares a mountain border, and India to the south, from which it is separated by a thin strip of a once malaria-infested jungle known as the Terai; really an extension of the Ganges plain. Between the mountains to the north and the forest to the south is a central belt of lower hills and valleys of which the Kathmandu Valley is the most important. This Himalayan kingdom of 147,181 square kilometres (56,831 square miles), of which almost half is heavily mountainous, supports an ever growing population of over 15 million.

The fact that Nepal was officially and strictly off-limits to westerners as late as 1949, long after other Himalayan regions had become a playground for European climbers, coupled with the fact that the country can boast of eight peaks over 8,000 metres, has resulted in the creation and sustaining of interest both in its cultural mystery and in its mountains.

Nepal remains a financially poor country in which earnings from tourism (including mountaineering) have only recently over-taken that of mercenary soldiers in the form of Gurkha pensions from foreign governments, as the major source of income. To this end mountaineering in Nepal is neither open nor free. Of the countless number of fine summits within the Nepal Himalaya only 104 expedition peaks are open to foreigners for which a fee has to be paid. On top of this an official liaison officer and sirdar must accompany the expedition, both of whom must be equipped and paid according to an official scale, as must all non-members going above base camp. As a result expeditions, especially to the higher, more prestigious peaks, can be very expensive so that large national, international and commercially-backed expeditions to the 8,000 metre summits have become the norm. This rigid control of supply and a growing demand has meant that many of the more famous mountains have a waiting list of several years and permits, it has been rumoured, have changed hands for considerable sums.

This all seems a far cry from the 1950s and early 1960s when expeditions roamed free, exploring remote valleys, crossing peaks, passes and glaciers, seemingly without let or hindrance in what might be termed the golden age of Himalayan mountaineering.

However, in 1978, under the control of the newly formed Nepal Mountaineering Association (NMA), 18 mountains between 5,587m (18,330ft) and 6,654m (21,830ft) were opened to foreign climbers without the financially restricting and administratively onerous regulations governing expedition peaks. This newly created list formed the so-called 'trekking peaks'; a misleading name that at one time was to be changed to 'alpine peaks', itself a misnomer since they are decidely not alpine. If it has to be changed perhaps 'small' or 'lesser Himalayan' is more descriptive; or perhaps 'non-expedition' would differentiate them from the other 104 peaks.

Overleaf is a full list of the trekking peaks, grouped according to their common geographical location, which is slightly different from the official listing reproduced elsewhere.

Manang Himal:
    Chulu West 6,419m (21,059ft)
    Chulu East 6,584m (21,601ft)
    Pisang 6,091m (19,983ft)
Annapurna Himal:
    Mardi Himal 5,555m (18,225ft)
    Hiunchuli 6,331m (20,771ft)
    Tharpu Chuli 5,500m (18,045ft)
    Singu Chuli 6,501m (21,328ft)
Ganesh Himal:
    Paldor 5,928m (19,450ft)
Langtang Himal:
    Naya Kanga 5,844m (19,173ft)
Rolwaling:
    Ramdung 5,925m (19,439ft)
    Parchamo 6,187m (20,298ft)
Khumbu Himal:
    Kusum Kanguru 6,369m (20,896ft)
    Kwangde 6,187m (20,298ft)
    Lobuje East 6,119m (20,075ft)
    Kongma Tse 5,820m (19,095ft)
    Pokalde 5,806m (19,048ft)
    Imja Tse 6,189m (20,305ft)
    Mera 6,476m (21,247ft)

What the trekking peaks actually provide is an opportunity to climb in some of the most important regions of Nepal with the exception of areas west of and including the Dhaulagiri Himal, Makalu Himal and the newly opened Kanchenjunga region, but hopefully new names will be added to this all-too-short list in the future. What they also provide, which has yet to be fully realised, is a potential for endless new route exploration at an altitude that will allow for extreme climbing in a style more closely related to alpinism than traditional Himalayan expeditioning. Whereas many were first climbed by the leading mountaineers of their day they have, apart from a couple of notable exceptions, been neglected by today's mountaineering élite or continue to be climbed by a standard route as acclimatisation for greater deeds. Things have begun to change and new routes, some extreme, have been climbed, re-flecting a change in style to a more adventurous and dynamic climbing ethic at the cutting edge of mountaineering. The Lowe/Brearshears route on Kwangde and the Ball/Curtis route on Kusum Kanguru are just two examples of the possible, whilst at the blunter end of things but still on the adventurous edge of exploration is the scope for routes, none the less new, pioneered at lower technical standards. One has only to look at recent developments on and around Paldor to realise that if the adventurous spirit is there, new things are possible.

Along with the climbing comes the opportunity for an individual or group of friends to take part in or organise their own expedition within the context of a few weeks' annual

Kusum Kanguru rises above the east bank of the Dudh Kosi. Seen from the west the peak rises above the Kusum Drangka.

Descending into a cloud-filled Khumbu Valley from the Mingbo La. On the left are the peaks of Kangtega and Tramserku.

holiday with the minimum red tape or expense. Today it is wholly possible to spend a month climbing in Nepal for a little over one month's average income whereas in the 1950s the fare alone was close to an individuals average annual earnings.

Within the pages of this book I have attempted to provide clear and accurate descriptions of what have become the 'trade routes', supported where necessary by photographs. Other important routes have also been included, sometimes as a full description, elsewhere as a note so that those interested in possible new routes will know where some of the gaps are. In all cases I have drawn up a simple line map to help clarify approaches and camps, not always clear when no accurate map is available.

As well as the route information I have included descriptions of at least one trekking route to and from the mountain and in most cases suggested others. Often I have opted to describe more remote approaches, far from the trekking crowd, the lodges and tea shops which require little description and in the context of an expedition are easily followed; remember that, unlike trekking, sooner or later to gain the summit you have to leave them all behind and support yourself either in the traditional style of an expedition with cooks and carriers or as a lightweight self-supporting team, climbing the mountain in true alpine, rather than lightweight Himalayan, style.

But an expedition to Nepal is so much more than climbing. A large part of the continuing

13

A traditionally dressed Tamang porter with a cane basket, tump line for carrying and Khukri.

footed or at best wearing thongs or Chinese pumps, pounding the trail beneath a giant load. But the porters are tradesmen and you pay for their skills, as do the local people when they want a heavy load taken to and from the bazaar or between home and village. I also have a suspicion that the locals might drive a harder bargain! Having said that, treat them with respect, you need their skills as much as they need your money. Learn from them, watch how they place their feet, try to catch their rhythm, see how they light their fires and blend so readily with the hills. They are the culture of Nepal.

One of the things that has always intrigued me on a expedition has been the social dynamics of the Sherpas and porters. Even on a lightweight expedition there is always a great number, or so it seems, bhandabhast, of people brought together to carry the food, fuel, equipment and other paraphenalia needed to travel to a remote area and remain self-sufficient for a month or more to climb a mountain. The porters, men and women, sometimes from the same village but often not, are then thrown together and become and essential part of the expedition. They carry, eat and sleep together under the leadership of a sirdar, invariably a Sherpa, who coaxes, cajoles, jokes with and generally manages them to wherever they were hired to carry. On the best trips, our culture and theirs come together, and feelings of friendship emerge. Interestingly enough, I've had the same porter on expeditions to the Ganesh, Langtang and Mera. Most recently he turned up on a expedition to Ama Dablam when there was a ritual handing over of pictures and quite a lot of drinking local beer (chang) to celebrate the meeting of old friends.

fascination is the people and culture of this mountain kingdom. An expedition provides a good vehicle for meeting the people of Nepal, for even as an employer of Sherpa and porters (whatever their ethnic background), you share for a while a common purpose which at the very least gives everyone concerned an insight into others' lives, and at best can consolidate into friendship and respect.

The open friendliness and physical toughness of Nepal's people is legendary. Porters are the 'Pickfords' of the Himalayas; there are few roads, and they provide the haulage system in the hills. Many trekkers I know get a great twinge of moral conscience when they see a pair of tiny, albeit muscular, legs, often bare

Do try to learn something of Nepal's culture and the social and religious taboos and expectations in order not to knowingly offend. Nepalis are getting used to foreigners, who they think of as being ritually 'polluted'. Actions on our part do and can offend and the dos and

Wherever you look in Kathmandu, people and gods are mingling. This is
Durbhar Square.

don'ts I have laid down elsewhere in this book have always stood me in good stead and our efforts at correct behaviour, apart from being good manners, are much appreciated by Nepalis. Once again, do relate to your Sherpas, many of whom have good English. They can help your Nepali language and in my experience are always happy to teach you the simple rules of their life.

In pulling together this information on the trekking peaks I quickly realised that many unofficial ascents had taken place about which only limited information is available. Even with legal ascents, reports fail to be sent to the Nepal Mountaineering Association (NMA) so that no official record of them exists. Hopefully, with the publication of this book things will change and new and old route information will emerge. To this end I would be grateful to hear of others' effort on these peaks so that in future we might have a more complete and accurate record of Himalayan mountaineering. Correspondence concerning route information should be sent to: Bill O'Connor, 10 South Drive, Harrogate, North Yorkshire, HG2 8AU, United Kingdom.

I TREKS AND CLIMBS

1 Khumbu Himal and the Everest Trek

The Solu/Khumbu is the most famous region of Nepal and quite possibly of the Himalaya. Not only is it the area of Everest, the world's highest mountain, it is also the home of some 3,500 Sherpas, undoubtedly the most legendary of mountain people. As well as Sagamartha (Mother of the Universe), as the Nepalis call Everest, the Khumbu also boasts other 8,000 metre peaks including Lhotse and Cho Oyu, whilst Makalu can be seen barely a ridge away.

In 1973 an area of 1,200 square kilometres (463 square miles) of mountainous land all above 3,000 metres, that included the upper basins of the Dudh Khosi, Bhote Khosi and Imja Khola, was declared the Sagamartha National Park in recognition of its unique status with regard to its mountains, people and their religious practices, as well as its flora and fauna. This was done in an attempt to protect and preserve these special attributes and to reconcile the conflicting pressures of modern tourism and traditional culture. Perhaps the most important factor affecting expeditions and trekkers is the restriction placed on the use of wood for fuel.

Several of the peaks covered in this book are to be found in the Khumbu Himal, they are: Lobuje East, 6,119m (20,075ft), Imja Tse (Island Peak), 6,189m (20,305ft), Pokalde, 5,806m (19,049ft), and Kongma Tse, 5,820m (19,095ft). There are also several peaks not in the Khumbu Himal that are best approached from the Solu/Khumbu. These are: Kwangde, 6,187m (20,298ft), Parchamo, 6,282m (20,610ft), Kusum Kanguru, 6,369m (20,896ft) and Mera, 6,476m (21,247ft). In all cases the usual approach is the one described; the Everest expedition route.

For all of the peaks mentioned, the quickest approach is to fly RNAC (Royal Nepalese Airline Corporation) to the STOL (Short Take Off and Landing) airstrip at Lukhla in the Dudh Khosi valley. This is less than two days' hike from Namche Bazaar.

The road from Kathmandu now extends as far as Jiri, which is only a short trek from Sherpa country; the Solu-Khumbu. In many ways this is a pity because the trek from, say, Dholalghat, although taking several days longer, is a much finer walk, giving those that take it a far greater insight into the landscape and people of the middle hills of Nepal. The long walk-in is also a great way to get into shape and acclimatise for the mountain ahead since it involves about 150 miles (242km) of hiking and over 61,000 feet (18,593m) of ascent and descent by the time you reach Namche!

Day 1: Kathmandu to Jiri

From Kathmandu it takes about six hours to drive the road to Jiri, a town that expanded rapidly with the advent of the Swiss extension to the Chinese road from Lamasangu. From time to time the odd land slip blocks the road and it might be necessary to portage bodies and equipment to the far side of the blockage. It all takes time and often a little more money, but as with all things in Nepal, if you add patience and good humour, things usually get sorted out.

Peaks in the Khumbu Himal. Looking south-east from below Thame toward the peaks of the Charpati and Hinku Himals beyond the Dudh Khosi. From left to right the summits are: Kangtega (6,779m 22,241ft), Tramserku (6,608m 21,680ft), Peak 43 (6,356m 20,853ft) and the triple summits of Kusum Kanguru.

Day 2: Jiri to Bhandar

From Jiri follow the trail leading up the east side of the Jiri Valley. You pass through several Tamang settlements and within two hours reach the Kharubas Pass (2,713m/ 8,900ft). Descend from the pass crossing the Yelung Khola and then cross a suspension bridge over the Khimti Khola to the village of Shivalaya (1,800m/5,900ft). In the springtime the rhododendron forests are a spectacular feature on this section of the trek. It takes between three and four hours to trek from Jiri.

The trail now climbs steeply, more or less, up the ridge to Pangbadanda (2,240m/ 7,350ft). Beyond the school the trail divides.

Take the right-hand branch for the more direct route which leads to the Sherpa settlement of Kasourbas continuing north of the Mohabir Khola through forest dense with rhododendron. You cross several side streams with watermills and mani-walls until you finally reach Buldars Pass (2,713m/ 8,900ft) marked by mani-walls and prayer flags – around two hours from the schoolhouse. For those who have worked up a head of steam the tea shops at the pass are a welcome sight.

Descend eastwards from the pass by the left-hand trail. Follow it through a sylvan forest of oak and rhododendron, passing a large chorten (religious shrine) into a beautiful valley that truly marks the start of Sherpa

A trader selling bamboo flutes, a common sight on the streets of Kathmandu.

country. The village of Chyangma (Bhandar) has a mixture of Tamangs and Newars, but is predominantly Sherpa. The mani-walls (prayer walls), chorten and small gompa (monasteries) welcome the trekker to the town as do the shops selling wooden chang bottles and Sherpa-style artefacts. Indeed I bought my first-ever ancient Tibetian antique here, which I notice as it sits on the bookshelf above my desk has all the marks of a twentieth-century machine lathe! It was here that I lost a Rolex wristwatch, left by a stream after bathing. I'm glad to say that was the last watch I ever wore. There is good camping just beyond the village. To reach Bhandar takes about six hours from Jiri.

Day 3: Bhandar to Sete

Descend, at first through forest and then through terraces, to Phedi, a Chettri village. Cross the suspension bridge and walk along the river to Kenja (1,634m/5,360ft), at the confluence of two rivers. Once again the village is a bustling combination of Sherpa, Newars and Chettris. There are fabric shops, a school and numerous lodges and tea shops. It is 3 hours from Chyangma.

Climbing steeply from the town follow the trail through oak and rhododendron forest to Sete (2,575m/8,450ft) with its lovely hilltop monastery which can be reached in about three hours from Kenja.

Tamang children near the village of Bhandar collecting animal fodder.

Day 4: Sete to Junbesi

The way to the Lamjura Pass (3,530m/11,582ft) is all uphill through oak and pine forests. The trail follows the line of the ridge, passing several houses. At a point where the ridge is marked by a mani-wall the way forks left to reach the pass. In springtime this is a mass of rhododendron. The views are limited but for those wanting to have a look at the Rolwaling peaks, the hilltop lookout north-west of the pass should be climbed, which will add about two hours. This pass marks your entry into Solu-Khumbu that lies ahead. I always feel a sense of pleasure when I cross the Lamjura; it's as if I've passed through the gateway to the mountains.

From the pass, descend through a forest of mixed fir and rhododendron to Thakdor (Tragdobuk), a Sherpa village that sports a huge, intricately carved, mani rock. The trail ahead contours on the north side of the valley on a hillside that is often covered with primula. After rounding the ridge the path descends to Junbesi (2,675m/8,775ft), a large Sherpa village with its chorten, monastery and a school built by Sir Edmund Hillary. I have camped several times above the village which has marvellous views down the Junbesi Khola to the south and to Numbur (6,959m/22,831ft) to the north, and is reached in about three hours from the pass.

Day 5: Junbesi to Trakshindu

After crossing the river below the chorten take the left-hand fork that climbs around the Shingsere Danda. The walking here is marvellous; along the hillside, passing through forests of pine, oak and rhododendron. At a point where you turn the ridge, often called the Solung Ridge, you sometimes get a glimpse of Everest's distant, dark pyramid. Within two hours you reach the Sherpa village of Solung (2,984m/9,790ft), with its waterspun mani-wheels.

Walking along this trail on bright sunny days I've twice been stopped, gladly, by a young Sherpani, whose cheeks were as full and red as ripe apples. She was selling suntala (mandarine oranges), which I willingly bought from her.

Below this is the valley of the Beni Khola, which flows from the Dudh Kund Glacier, beneath the southern flanks of Numbur, Khartang and Karyolung, peaks that will become familiar to those heading towards Lumding and the southern flank of Kwangde. The way, however, leads to Ringmo on the far side of the river with its apple orchards, always a treat, especially if your expedition cook can turn them into an apple-pie or fritters!

For those with an interest in Tibetan Buddhism who would like to get off the main trail there is an attractive alternative hike from Junbesi which heads north up the west bank of the Junbesi Khola until it is possible in just over one hour to cross the river to the east bank and ascend to the village of Mopung. North-west of this settlement, before Pangkarma, is the Gompa of Thubten-cho-ling, a monastery which was established after the Chinese invasion of Tibet. It now has over one hundred monks, who are predominantly Tibetan rather than Sherpa and it can be regarded as the most important monastery in the Solu/Khumbu. The Gompa is headed by Tul-shis-rimpoche himself, regarded as the spiritual leader of Buddhism in the Solu/Khumbu.

From the Gompa a trail climbs eastwards, crossing the Shingsere Danda by a pass at 3,476m (11,404ft) before descending into the Beni Khola and meeting the main path near Gonbo before Ringmo.

A dancing demon during the drama of Mani Rimdu at Thyangboche Gompa.

From Ringmo (2,005m/9,200ft), climb steeply up the west flank of the Kemche Danda to the Trakshindu La (3,071m/10,075ft), marked with mani and chorten. As you pass through an arch of prayer flags you will have your first view of several striking peaks including Kusum Kanguru, Tramserku and Kangtega to the north-east.

The Lumding Valley from the south:
There is a trail going north from Ringmo along the Kemche Danda that turns north-east, traversing several ridges to the pastures around Lumding Kharka beneath the southern flank of Kongde. I have no details of the trail but several Sherpa sirdars who know it say that it presents no real problem, as long as there hasn't been recent snowfall. It goes without saying that a party taking this route would have to be independent with regard to food and shelter. If your sirdar doesn't know the route I would suggest getting local help in Ringmo.

23

On the east side of the pass you will descend to Trakshindu Gompa, which was set up around 1946 by a lama from Thyangboche. A great deal of development has taken place at the monastery in recent years including the introduction of solar energy panels and a piped water system which was the result of a project headed by John Martinek and Tom Nowell in 1981. On one visit, several years ago, I was amazed to see the head lama conducting a Mani-Rimdu style festival wearing a UCLA (University College Los Angeles) sweatshirt beneath his robes. Kon-chhok Lama had apparently been teaching a class in Buddhism at Berkeley during the monsoon semester! Recently Kon-chhok made the unprecedented move of standing down as head lama and now runs a small restaurant. There is camping near the Gompa, which is six hours from Junbesi.

Day 6: Trakshindu to Kharikhola

Far below you is the valley of the Dudh Khosi, a real milestone for any mountaineer who has dreamed of climbing in the Himalaya. The river that drains from Everest is the gateway to untold adventures. I had read, heard and dreamed of it for years before I first visited the Khumbu. I had high expectations, which the river and its valley still fulfill.

Descend steeply through forest to Manidingma, a Rai and Sherpa village; this takes just over an hour. Then continue down through terraces and forest, where you can often see Langur monkeys, to the suspension bridge crossing the Dudh Khosi.

Now on the east bank, climb to the Rai settlement of Jubing (1,676m/5,499ft). The path meanders through stands of bamboo near to the houses. Continue to Kharikhola (2,004m/6,575ft), a village of predominantly Sherpa and Magyar inhabitants. This is a village of mani-walls and water-wheels, that every Wednesday has a thriving market, pedlars from which then head off to Namche in time for the Saturday morning bazaar there. This is a relatively short day.

Hinku Drangka and Mera Peak from the south:
Those wishing to climb on Mera Peak and wanting to enter the Hinku Drangka from the south leave the Everest trek here and head east to Pangkongma. Details of this trek can be found in the section dealing with Mera Peak, page 32.

Day 7: Kharikhola to Surkya

Cross the river tributaries of the Kharikhola and climb steeply to Kharte through a mixed forest of oak, rhododendron and the fragrant Dhaphne bholua; the Nepalese paper plant, which the Sherpas always warn against smelling too closely because it will give you headaches. Bird life, including pheasant, is abundant along this section of the trail. Continue traversing the flank of the Kharte Dande high above the river to a notch in the ridge, the Kharte La (3,081m/10,108ft). Descend north-east to the Poyan Khola which is about four hours from Kharikhola. There is good camping in the forest near the stream, which is a mixture of oak, pine, bamboo and birch.

The trail continues through Puiyan (2,800m/9,186ft), rising slowly on the flank of the Sebuk Danda to the Chutok La (2,945m/9,662ft). This ridge leads eastward to the Zatrwa La, the pass giving access to the Hinku Valley. Descend nearly seven hundred metres to Surkya (2,293m/7,525ft), astride the Surke Drangka which is merely two hours from Puiyan.

Hinku and Mera Peak via the Zatrwa La:
Thirty minutes beyond Surkya there is a trail forking right that leads to Lukhla. The trek from there is described in the Mera Peak section, page 32.

Day 8: Surkya to Monjo

Those heading north should stay on the main trail which traverses a gorge with a waterfall before reaching Chaurikharka (2,652m/8,700ft), which is about two hours from Surkya. The main trail from Lukhla joins here.

If you arrive by air, cross the runway, having now opened your eyes and walk through the urban disaster of this ever-expanding airport town. There are plenty of lodges and tea shops and, at times when flights fail to arrive, a mass of ill-mannered tourists. Of Lukhla legends abound, of bribery and corruption, fist-fights and near starvation and of various dirty deeds done to secure a seat on the next available flight. In the end it's really only a problem of western travellers' schedules not fitting in with the reality of Himalayan travel, and air travel in particular.

The trail now descends north, with marvellous views of Nupla, to meet the main trail at Chaurikharka. Continue on the main trail northwards and cross the Kusum Drangka a tributary of the Dudh Khosi.

Those wishing to climb on the South-West Flank of Kusum Kanguru should head up the faint trail leading eastwards up the valley.

All others should continue to the river at Ghat.

Lumding Valley and Kwangde from the south:
Those heading for the Lumding Valley via the Moro La should cross the river and pick up the Moro La trail which climbs steeply through Moro Kharka following a ridge line, to cross the divide of the Tragkarmigo and descend to Lumding Kharka.

Otherwise, continue to Phakding. Cross by a rickety, cantilever bridge to good camping and a lodge on the west bank. Traces of a once sturdier Hillary-built bridge still drape the bank.

On 5 August 1985, an ice lake above the village of Thame burst from the moraine, causing a massive wall of water to flood down the Bhote Khosi. This flood destroyed the Austrian hydroelectric power scheme below Thame and washed away all of the bridges to Phakding, many of which were substantial structures, built by Hillary and others as part of an aid programme. Along with the bridges went much of a newly constructed trail and many large carved mani-boulders along the river bank. Some of these commemorated Sherpa families that had been washed away by a similar accident that occurred previously, when a moraine lake burst near Mingbo below Ama Dablam. Fortunately there was no loss of life in 1985.

Continue northwards on the main trail, where you will notice the massive erosion caused by the flooding. In many places the path has been undercut and has slipped into the river; taking the old path you often come to a dead end. But this will improve with usage.

In a short while you will pass through Gomila (Romishung) where the trail to the Lumding La climbs steeply westward. If there is a lot of snow lying on the ridges the Moro La is a better alternative for crossing the Tragkarmigo.

Those heading for Namche continue to Benkar and eventually cross back to the east bank on a makeshift cantilever log bridge. These will undoubtedly be improved in time. Stay on the east bank, passing the Japanese vegetable garden and lodge at Chumoa. The food is fresh and the salad a real treat.

Kusum Kanguru, North Face routes:
Cross the Kyashar Drangka before Monjo where those heading for the north side of Kusum Kanguru follow a trail east up the river.

The Sherpa capital of Namche Bazaar, an amphitheatre filled with houses beneath the towering north flank of Kwangde Ri.

There are tea shops in the small village. The National Park entrance is nearby. A small entrance fee is charged and permits checked.

Day 8: Monjo to Namche Bazaar

The trail now continues up the east bank, whereas before the flood it crossed the Dudh Khosi by a large suspension bridge at Jorsale where you used to enter the National Park. It then stayed on the west bank, crossing the Bhote Khosi near its confluence with the Imja before climbing steeply to Namche.

Now the trail continues up what Sherpas call the 'old path' on the east bank, making sharp ups and downs before descending steeply to a gorge of the Imja Drangka where a log bridge provides spectacular views northward to Taweche. Over the bridge the path makes a right turn, climbing steeply beneath rock overhangs before zig-zagging up through forest to a tea shop, where it joins the wide track leading to Namche Bazaar. Those with an interest in the north side of Kwangde will now have a chance to view the mountain, rearing up, across the Bhote Khosi.

Namche Bazaar (3,446m/11,306ft) is the traditional trading centre for the Sherpa; the market comes to town every Saturday. From above the village you look down on a horse-shoe of houses that gives a feeling of an ancient Greek theatre. Land is scarce in this dusty amphitheatre and the stony main street connects a maze of side alleys with small plots of land and long houses built on terraces. Centre stage is a small patchwork of dirt squares that grow a meagre crop of potatoes and buck-wheat, but more often are home for a multitude of tents, that with the lodge vie for space and trade during the busy trekking season. Just about everything you need, plus much that you don't, can be bought in Namche. The lodges have sophisticated menus, hot showers and electric lights thanks to a small hydro-electric power scheme, abundant trekking food, a multitude of ex-expedition gear should you have forgotten something, and yet more 'Tibetian antiques'. You will need to check in at the police check post on the east side of town. There is also a bank and a post office.

The Sagamartha National Park Centre is well worth a visit and in any case the walk up the hill will help you acclimatise. It's also as good a place as any to watch the sunrise on the 'Mother-Goddess of the Earth'. A Sherpa sirdar recently explained to me that Chomolungma, the Tibetian name for Everest, actually meant a chicken's knee joint rather than the Mother Goddess of the Earth; but that can't be true, can it?

Kwangde North Face routes and Parchamo:
Those heading for the north side of Kwangde or the Trashi Labtsa and Parchamo go west, following the main trail from Namche to Thame.

If you have just arrived in the Khumbu, having flown to Lukhla, it would be advisable to spend a day or so in or around Namche, perhaps going up the hill to explore Kunde and Khumjung, the other major villages in the area.

Day 9: Namche to Thyangboche

In my opinion this is one of the loveliest day's hiking on the Everest trek. The path forks left from the trail to the National Park Centre, contouring north-east high above the Imja Khola Gorge. Despite the fact that this side of the valley is heavily deforested and grazed, the open hillsides are attractive, covered as they in sweet smelling dwarf rhododendron, berberis and a multitude of alpine plants, including at least two varieties of gentian, one a stunning striped, trumpet gentian, quite unlike anything one normally sees in the alps. I've also seen more edelweiss on this leg of the trek that ever I've seen in more than twenty-five European alpine seasons.

As you round the corner, the panorama of Kusum Kanguru, Tramserku and Kangtaga gives way to an even more striking form, that of Ama Dablam, surely one of the most beautiful of mountains. From this angle the mountain is at her most benign, sending down ridges like welcoming arms, whilst high on her South-West Face a hanging glacier resembles a Dablam, the sacred ornamental box worn by Sherpini, and from which the mountain takes her name.

Not long after, this marvellous view becomes even more extensive, with a panorama that extends from Cholatse and Taweche to the massive south wall of the Nuptse and Lhotse, with the peeping black triangle of Everest looking quite insignificant above the ridge, unless of course there is a pennant of ice blowing in the jet stream far out over Tibet from the summit. Look out for Himalayan griffons and Lammergeirs quartering the hill-side above your head as you stride along this open trail.

The way descends, through rhododendron woods, past large boulders where it crosses a stream and meets a path descending from Khumjung and the Everest View Hotel. A little

Monks at Thyangboche blowing telescopic horns that give the deep, droning 'om' to Buddist ceremony.

further on a gaggle of tea shops and Tibetian traders selling all manner of things bar the trail. This is Sanasa, where the route up the Ngozumpa Valley to Gokyo can be joined by a detour up the path towards Khumjung.

The trail continues through pine and rhododendron woods, past a forestry nursery and the settlement of Trashinga to the bridge at Phunki Tenga. There are tea shops both before and after the bridge. The path now climbs past water-driven mani-wheels, up the wooded ridge to Thyangboche Gompa, the most important monastery in the Khumbu. The 600 metre climb is through marvellous woods of pine, rhododendron, juniper and fir. There are several lodges, some owned by trekking agencies, and a lot of camping space, for which the monastery charges a small fee.

There is a very good lodge beyond the gompa that you will find if you follow the ridge to the west. The whole site is rather fantastic. It is built on a spur high above the confluence of the Imja and Phunki Drangkas, at the foot of Kangtega and Tramserku. But it has always seemed to me that it was built more in homage to Ama Dablam which rises loftily north-east of the gompa and seems omnipotent when compared with the nearby giants of the Everest group.

Like the thankas (religious scroll paintings) on sale in Kathmandu, the monastery at Thyangboche has been aged by smoke and dust. In fact the present building dates from the mid-1930s. The original gompa was destroyed by earthquake in 1934, but even that only dated from around 1915.

Day 11: Thyangboche to Pheriche

If any of your party is not acclimatising, either stay at Thyangboche or return down the hill to Phunki Tenga. If you simply want a short day, rather than go on to Pheriche, the village of Pangboche has plenty of lodges and campsites.

From Thyangboche follow the main trail down past the stream, through a haunting wood of juniper, rhododendron and curly barked silver birch, that the Sherpas tap for its sap. In the early morning I've often seen blood pheasant and twice startled musk deer near here.

The trail passes by mani-walls leading to the nuns' settlement of Devoche and Milingo, all part of the religious establishment. Shortly afterwards an airy suspension bridge spans the narrow, rocky gorge of the Imja, giving stunning views of Ama Dablam. The stream and waterfall on the opposite bank can provide a sheltered shower before continuing the climb past a large chorten. The trail continues through an entrance arch to a small notch between large boulders. Here the trail divides, the lower path leading to lower Pangboche whilst the left-hand trail leads to the upper village with its ochre-coloured gompa set in a sheltered hollow of ancient Juniper trees. This is the oldest gompa in the Khumbu, built some 300 years ago, alas no longer active. However, it's well worth a visit, so seek out the villager who has the key and who will willingly open up. As well as the paintings and statues, the upper room also houses the infamous Yeti hand and scalp. Do remember to leave an offering, which is quite normal even for locals when they visit a temple or monastery.

The trail skirts round the back of the gompa, through the trees and past intricately carved mani-stones, and joins the main trail. Below the village the river still shows evidence of the damage caused in the 1977 flood. On the hillside opposite the side of the moraine below Ama Dablam and Mingbo are the white scars where the burst lake waters flooded down the narrow valley.

Less than two hours from Pangboche, the trail divides at a mani-wall. The right-hand trail leads to Dingboche, the left continues to Pheriche.

Pokalde, Kongma Tse and Island Peak:
The trail for these peaks breaks off right at this point and leads initially to Dingboche.

The left-hand fork climbs a rise past a house and crosses a ridge from where you can see Pheriche. Those interested in Lobuje Peak will also get their first view of that mountain. Pokalde is the fairly insignificant rocky mountain behind Pheriche. The path now descends and crosses the river, the Khumbu Khola. The Imja Khola, like the footpath, goes to the right towards Dingboche and the imposing Imja Glacier.

A chorten on the path to Pangboche echoes the pyramid of Ama Dablam.

In a short while the trail becomes Pheriche's main street, a dusty settlement with intricate stone walls enclosing the houses and lodges. The larger building is the Himalayan Rescue Association Hospital, where a lot of marvellous work on mountain sickness has been done and trekkers cared for. In the time of Dr Peter Hackett there were some marvellous parties for expeditions and trekkers alike. In 1982, after our Cholatse Expedition celebrations one missing member was eventually found in the hospital's decompression chamber!

Pokalde South Face and Ridge:
Anyone interested in these will find Pheriche the best place to establish base. The mountain can be and has

29

been climbed in a day from here although the route mentioned isn't very good. However, the long South-East Ridge might provide better climbing along its many-summited crest.

Pheriche is dominated by Taweche and its near neighbour Cholatse, best seen by climbing the moraine behind the village. Some people might benefit from an extra night here, especially if there are any signs of altitude-related problems.

Day 12: Pheriche to Lobuje

The main trail leads up the valley over springy turf and grazing meadows carpeted with small alpine flowers to the kharka (summer pasture) at Phulung Karpo, where the trail begins to steepen. Ahead is the terminal moraine at the snout of the rubble-covered Khumbu Glacier. Cross the glacier stream and moraine to Duglha with its welcome tea shop and lodges.

This is the parting of the ways for those going to the west and north flanks of Kongma Tse and Pokalde. This route goes up the east bank of the Khumbu glacier.

Lobuje East Peak – South Face:
The route to base camp leaves the main trail here, details of which are given under Lobuje Peak, page 63.

Shortly after Duglha the trail levels out and a chorten stands as a memorial to sherpas killed on Everest. The trail now climbs along the lateral moraine of the Khumbu glacier and arrives at Lobuje (4,887m/16,000ft), where there are lodges and camping places. This provides an ideal base for those interested in the east and north flank of Lobuje East. In all it is about four hours walking from Pheriche, but for the unacclimatised it may seem, and indeed be, a lot longer.

Lobuje is cold and austere – set amid huge moraines and grand peaks, it is the last habitation before Everest Base Camp, although there are stone huts at Gorak Shep which sometimes cater for trekkers.

From Lobuje it's possible to cross the jumbled Khumbu Glacier to the yak pastures at the foot of the Kongma La.

Day 13: Lobuje to Kala Pattar

Although there are no more listed trekking peaks north of Lobuje there is a very fine viewpoint above Gorak Shep called Kala Pattar. In the minds of many this is what they think of when someone talks about trekking peaks; something that a strong hiker can aspire to, providing a good summit but without technical difficulty or objective danger.

The trail from Lobuje follows the mulde, a geographer's name for the trough at the edge of a glacier's lateral moraine. A tributary glacier has piled another moraine across the trail; this has to be crossed, giving a good view of Pumori (7,145m/23,441ft). This section of the trek provides good views of the north and north-west flank of Lobuje Peak, whilst across the Khumbu Glacier, Kongma Tse is seen as a knuckle on the bony finger of Nuptse's South-West Ridge.

The black hill with a small lake, rising from the sandy flat, is Kala Pattar and the flat is Gorak Shep. A trail leads to the cairned summit of the hill giving striking views of the Everest group and Pumori, while Nuptse (7,879m/25,850ft) takes on its most striking profile from Kala Pattar. The great Lhotse/Nuptse Ridge, now seen end-on, is a shapely peak and is quite unrecognisable as the flat-topped flank of rock and ice that dominates the hike up the Khumbu Valley.

Gokyo and the Chhugyima La Route

Those with more time may prefer approaching the peaks in the upper Khumbu by going to Gokyo where the turquoise-blue lakes provide a scenic base for an ascent of the Gokyo Ri (5,360m/17,585ft), a good acclimatisation hike and a spectacular view-point, looking directly at the South Face of Cho Oyu (8,153m/ 26,749ft) and Gyachung Kang (7,922m/ 25,990ft). But that's not all; this splendid hill also provides a panorama of peaks that includes Everest, Lhotse, Nuptse and beyond to Makalu, whilst southwards it takes in Cholatse (6,440m/21,129ft), a peak that John Roskelly, Vernon Clevinger, Galen Rowell and myself made the first ascent of in 1982. On the Schneider Khumbu map this peak is called Jobo Lhaptshan, a name that no local seems to know it by.

From Gokyo it is possible to cross the snout of the Ngozumpa Glacier to the kharka of Dragnag and continue ascending over moraine to beneath the pass. Although most people seem to refer to this as the Tsho La, the Sherpas actually call it the Chhugyima La (5,420m/ 17,782ft). A camp can be made below the pass if required. Looking up at the pass, ascend at first on steep scree and boulders on the right-hand side. Cross diagonally to the snow on the left-hand side and reach the crest of the col without much difficulty. Sometimes this section is a snow-slope and steps may need to be kicked for porters. Although this is a glacier-capped pass, it traverses without difficulty and Sherpa porters cross it in gym shoes. In a dry year it may of course be icy and more difficult for porters. Care should be taken, however, to find the right descent, especially in poor visibility or soft snow. Stay on the south side of the pass and gradually descend by trending round to the right, well clear of crevasses, and so reach a series of rocky terraces. Find a way through these (marked with cairns), to even-

Lobuje East (6,119m 20,075ft) viewed from the south-west, from high on the Tsho La. The left-hand skyline is the North-West Ridge, the right-hand skyline, the South-East Ridge; between is a mass of unclimbed mountain!

tually reach pastures above Dzonglha and a good campsite. The views are again spectacular with Lobuje Peak, Cholatse, Taweche and Ama Dablam dominating the scene.

The Lobuje South Ridge base camp is to the north, climbing the hillside near the stream flowing into the lake south-east of Tshola (4,665m/15,305ft).

The main trail now continues past the glacial Tshola Tso (lake), to Duglha, where it meets the main Everest Base Camp trail.

2 Mera Peak (6,476m/21,247ft) and the Hinku Valley

The bulk of Mera, officially the highest of Nepal's permitted trekking peaks, rises to the south of Everest and dominates the watershed between the wild and heavily wooded valleys of the Hinku and Hongu Drangkas and is not truly speaking part of the Khumbu Himal. It should also be noted that there is a discrepancy between the official height given by the NMA (6,654m/21,831ft) and the Schneider Map (6,476m/21,247ft); my own reading on the summit was wildly innaccurate.

The first ascent of Mera was made by J.O.M. Roberts and Sen Tenzing on 20 May 1953, by the now standard route from the Mera La. It was during this season that Roberts made the first western exploration of the Lumding, Hinku (Inukhu) and Hongu valleys. It would appear that Mera did not receive a subsequent ascent until 1975 when French climbers Marcel Jolly, G. Baus and L. Honills climbed the North Peak, following the same route as Roberts but traversing along the connecting ridge to the further summit.

Both the Hongu and Hinku valleys remain uninhabited although there are kharka in the upper Hinku basin where Sherpa from the south, near Pangkongma, graze their animals during the grass-growing monsoon.

By its standard route from the Mera La, the ascent is technically straightforward; however, after a heavy fall of snow or when the maze of crevasses are open, the way can be long and demanding. Far and above the most rewarding aspect of a trip to Mera is a chance to venture into a little-visited and as yet unspoilt region of Nepal where the hillsides are still densely forested and a need to be self-sufficient is essential. There is also, of course, the pleasure of going above 21,000 feet.

There are many approaches to Mera; none are easy and some require the crossing of high and difficult passes, making a trek to the peak a real mountaineering adventure for which effort is rewarded with spectacular scenery and ultimately one of the finest viewpoints in Nepal.

The upper Hongu Basin is truly a mountain wilderness, a place of massive moraines, glacial lakes and spectacular peaks that include Chamlang and Baruntse. The valley terminates in a crescent of ridges, peaks and passes that includes West Col (6,135m/20,128ft), Amphu Labtsa (5,780m/18,963ft) and the Mingbo La (5,817m/19,085ft). All of these crossings provide magnificent, albeit difficult, entries and exits to and from the Hongu Basin. Interestingly, a group of lakes (generally referred to as Panch Pokhri) set just below the Amphu Labtsa and near the snout of the Mingbo Nup Glacier on the approach to the Mingbo La is a sacred site and a place of pilgrimage.

On my first visit to the lakes I had just led a group up Mera and we were on our way to the Mingbo La hoping to get to Thyangboche Gompa for the start of Mani Rimdu, a dance–drama depicting the struggle of good over evil, and a major social event in the Sherpa calendar. It was November, the sky was deep blue and cloudless. As the sun sank it became intensely cold as I sat on a white granite boulder watching ice blocks calve into the lake. Co-cooned in down, I saw the final kaleidoscope

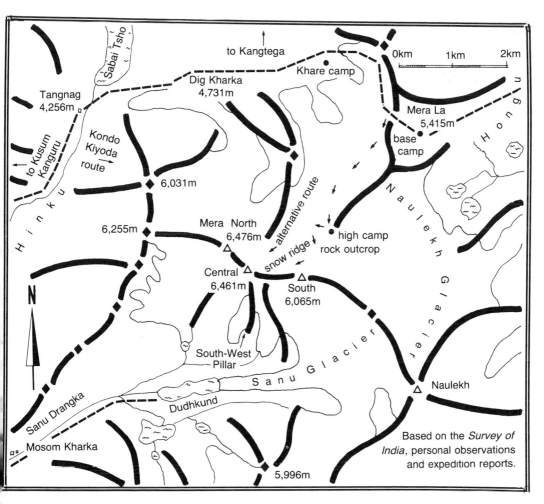

to Kangtega

Sabai Tsho

Khare camp

0km 1km 2km

Dig Kharka
4,731m

Tangnag
4,256m

Mera La
5,415m

Kondo
Kiyoda
route

6,031m

base
camp

to Kusum Kanguru

Hinku

Hongu

Nauiekh Glacier

6,255m

Mera North
6,476m

alternative route

high camp
rock outcrop

snow ridge

Central
6,461m

South
6,065m

N

South-West
Pillar

Sanu Glacier

Sanu Drangka

Dudhkund

Naulekh

Mosom Kharka

5,996m

Based on the *Survey of
India*, personal observations
and expedition reports.

MERA PEAK

of colours on Chamlang as the moon, almost full, rose above the Hongu. Dotted on the pale granite boulders were small cairns of stones, a bell and strings of flowers, dried in the cold, thin air. I was impressed by the pilgrim whose progress had brought him to Panch Pokhari.

THE TREK

The most straightforward approach to Mera is from Lukhla. For those not flying into the

STOL airstrip, the traditional Everest Trek is followed.

Behind Lukhla, to the east, is a magnificent mountain ampitheatre that few of the trekkers who are forced to hang around the airstrip visit. It's a bit like the Sunday drivers who venture into the country only to picnic in a car park!

For those venturing into the Hinku and Hongu basins, it is essential that you are totally self-sufficient and that you have enough food and clothing to remain self-contained for the

Mera Peak, with a climbing party below the central glacier bay. The Central
Peak is on the left and the North Peak in the centre; the beautiful fluted summit
is the North-West Peak.

duration of your expedition, and in the case of
poor weather conditions that you are able to
look after your porters as well as yourselves.
This becomes even more important for those
going beyond the Mera La into the Hongu
Basin. In the event of heavy snowfall, crossing
back over the Mera La, or pushing up into the
Hongu Basin hoping to cross the Mingbo La
or Amphu Labtsa may prove impossible,
especially to a poorly equipped or inexper-
ienced party. You should also bear in mind
that in the case of an accident or serious illness
helicopter rescue from the upper Hongu, could
you summon it, should be ruled out.

Entering the Hongu from the South

It should be noted that the Hongu Drangka
can be approached from the south via the
Kemba La (3,913m/12,912ft), a pass on the east
rim of the Hongu Gorge to the south of the
Chamlang massive. This route is little used, ill-
defined and follows a high ridge with little
water, the Kal Pokhari Danda.

The Kemba La can be reached from Lukhla
in a few days via the Sherpa village of Pang
kongma and the Rai settlement of Chemsing
The pass can also be reached by a little-used
trail from the Arun Valley. The Kal Pokhar
Danda trail climbs to around 4,390m (15,000ft)
above the precipitous gorge of the Hongu
before descending through dense bamboo

and rhododendron forest to Urpa (4,090m/ 13,419ft). A crossing point just beyond that leads north-west to Kongme Dingma and a steep climb to the east side of the Mera La. The views of Chamlang's south and west flank from the trail above Kongme are spectacular.

Day 1: Lukhla to Chutanga

This airport town is forever growing and has abundant campsites (scruffy) and numerous lodges should you have to spend time organising porters or waiting for a flight out. For those interested in people-watching and the full gamut of human emotions, a doctorate could be had on these subjects based on a few days' observation of crowd behaviour when the planes can't land.

Camp below the Zatrwa La on the approach to Mera. To the north-west are the peaks of the Lumding Himal.

From Lukhla the path traverses south-east through forest, crossing several cascading streams. Above are a semi-circle of attractive rock peaks that form the ridge of the Kalo Himal, dividing the Khumbu Valley from the Hinku. This unlikely-looking ridge has two passes, the Zatr Teng (4,943m/16,311ft) and the Zatrwa La (4,600m/15,000ft). The latter, with its gentler approach, is the more reliable – but be wary of the Zatr Teng when there is fresh snowfall on the Kalo Himal Ridge.

For those flying into Lukhla, I would recommend a couple of nights camping below the pass, exploring this wonderful cwm and so giving yourself a chance to acclimatise. The peaks are reminiscent of the Bregaglia and I'm sure would offer some good climbing.

On the route to the pass there are numerous possible campsites with good water. In a forest clearing between streams near Chutanga are some huge boulders where I made camp and spent a day exploring the slopes towards Gonglha. There is also a good site for numerous tents near the last stream before the Zatr Og. It has a magnificent position that looks out over the Dudh Khosi towards Karyolung (6,511m/21,362ft), Numbur (6,959m/22,831ft) and the south-east flank of Nupla.

Day 2: Chutanga to Tuli Kharka

The trail passes through a small notch just east of the Zatr Og on the Sebuk Danda Ridge. This is quite well defined, although care should be taken in poor visibility. From the notch the path traverses rugged, rocky country south-east below the ridge, rising gently to the Zatrwa La, marked by mani and chorten. The landscape is wild, rocky and impressive. On the far side of the pass the hillside falls steeply to the Hinku Dranka. The path, not so well defined at first, drops toward a rugged, stream-filled, boulder strewn valley. Tuli Kharka (4,400m/ 14,436ft) is a good site for camp.

Day 3: Tuli Kharka to Tashing Ongma

From Tuli Kharka the path traverses the hillside, first south-eastwards, crossing several spurs. The path is steep, and care should be taken crossing scree-filled washouts where the path may be ill-defined and loose. There are several points on the trail that give good views up the steep sided Sanu Drangka to the South Face of Mera. Unlike the well-populated valleys of high Nepal, the Hinku hillsides hold abundant forests of tall blue Himalayan pine, hemlock, birch and luxuriant rhododendron.

Before the trail re-enters the forest after crossing the streams near Tashing Dingma, a multitude of alpine scrub zone plants decorate the hillside including the unusual 'snowball flower' (*Saussurea gossypiphora*). This plant somehow survives despite the extremes of heat and cold, by mummifying itself within its own fibres and so producing a protective microclimate in which to live – a skill we might all wish we could emulate high on Mera!

After traversing for a while the path descends steeply through dense forest to the river. Branching rhododendron crouch over the trail swathed in tattered Usnea lichen which hangs like an old man's beard from their limbs, filtering the sunlight and waving like weathered prayer flags in the wind. Tashing Dingma (3,500m/11,489ft), provides a good lunch or camp spot.

Day 4: Tashing Ongma to Tangnag

The path now follows the west bank of the Hinku Drangka northwards, gradually climbing via the kharkas of Godishung, Dupishung and Lungsamba. These are no more than a few buildings that are used during the monsoon when the valley provides good grazing for animals driven up from the south.

Approaching the Mera La from Khare. On the right is the stunning South-East Face of Kangtega.

Not far from Godishung, beneath a great rock overhang, is a small gompa with a buddha and several buddsatva and prayer flags. The statues seem especially fine for such a remote setting. Lakpa Dorje, my sirdar, told me there was once a larger gompa here.

Mera Peak, South-West Face:
The trail to the South-West Face of Mera goes up the Sanu Drangka, following the south bank of the river. Reach this by crossing the Hinku River at a bridge before Godishung and backtracking to Mosum Kharka. A trail follows the Sanu Drangka Valley east towards the Dudh Kund lake. This is a hard four hour climb from a campsite at Mosum Kharka.

Beyond Lungsamba the valley narrows between the flanks of Kusum Kanguru (6,369m/20,896ft), to the west and the truncated far western peak of Mera (6,255m/20,522ft) to the east, a magnificent 1,800 metre rock face cut by diagonal snow bands and draped with fingers of ice – some trekking peak! This was first climbed by Japanese climbers Kunihiko Kondo and Michiko Kiyoda in the spring of 1985.

For those with the time, it's well worth spending an extra day at Tangnag. It's in a superb setting, surrounded by stunning peaks. In particular, Peak 43, which rises to 6,769 metres (22,208 feet) north-west of Tangnag, will make the pulse quicken and the palms sweat of anyone with an eye for a line. Tangnag is also the base for those interested in the east and north-east side of Kusum Kanguru.

Just north of Tangnag is a huge moraine behind which is dammed a beautiful glacial lake; the Sabai Tsho, into which plummets the hanging Sabai Glacier. This is well worth exploring and the time thus spent will go a long way to helping you acclimatise.

Day 5: Tangnag to Dig Khare

From Tangnag the valley steepens and bends sharply to the east where the path follows the lateral moraine of the Dig Glacier to Dig Kharka. Once again the setting is spectacular with the view dominated by the abruptly terminated crest of the Charpati Himal that forms Peak 43. Those with a lust for exploration will take time to stay a little longer at Dig Kharka to explore northwards along the Hinku Glacier and the approach route to Kangtega which was climbed by a joint American/New Zealand expedition in 1963.

Some may prefer to place a base camp below the pass on the Hinku side at Khare. I much prefer, however, to climb to the col and site it 100 metres below the col on the Hongu side.

From Dig Kharka the path finds a way through moraines and across streams at the snout of the Hinku Nup and Shar Glaciers and then climbs more steeply to Khare (5,099m/16,729ft), at the start of the glacier that leads to the Mera La.

Day 6: Khare to Base Camp

Depending on the state of the snow and condition of the glacier, getting on to the ice can prove tricky. Once established on the glacier, a well-defined snow ridge on the true right bank of this ice tongue usually leads in an arc toward the Mera La (5,415m/17,767ft) without difficulty – other than increasing altitude. However, as the glacier levels out near the col care should be taken with snow covered crevasses. Look out for porters who may trail behind or, as is more often the case, stomp ahead, despite carrying a heavier load. Once again the views from the pass are magnificent. From the col descend for about 100 metres on the Hongu side and site base camp in a gravel and silt flat in the moraine below the ice (5,300m/17,388ft). It's a good site for early morning sun and there's plenty of running water during the day.

THE CLIMBS

North Face Glacier from the Mera La

From base camp it is possible for a fit party to make the summit and return in one day, given good conditions. A skilled party on skis, for which Mera is suited, would certainly be able to ski to the summit ridge, traverse the summits and descend that same day. However, if the snow was breakable crust the descent would be a nightmare.

Perhaps the most rewarding style of ascent is to establish a high camp at 5,800 metres (19,028 feet), near a rocky outcrop on the

A climbing party on the Mera La with the massive South-West Face of Chamlang on the right and the pale granite peak of Makalu beyond.

Mera Glacier. From the Mera La wide snow slopes lead south and south-westward to a rock outcrop that marks the divide between the Mera and Naulekh Glaciers. A high camp can be established here, providing one of the most glorious viewpoints in Nepal, with a panorama that takes in Kanchenjunga, Chamlang, Makalu and Baruntse sweeping round from the east, whilst due north Everest peers over the crumpled sedimentary rock bands that make up the massive unclimbed South Face of Lhotse and the Nuptse/Lhotse ridge. Continuing westward, the peaks of Ama Dablam, Cho Oyu and Kangtega fill the view. Sitting on that rock outcrop, listening to the wind and looking out across untracked glaciers remains a highlight of my Mera expedition.

Above you, the Central Summit stands at the head of a wide glacier bay flanked by two ridges. Ascend towards the main bay over open snowfields but beware hidden crevasses. The way then swings back south-east, skirting below and to the east of the left-hand ridge. This is really a continuation of the ridge and rocky outcrop on which the high camp stands. The way now leads back south-west toward the main summit ridge of Mera. The route actually joins this ridge between what in fact turns out to be two of the mountain's three summits. All three are climbable without much difficulty, although at the time it does seem quite a lot of effort. The South Summit (6,065m/19,828ft), is the most accessible with the Northern Summit (6,476m/21,247ft), the highest, which can be reached by skirting the Central Summit (6,461m/21,198ft) to the

Climbing from the Mera La towards high camp. Base camp was placed about 100 metres below the col on the right.

north and following a classic snow ridge to its top. The middle summit provides a slightly more technical ascent up steep snow with the possibility of a cornice to overcome on the north side. Descend by the same route.

The main glacier bay below the Central Summit can also be climbed, but appears to give a lot more crevasse problems.

Technically Mera North is a straight-forward climb, little more than glacier walking, albeit at relatively high altitude. In poor conditions, however, with little visibility, the broad featureless slopes could present grave problems to an ill-prepared or equipped party.

West Face

First ascent was by Kunihiko Kondo and Michiko Kiyoda in spring 1985. The face was climbed in alpine style from a base camp at Tangnag. The route initially follows a couloir in the centre of the face and then a diagonal ramp line that runs from the centre of the face to the left-hand skyline ridge. This was then followed on steep ice to the summit. No detailed route description has been made available and from what information there is the climb would appear to give technically difficult climbing.

South-West Pillar

First ascent by Mal Duff and Ian Tattersall over three days between 27 and 30 March 1986. This is a technically difficult climb with an Alpine grade of ED inf. Approximately 1,800 metres (5,906ft), to the East Summit from the base.

Base camp can be established in the Sanu Drangka valley from which the base of the pillar

Looking east from the rocky ridge at high camp across the Chamlang Lekh to the distant peak of Kanchenjunga.

can be reached by a difficult glacier crossing. The base of the pillar is a series of stepped overhangs of poor rock; gain the pillar from the left by a rising traverse from the icefall.

Much of the climb follows the crest of the pillar except where excursions on to the flanks are necessary to avoid sections of overhanging rock. A lot of the climbing is mixed; on hard ice or bad rock. When first climbed, the expected easy snow arête on the last day was in fact hard 70 degree ice.

The route is serious and threatened by seracs from the eastern icefall. It also involves precarious climbing through the western icefall to gain the pillar. Retreat would be a problem because of poor belays on loose rock and because of the overhanging nature of the pillar's base.

THE RETURN TREK

For those not wishing to return by the same route there are several options, all of which are through uninhabited country, which means the whole party needs to be self-sufficient.

To the North

For those opting to cross the high snow and ice passes of the upper Hongu it seems sensible in the light of my own experience to do this as lightly loaded as possible, perhaps sending back some equipment or stores to Lukhla, thus avoiding the need to take porters with limited experience on a potentially dangerous and difficult crossing. At the end of the day a small lightweight group moves faster and can

Climbers on the summit ridge of Mera Peak approaching the West Summit with the Central Peak behind. To the right is the Peak of Naulekh.

Descending from the summit of Mera in strong winds and spindrift.

be more flexible with regard to route options.

Of the passes, the Mingbo La is the most direct to Khumbu, and the least dangerous. The landscape is superb; all above 5,000 metres, with constant views of magnificent mountains, dominated in the last few days by Ama Dablam. The Khumbu side of the Mingbo La is quite steep as you descend between ice flutings for about 100 metres, with the final glacier section through the seracs of the Mingbo Glacier quite stunning. A further day descending moraines below the South-West Face of Ama Dablam leads to Pangboche and the main Everest Base Camp trail. Expect to take three days to travel from base camp to a camp on the Hunku Nup Glacier, on the east side of the Mingbo La, with a further two days to Pangboche.

To the South

Parties not wanting to cross the high passes to the north can return south down the Hinku Drangka to Pangkongma, going west to the Dudh Khosi and so return to Lukhla or Kathmandu along the traditional Everest trek.

Day 1 and 2: Base Camp to Mosum Kharka

From the Mera La, return to Tangnag and the Hinku valley. Continue downstream to Gandishung, the site of the old gompa. A short way downstream cross via a bridge to the east bank of the river and follow the trail to Mosum Kharka (3,691m/12,100ft), at the confluence of the Hinku and Sanu Drangka.

Day 4: Chanbu Kharka to Gay Kharka

The trail continues across the stream, heading south by an ill-defined path that passes between some lakes (Panch Pokhari) and climbs to the main crest of the ridge, passing to the east of the high point (4,503m/14,774ft), before descending to a pass (3,900m/12,900ft). The views along this section are superb and welcome after the restricting confines of the valley. Eastward you can see Kanchenjunga and Jannu, whilst to the north the Hinku and Hongu summits dominate.

Continue steeply down between two bluffs near Danda Kharka before traversing to the west side of the Surkie Danda through scrub rhododendron to a delightful campsite in a forest clearing at Chalem Kharka (3,200m/10,496ft).

Continue the descent down the ridge on its south-east flank, meeting the trail coming from east Nepal below the Surkie La (3,085m/10,200ft). The path then drops steeply westward through pasture land to Nashing Dingma (2,500m/8,300ft) then to Gay Kharka, where there is a good campsite.

Day 5: Gay Kharka to Kharikhola

The trail continues steeply to the Hinku Khola and crosses by a bridge (1,856m/6,089ft). It then climbs for nearly 1,000 metres to Pangkongma La (3,173m/10,400ft) via the lovely settlement of Shibuje. The panorama on this section is superb, with endless views of the Himalayan foothills to the south and a glimpse back at Mera up the Hinku Drangka. From the pass, the route descends through thick rhododendron and bamboo to Pangkongma (2,846m/9,337ft), a Sherpa village spread out along the trail. The views are now across the Dudh Khosi to the Lamjura Pass, the Lumding Himal and Kwandge. The Sherpa culture here

Descending the fluted west side of the Mingbo La from the Hongu basin.

Day 3: Mosum Kharka to Chanbu Kharka

Cross the Sanu river by a small bridge and continue south along the main valley on a rough path. Going south, the rough, boulder-strewn trail through forest leads along the east bank of the river to Rondruk Dingma before it climbs the spur and traverses into the valley of the Mojang Drangka and crosses the stream (3,550m/11,647ft). The trail leads steeply through the forest, traversing high above the main valley. It is a difficult hike. Eventually it traverses into the valley of the Chanbu Drangka climbing out of forest into scrub and rhododendron by a path that traverses and finally descends to Chanbu Kharka (4,200m/13,780ft).

has been modified by the influence of the Rai who come from east Nepal and have traditionally been trading partners with the Sherpa. This trail is an important link with east Nepal in the trans-Himalayan trade carried out between these peoples.

There is a high-level trail that traverses to Pangkongma from Nashing Dingma (marked on the Schneider map) that avoids some of the big descents and climbs, and, although I have no details or personal experience of it, it looks very straightforward. Your sirdar or the local people may be able to tell you about it.

For those returning to Lukhla, there is a high level traverse from Pangkongma to Kharte. Otherwise make the long descent (900m) to Kharikhola (2,073m/6,800ft), a Sherpa village much influenced by Rai and Magar settlers.

Those walking to Kathmandu should continue westwards to the Rai village of Jubing and cross the Dudh Khosi. The route is described in the Everest Base Camp trek (page 19). The route to Lukhla is also described in this trek.

3 Kusum Kanguru (6,369m/20,896ft)

This impressive rock and ice peak dominates the southern end of the Charpati Himal, which separates the valley of the Dudh Khosi from the upper reaches of the Hinku Drangka. The northern end of this chain is dominated by the spectacular fangs of Kangtega (6,779m/22,241ft) and Tramserku (6,608m/21,680ft). Kusum Kanguru is well hidden until you get out of the valley, although it can be glimpsed from the Namche trail at Ghat, from where the West and South-West Faces can be seen up the valley of the Kusum Drangka. For those approaching from Jiri on the Everest trek the peak can be viewed from the Trakshindu La.

A complex, triple-summited mountain, Kusum Kanguru, also spelt Kusum Kangguru, has at least five major ridges, and as many faces, of which the North Face of the main summit is the most awesome. The name Kusum Kanguru (or more correctly Kusum Kangri) comes from the Tibetian, meaning 'three snow peaks'.

Of all the peaks in this book, Kusum Kanguru has the reputation for being the most difficult, without doubt increased by the label 'trekking peak', with all that that entails. It can in no way, even by its most moderate route, be compared with the more straightforward climbs on summits such as Island, Mera, or Pisang for instance. The climbing is technically difficult, needing a high degree of commitment and experience. Whereas many Nepal peaks are ideal for well-led groups with limited experience, this mountain is not.

Prior to its first ascent by a Japanese team in the autumn of 1979 there were four unsuccessful attempts on the mountain by British, New Zealand and two Japanese expeditions.

THE TREK

For those using air transport this is the easiest mountain to reach. By flying to Lukhla you can trek to base camp at the snout of the Kyashar Glacier in two days, however at that rate you're unlikely to get much higher. If you are flying into Lukhla you might consider doing some trekking before going on to the mountain. The valleys, mountains and villages of the Khumbu are well worth exploring and acclimatisation will be essential.

For those trekking in from Kathmandu follow the Everest expedition route. For climbs on the east side of the mountain, the Mera trek to the Hinku should be followed from Lukhla, or alternatively, from Kharikhola follow the southern route to Pangkongma and then head up the Hinku Drangka. For routes on the north side you leave the expedition trek at Monjo. Base camp at the snout of the Kyashar Glacier can be reached in a long hard day from Monjo, but most parties will want to take two.

THE CLIMBS

South-East Face

First ascent was in 1979 by Takeshi Kanazawa, Hideako Naoi, Hajime Vematsu, Mansanori Miyano and Tomooh Toyoda. This ascent was made soon after Doug Scott's expedition came close to reaching the summit, and was the first complete ascent of the mountain.

From a base camp at 4,358 metres (14,300 feet) they climbed the face with two bivouacs;

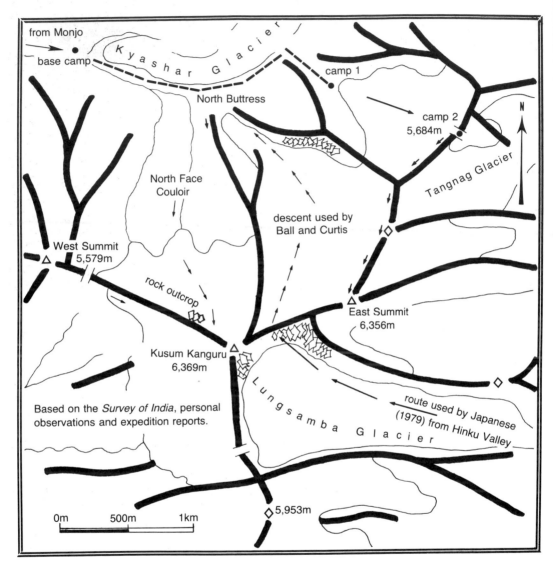

from Monjo

base camp

Kyashar Glacier

North Buttress

camp 1

camp 2
5,684m

Tangnag Glacier

North Face
Couloir

descent used by
Ball and Curtis

West Summit
5,579m

rock outcrop

East Summit
6,356m

Kusum Kanguru
6,369m

Based on the *Survey of India*, personal
observations and expedition reports.

Lungsamba Glacier

route used by Japanese
(1979) from Hinku Valley

0m   500m   1km

5,953m

N

KUSUM KANGURU

one in a crevasse at 5,403 metres (17,725 feet),
and another on the North-East Ridge at 6,203
metres (20,350 feet).

South-East Face
(Alternative Route)

During the post-monsoon period of 1981 the
Hoyu Shigaku-Kai Club Expedition led by
Minoru Kato climbed the South-East Face. In

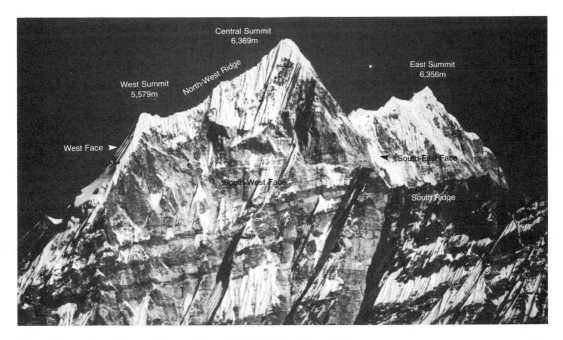

The triple summits of Kusum Kanguru. In profile is the West Face and the
North-West Ridge leading through the West Summit to the Central Summit. On
the right is the East Summit.

all, six climbers reached the summit after two camps.

This route, via the Lungsamba Glacier, is approached via the Hinku Drangka and appears to be the most reasonable route to the main summit, although a detailed description has not been made available. This is similar to the original route and the descent route taken by Bill Denz in 1981.

North Face of Main Summit

In April 1985 Takao Kurosawa with Hirosho Aota reached a high point of 5,600 metres (18,373 feet). Kurosawa, then alone, traversed off right to what could be called the West Summit. After making a bivouac he then continued along the knife-edge ridge to the true summit. This was a very impressive effort. In November 1985 a complete and more direct route on the face was climbed by John Ball

and Tom Curtis in true alpine style over four days (4–8 November 1985). Their ascent was made after a period of poor weather when there was a large amount of fresh snow on the face which undoubtedly made sections of the route more difficult.

The face forms a large amphitheatre between the North Buttress and the North-West Ridge approximately 1,500 metres (5,000 feet) high. The main feature of the face is a large central couloir rising from a massive avalanche cone. In the upper half of the face a network of flutings fan from the central runnel to the summit ridge. An important feature and landmark on the route is a rock buttress, outcropping to the right of the main couloir, west of the true summit and just below the main ridge; this is obvious in all photographs of the face. The climb exited on to this ridge to the left of this rock buttress.

Ascend to the foot of the face from base

The North Face of Kusum Kanguru forms an impressive amphitheatre between
the Central Summit on the left and the West Summit on the right.

camp at the snout of the Kyashar Glacier. Camp was made by the side of a huge boulder, which also makes a useful landmark. The central couloir can be reached by climbing to the left of the obvious snow cone. On the first ascent, because of deep snow, this was approached from the North Buttress and a bivouac was made near the top and to the left of the cone at around 5,000 metres (16,404 feet).

Continue up the central, twisting couloir which has a number of steep steps of 60–70 degrees, although the majority are 45–50 degrees. This continues for almost half the height of the face. A bivouac ledge was cut beneath a small rock outcrop. On the first ascent this was climbed unroped. Above, the route steepens considerably and flutings lead toward the summit ridge, with the rock buttress mentioned to the right.

From the bivouac, a steep ice corner leads to a small snowfield above which there are rock slabs with a veneer of névé. To the left of the slabs a narrower twisting gully can be followed for three difficult pitches. Eventually a diagonal abseil can be made to regain the slabs, which are then climbed. It would appear to be better to follow the slabs direct. A lot of 70 degree ice is encountered on this section of the climb; a bivouac ledge can be cut in the side of a fluting above the slabs.

Keeping to the left of the rock outcrop, steep ice flutings can be followed to the summit ridge. On the first ascent this was made both difficult and dangerous by a large amount of fresh powder snow. The summit ridge is then followed to the final summit mushroom. On the first ascent a further bivouac was made in an ice cave dug in and through this narrow corniced ridge.

Descent was made by abseil down the hanging glacier on the North-East Face between the main and the East Summit that makes up the North-East Face; this was both difficult and dangerous. Ball and Curtis had hoped to

Looking down the North-West Ridge of Kusum Kanguru toward the West Summit and the Dudh Khosi. The rock outcrop near the top of the North Face route can be seen behind the climber.

descend the North Buttress but dangerous snow conditions on the upper ridge made this impossible. It would appear that these same conditions had stopped Doug Scott's party from reaching the summit in 1979. Alpine TD+ seems a reasonable grade for the route.

North Ridge

This was first attempted in September 1979 by Georges Bettembourge, Mike Covington and Doug Scott who are reported to have climbed to within twenty metres of the summit over a period of three days. The following account was taken from the NMA, but I have been

49

Kusum Kanguru seen from the Moro La. The left-hand skyline is the North-East Ridge of the East Peak. The ridge in the foreground is the North-West Ridge leading to the West Peak, whilst in shadow on the left is the North Face.

unable to verify the ascent or the description given by Colin Jamieson.

From base camp ascend steep grass and scree and finally a ramp leading to the ridge proper. At the end of the ramp climb a steep, short chimney on to the crest of the ridge and continue along this more easily to an obvious overhang where there is also a good bivouac ledge.

Turn the overhang on the right and so gain the ridge crest once again. Follow the ridge by more moderate climbing with two sections of more difficult, steep ground until at last you reach a small col.

Climb the crest of the ridge to the right of the col for two pitches to a good bivouac ledge. Above the ledge, climb slabs more easily for several pitches which in turn are followed by snowy ramps leading to the final ridge

which is both difficult and precarious and leads to the Central Summit.

South-West Buttress and West Face

In October 1981 Bill Denz from New Zealand made a solo traverse of the mountain via the West Face. He continued his traverse over the main summit to the East Summit and descended the South-East Flank.

West Ridge

During May 1982 the Gumma Tomioka Himalayan Expedition from Japan climbed the West Ridge. On May 2 Ikuo Yoshita and Anu Temba reached the summit whilst Keichi Suto and Lhakpa Sherpa went to the summit on the following day. Although this obviously follows the same line as the Denz route in the upper section, the lower line is new.

East Summit
North-East Ridge

The North-East Ridge to the East Summit provides a fine climb at a reasonable, albeit high, standard. The first ascent as far as the East Summit was climbed by an Anglo–Canadian–Nepalese Expedition in 1983 led by Dr David Hopkins, including members Guy Neithardt (Swiss) and Andrew Wielochowski (British), who reached the top on 16 September 1983. The route was graded Alpine D (serious). The climb was completed in alpine style during a one week absence from base camp and involved major difficulties on both rock and ice.

The complete ridge to the main summit was climbed in 1985 by the Spanish climbers, Anton Zamabide, Eduardo Emmanuel Arrantz and Alejandro Arrantz.

A base camp (4,280m/14,041ft) is found in a grassy, rock hollow at the snout of the Kyashar Glacier. From base camp the route can be divided into six distinct sections:

1   Follow the south-east moraine of the Kyashar Glacier until a steep ascent can be made towards the col between Kusum Kanguru and Peak 43 to the North Peak 6,769m (22,208ft). A bivouac can be established (cave camp 5,180m/16,994ft) under a large boulder on the east side of the moraine, below the glacier that drops from the col.
2   Climb the glacier leading to the col which, although small, is complex and troublesome.

Kusum Kanguru, seen looking due east from Pangchung Kharka across the Dudh Khosi. The North-West Ridge forms the left skyline, whilst the South Ridge falls to the right.

It leads to a flat basin below the col (5,400m/ 17,716ft).

3   A 45 degree snow rib is followed for 250 metres (800 feet) to the col (5,654m/18,580ft). On the first ascent 200 metres (650 feet) of fixed ropes were left in place. A camp was established on its narrow and precipitous low point.

4   The North-East Ridge leading from the col is followed to the base of the summit pyramid (6,194m/20,321ft). The ridge presents rock and snow difficulties, to begin with following ledges on the South-East flank and then along the crest.

5   The steep face leading to the top of the North-East Buttress of the East Summit provides the most concentrated difficulties combined with complex route finding on loose rock and variable snow.

6   Finally, traverse the knife-edge snow ridge to the East Summit (6,356m/20,858ft).

Descent was made by the same route.

4 Kwangde Ri (6,187m/20,298ft)

Kwangde Ri is also called Kongde Ri and Kwande on various maps. Despite the fact that the Schneider Shorong/Hinku 1:50,000 map calls it Kongde Ri, I have opted for the more generally used name of Kwangde, which seems phonetically closest to the Sherpa pronunciation.

This difficult mountain forms an impressive multi-summited ridge on the eastern end of the Lumding Himal, which in turn can be regarded as part of the Rolwaling Himal. Rising south-west of Namche Bazaar above the Bhote Khosi, the mountain's northern flank forms an impressive barrier that throws down several steep ridges to the north.

Its glaciated southern flank is more aloof. It is hidden at the northern end of the Lumding Drangka, a high and remote valley bounded to the west by the tumbling glaciers of Karyolung (6,511m/21,361ft), Khartang (6,853m/22,484ft) and Numbur (6,959m/22,831ft). The Lumding valley is rarely visited by trekkers or expeditions. At the northern end of the valley the stream cascades down a natural rocky barrier above which is a moraine-bound lake, the Tsho Og, at the snout of the Lumding Glacier. North of the Tsho Og, itself hidden in a huge rocky cwm, is the massive Lumding Tsho Teng (5,151m/16,899ft).

Surrounding the lake are the peaks of the

Kwangde Ri seen from Thyangboche Monastery. Left of centre is the obvious inverted 'Y' of the North-East Ridge of Kwangde Shar. To its right is the impressive North Face, climbed by the Lowe route, and right of this is the summit of Nup.

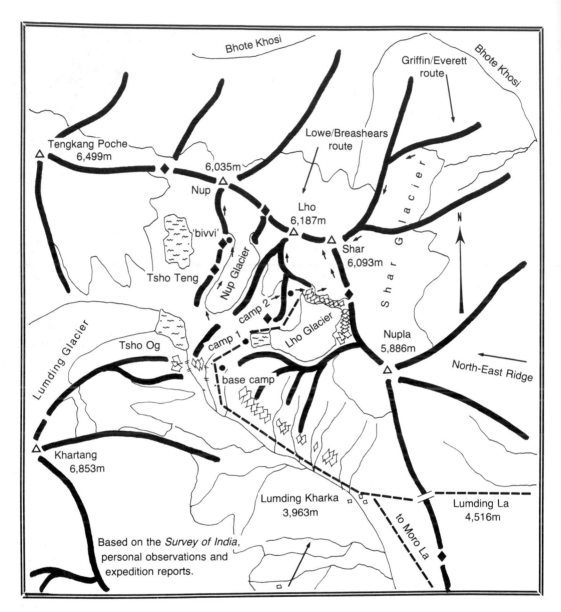

KWANGDE RI

Lumding Himal which begin with Panayo Tippa (6,696m/22,952ft) at the western end of the range and continues through Panayo Shar (6,549/21,486ft), Teng Kang Poche (6,499m/21,322ft) and Kwangde Ri (6,187m/20,298ft). The ridge continues in a south-east sweep to terminate in the summit of Nupla (5,885m/19,307ft), above Gumila in the Dudh Khosi valley.

The actual mass of Kwangde Ri is a five kilometre ridge running from the summit of Nup (6,035m/19,799ft) south-east through the

Prayer flags and mani-stones on the Moro La with the peaks of Everest, Lhotse and Nuptse beyond.

summits of Kwangde Lho (6,187m/20,298ft) and Kwangde Shar (6,093m/19,990ft), after which it turns sharply south-south-east through several lesser summits to terminate in Nupla (5,885m/19,307ft), whose fine North-East Ridge is well seen from Namche Bazaar. All of these summits are included in the peak permit. What is also clear from various expedition reports is that the height differential of the Lho and Shar summits is less than that given officially and in fact there seems little discernable difference.

In 1953, after organising oxygen loads to Everest Base Camp, Jimmy Roberts made the first exploration of the Lumding Valley. He was followed in 1954 by Fred Becky who made an attempt on Kwangde Shar during which he discovered the Lumding Tsho Teng, one of the highest lakes in the world.

All of the routes climbed to date on the Kwangde Peaks are difficult, none have proved suitable for commercial trekking peak expeditions. The routes on the North Face are particularly difficult and reflect recent developments in lightweight Himalayan climbing, with an emphasis on technical difficulty and a high degree of commitment. They have invariably been made by two climbers without support camps or fixed ropes, although in at least one case a subsequent ascent has seen a return to traditional siege style tactics with masses of fixed rope and camps. Even the routes on the South Face are committing and difficult, although the climbing is more traditional in character.

The first ascent of Kwangde Lho was made by a Nepalese expedition in 1975 which was led by Kumar Khagdar and Bikram Shar. The actual summit was reached on 17 October by Lhakpa Tenzing. Sonam Gyalzen, Shambhu Tamang and Sonam Hisi via the South Ridge.

THE TREK

From Kathmandu the normal Everest Base Camp Trek is followed. Flying to Lukhla is the quickest approach to the Khumbu. For those interested in climbs on the north side, the route goes to Namche Bazaar and then towards Thame in the Bhote Khosi (Nangpo Dzangpo) valley.

Those wishing to climb on the South Face will need to cross the Dudh Khosi to Gomila (marked Rimishung on the map) and then trek steeply over the Tragkarmigo Danda either by the Lumding La (4,516m/14,816ft) or the Moro La (4,343m/14,248ft) further to the south, to gain entry to the Lumding Drangka. The Moro La seems to be the most reliable pass, especially after snowfall.

Those walking in from Jiri can either follow the route described over these passes or follow an alternative route from the south leading in to Lumding Kharka from Ringmo and Trak-shindu La. I have spoken to local Sherpas that know the trail who say it presents no real problem under good conditions, but deep snow often remains on the north facing flanks of ridges, making it a difficult and dangerous route after recent heavy snows. However, with regard to conditions, you should check with your sirdar or local people near Ringmo.

All of the trails mentioned lead to Lumding Kharka, a small group of huts, below the Lumding La.

THE CLIMBS

Kwangde Lho (6,187m/20,298ft)

South Ridge

First ascent was in 1975, by Lharkpa Tenzing, Sonam Gyalzen, Shambhu Tamang and Sonam Hisi. The route described here follows the same line as the Kwangde Shar route in the lower half but, instead of traversing the ledge line above the polished slabs, it gains the south ridge of Kwangde Lho by a direct line from the rocky cwm. This is the line taken by John Ball and Trevor Pilling in 1984.

On the Nepalese ascent in 1975 the Sherpa team climbed the polished rock slabs on the far right-hand side of the Kwangde Lho Glacier and so gained the South Ridge by traversing the glacier above the rock barrier. However, there seems no point in taking such an indirect and potentially dangerous line.

Base camp (4,700m/15,420ft), was established south-east of the Tsho Og, at the snout of the Lumding Glacier. Traverse north-east, climbing moraines to gain a rocky ridge, from where there are good views of the southern flank of Kwangde Ri. Continue along rubble-covered ledges and descend to a small moraine lake at the snout of the Kwangde Lho Glacier. Camp 1 (5,100m/16,732ft) can be established here.

Climb over snow and rocky slopes to gain the rocky hollow below the ice cliffs of the upper Kwangde Lho Glacier. Above, the curving snow arête of the south ridge sweeps down to meet these ice cliffs. The ridge proper continues as a rocky arm that terminates in Point 5,457m, north of the lake at Camp 1.

A snow slope at the head of the hollow leads up towards a broken rock barrier below the curving snow ridge. Climb the snow cone and some awkward mixed ground through the barrier to gain the snow arête above. Instead of a camp in the rocky hollow, a bivouac site can be found in large boulders above the snow slope. Alternatively, instead of ascending the snow slope climb the boulder slope to the west and so join the rocky continuation of the South Ridge at a col. A camp can be made here. The ridge can then be followed via a short section of mixed climbing to the snowy arête of the ridge proper.

Once on the South Ridge proper, follow this in a sweeping arc towards the summit. Snow conditions will obviously have big effect

Kwangde Lho

South Ridge

bivvi

obvious avalanche danger

German route

approach to
South Ridge

polished slabs

rocky hollow

Camp 2

Lower Kwangde
Lho Glacier

*Kwangde, South Face, seen from the lower Kwangde Lho Glacier. The South
Ridge is the obvious left-hand skyline.*

Kwangde Lho with the beautiful curving line of the South Ridge running directly toward the camera.

on the difficulty of the route. Steep, exposed climbing leads to a final mixed section near the summit. At least one party found an easier line climbing on the east side of the ridge crest. Graded Alpine AD+to D.

North Face

First ascent was by Jeff Lowe and Dave Breashears in November 1982. This is a thoroughly modern climb of extreme difficulty, involving four bivouacs from the foot of the face to the summit ridge. The route climbs the face behind Hungo, following a steep ice couloir to a central ice ledge system, after which it traverses right to gain more steep ice. This follows a difficult line through the central rock band. After the central rock band, steep ice is then followed, leading diagonally right to the summit ridge.

Another route was made on the North Face in 1985 to the right of the Lowe/Breashears

route by Spanish climbers Angel L. Minoz and Juan Antonio Lorenzo. Again, four bivouacs were taken to reach the west ridge which was followed to the top. The climb is Grade 6, with 65 to 90 degree ice.

Kwangde Shar (6,093m/19,990ft)

South Face

This was the first route to the summit of a Kwangde peak and was first climbed by the Allgauer Himalayan Expedition of 1972 made up of Dr Karl-Dieter Fuchsberger (leader), Helmut Schaefer, Franz Bischof, Wolfgang Reichart and Franz Durschmidt.

The following route uses the same approach as the South Ridge route (page 56) as far as the rocky hollow below the ridge. From a base camp established at the south-eastern end of the Tsho Og at the snout of the Lumding Glacier (4,700m/15,420ft), traverse north-east over large glacial moraines to gain a rock ridge from where there are good views of the glaciated southern flank of Kwangde. Continue along rubble-covered ledges and descend to a small glacial lake at the snout of the Kwangde Lho Glacier. Camp 1 is placed at the southern end of the lake (5,100m/16,732ft). Camp 2 can be established in a rocky cwm between Point 5,457 and the Kwangde Lho Glacier at 5,300 metres (17,388ft). This is directly below the snowy South Ridge of Kwangde Lho.

The upper and lower sections of the Kwangde Lho Glacier are separated by a rock barrier of glaciated slabs which are overhung by ice cliffs. It was these rock slabs that were reported to have been climbed barefoot by the Sherpa team making the first ascent of Lho!

Traverse right across a snow slope to gain a broad terrace dividing the upper rock wall from the polished slabs below. Cross to the right-hand end of this terrace to the edge of the upper glacier where it presents a vertical ice barrier of 25 metres (90 feet) that has to be climbed to gain the upper glacier. The traverse of the terrace, although straight-forward, is menaced by icefall from the seracs above. The ice nose presents the technical crux of the climb.

Beyond, cross broad glacier slopes to below the western flank of the South-East Ridge of Kwangde Shar. Ahead there are two possibilities for gaining the summit: either climb directly up steep mixed slopes to gain the narrow crest of the South-East Ridge and follow it to the summit; or traverse the glacier to the saddle between the summits of Kwangde Lho and Shar, then traverse east along the West Ridge of Kwangde Shar to its summit.

It is worth noting that Griffin and Everett descended directly to the glacier from the summit of Kwangde Shar after their ascent of the North-East Ridge, reporting a 150 metre (500 foot) slope of perfect névé. Your descent can be made either by the same route or by continuing over the summit and descending by the South-East Ridge. It is possible to continue along the ridge to another summit on the ridge, 5,734m (18,812ft). This traverse was done solo in 1972 by Franz Durschmidt.

From the saddle (5,950m/19,521ft) between the main summits, the West Summit, Kwangde Lho, may have been climbed from the saddle by its East Ridge, which has a marked step that may present difficult ice climbing. This ridge divides in its lower half and the south-eastern spur appears to give the least difficult alternative and avoids the step. This ridge may have been climbed in 1978 by a Japanese expedition. The summit ridge is narrow and exposed.

North-East Ridge

The first ascent was made in October 1978 by Lindsay Griffin and Roger Everett, climbing alpine style from a base camp above Pare and below the Kwangde Shar Glacier. Descent was made down the South Face into the Lumding Valley. This same ridge had a winter ascent by a Japanese expedition in 1983, who made two camps and fixed ropes on the final headwall.

The sharp North-East Ridge of Kwangde Shar, falling directly from the summit to the Bhote Khosi, splits in its lower section to resemble the shape of an inverted 'Y'. The difficulties occur in the last 900 metres (3,000 feet) where, on the first ascent, unconsolidated snow lay on top of good, sound granite and gave interesting mixed climbing. Belays are good, but comfortable bivouacs sites are rare.

From Namche Bazaar a short day on a good path leads, via the bridge at Samde, to the small hamlet of Pare (3,700m/12,139ft). Continue east above the Bhote Kosi on good yak tracks until a steep valley, festooned with scrub rhododendron and tangled undergrowth, rises towards the left arm of the inverted 'Y'. There is no path, and several overgrown rock barriers require careful negotiation. A base camp can be sited in a small hollow at 4,600 metres (15,091ft).

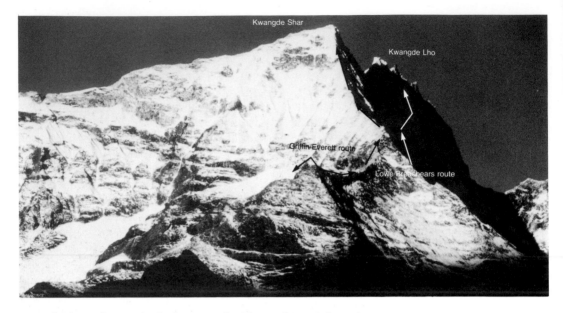

Kwangde Shar and Kwangde Lho from Namche. The North-East Ridge is the obvious inverted 'Y' and the face in shadow is the one climbed by the Lowe route.

Reach the base of the left arm of the ridge and scramble relatively easily up its left side. On reaching the top one can descend a little on the south side and follow the edge of the glacier into a basin which lies below the foot of the sharp ridge dropping directly from the summit. Camp/bivouac at 5,200 metres (17,060 feet). The glacier also leads directly down to the east and an easier approach can be made this way.

The lower section of the ridge is not steep but is wafer thin with sharp flakes of perforated rock. Slant up the face on the left to reach the crest of the ridge above this point, where it steepens. Continue up the ridge on mixed climbing with considerable snow (on the first ascent) overlaying good granite. Before the final steep section at 5,800 metres (19,029ft), there is a small shoulder and room for a camp or bivouac.

The climb now becomes steeper and more sustained, with snow over more compact rounded granite, easing slightly below the summit. The exit is abrupt and surprising as

the summit lies on a very sharp crest. Descent was made down the south face via the Kwangde Lho Glacier.

It should be pointed out that this ascent was made after a lot of snowfall.

Kwangde Nup (6,035m/19,800ft)

South Face and Ridge

First ascent was by John Ball and Kurt Arenoe in 1984. From a base camp near the snout of the Kwangde Lho Glacier traverse west to the Kwangde Nup Glacier where a rocky gully leads on to its west side.

Follow the west (true right) bank of the glacier with few crevasses, below the rocky, bounding ridge on the left with its obvious pinnacle, 5,515 metres/18,094 feet (marked on the Schneider map). Follow the glacier to a notch in the ridge at about 150 metres (500 feet), below an obvious rock pillar. On the first ascent a bivouac was made here.

Traverse the glacier to the right of the rock

pillar, avoiding crevasses and seracs, and so gain the foot of a loose rock buttress. This is climbed by a series of diagonal, linking terraces. Small cairns were built at the end of each of these connecting shelves. The buttress is followed until snow can be regained near its top right-hand side.

The snow face is then followed to a steep ice arête. This gives several pitches of 45–50 degree ice climbing. The arête in turn leads to a highly crevassed section of glacier. The glacier becomes more broken and a way has to be found around the seracs. The slope above presents fewer problems, leading first to a false top and finally to the large snowy dome of the true summit.

The ice arête provides the major technical difficulties. Route finding or descent in poor visibility would be particularly difficult. Marker flags were left on the glacier during the first ascent to aid the descent.

Nupla or Kwangde South (5,885m/19,308ft)

North-East Ridge

First ascent was by Rob Burnoe, Pemba Norbu Sherpa, Jim Traverso and Eric Bland. This is reported to be a fine climb on good granite with sections of pure rock, mixed ground and finally ice climbing near the top of the ridge.

From Phakding cross the Dudh Khosi and follow the trail to Nyambua Thyang and around the spur to Kwangde Yersa (4,132m/13,556ft on the Schneider Shorong/Hinku map). Continue climbing westwards to a lake. Base camp can be placed beyond this.

From base camp, climb two snow fields separated by easy rock climbing (UIAA III). Continue climbing to the first rock tower. Camp below this.

Pass this tower and then a second rock tower low on the right. This is the most difficult section of the route; difficulties are concen-

View south down the Lumding Valley. The Lumding La and Moro La cross the ridge on the left.

trated in the first 150 metres (500 feet) of climbing. Climb an overhang (VI–) free, although it is considerably easier if aid is used. After the overhang, exposed but moderate rock then leads to a more broken section of mixed climbing on steep snow and loose rock. The ridge to the right is gained as soon as possible over ground where many variations can be used.

A snow slope is then followed to an overhanging rock wall, until a notch is reached. Above, more snow slopes lead to the summit. There are short sections of more difficult mixed ground between the summit snowfields. Fixed ropes were placed on the difficult sections on the first ascent, and descent was made by the same route.

RETURN TREK

The quickest return is obviously via Lukhla, that is of course based on the assumption that you have a confirmed flight and that it takes off. Delays in high mountains inevitably occur and anyone using STOL airstrips in the Himalaya should be prepared to wait, although at Lukhla you get so much more; all kinds of schemes, plans and plots to overthrow RNAC have been hatched there and from time to time outright aggression erupts at the surface. You can, of course, walk out to Jiri which, even with equipment, can be done in under a week.

5 Lobuje Peak East (6,119m/20,075ft)

There exist two distinct summits to Lobuje Peak: Lobuje East (6,119m/20,075ft) and Lobuje West (6,145m/20,161ft). Although they are connected by a continuous ridge there is a sharp gap and a considerable distance between them. The trekking peak permit is for the East Peak, whilst Lobuje West, well seen at the head of the Lobuje Glacier, requires an Expedition Permit. Lobuje is also spelt Lobuche on some maps.

Lobuje Peak is an attractive summit, offering a variety of existing routes and wide scope for new lines. Seen from near Pheriche, the dark triangle of its rocky East Face rises above the moraines of the Khumbu Glacier to an icy skyline. This skyline forms the South Ridge, the junction of the East Face with the glaciated South-West Face and the line of the normal route of ascent. This in turn leads to the summit ridge running north-west from the top of the East Face through several small summits to the East Peak.

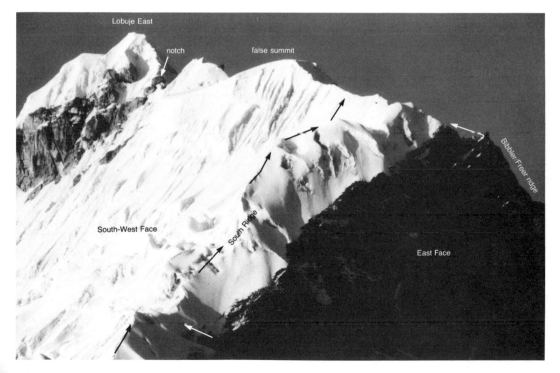

Lobuje East with the glaciated South-West Face on the left and the top of the East Face on the right. The notch before the main summit is obvious.

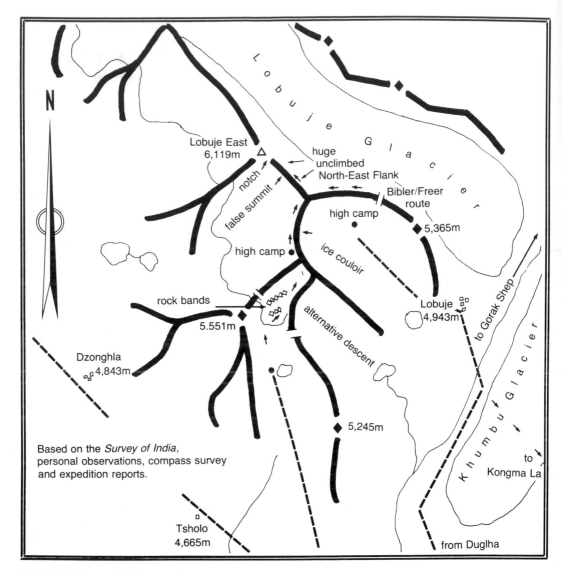

Based on the *Survey of India*,
personal observations, compass survey
and expedition reports.

LOBUJE EAST

The true East Peak is quite striking and is
reached by descending into a marked notch
and climbing steep snow/ice slopes to the top.
This is rarely climbed and is often mistaken for
Lobuje West. Most attempts on the mountain
climb the summit ridge only as far as a subsidiary snow summit, before the notch, south-
east of the true peak. The false summits east of

the notch have been attained by numerous
parties, including my own, but the first recorded ascent of the true Lobuje East seems to
have been made by Laurence Nielson and
Sherpa Ang Gyalzen on 25 April 1984. It seems
likely that others may have reached the true
summit before this date but no record exists.

Porters approaching the 'hidden lake' at base camp below the South-East Ridge of Lobuje. Ama Dablam is behind.

THE CLIMBS

South Ridge

Base camp for the South Ridge is best established near a hidden lake in a rocky hollow at the base of the glaciated South-West Face near Point 5,551 metres (18,212 feet).

To reach this lake follow the lower trail from Pheriche through Phulung Karpo and on to the tea shops at Duglha (4,620m/15,157ft), set in the chaos of moraines at the snout of the Khumbu Glacier. Follow the trail westwards towards Dzonglha, traversing the hillside above the Tshola Tso. At a point where a main stream descends from Lobuje Peak into the lake, ascend a vague trail up grazing slopes near to the stream, into a rocky hollow wherein lies the hidden lake. The views of Ama Dablam and Taweche are spectacular, and this spot provides a superb site for base camp.

From the northern end of the lake climb steep slabby terraces and snow slopes leading rightward beneath the main glaciers on the South-West Face of Lobuje East and so gain access to the ridge overlooking Lobuje and the Khumbu Glacier. These snow/ice slopes can be quite steep (45–50 degrees) and provide several difficult steps. Many parties have fixed rope on these steps. This point has also been reached from the Lobuje side without great difficulty.

At this point the glacier face and the ridge meet, leaving a rocky/snow-covered corridor to the right (east) of the ridge crest. A high camp can be placed here or higher on the ridge.

Depending on conditions, the sinuous snow arête can be followed, more or less, to its junction with the summit ridge. Some parties have found it easier to leave the arête for the broader snowslopes on the face to the left.

Diagonal snow ramps lead from above base camp to the arête of the South-East
Ridge of Lobuje.

Climbing party on the South-East Ridge of Lobuje after heavy snowfall. Ama
Dablam is the obvious spire whilst the peak on the left with the rocky summit is
Pokalde.

66

Lobuje East showing the rocky East Face with the South Ridge forming the snowy left-hand skyline, and the Bibbler/Freer route the right-hand ridge. The Lowe/Kendal couloir rises from the left-hand snow cone.

Mark Twight leading one of the ice pitches on the East Face Couloir.

Snow conditions and crevasses will obviously dictate the best line.

The route to the East Peak then follows the summit ridge north-west. There are several snow bumps along the way and parties have recorded problems with crevasses cutting the ridge and presenting difficulties. It would appear that most parties go only as far as the snow summit before the obvious notch, what might be termed the Far East Peak! The true East Summit is reached with some difficulty by gaining the notch by abseil and climbing the steep and quite difficult snow slopes to the summit on the far side.

East Face Couloir

First ascent was by Jeff Lowe and Henry Kendal in spring 1986; it received a second ascent one day later by Alison Jane Hargreaves and Mark Twight.

The East Face is the dark pyramid of slabby rock overlooking the lodges of Lobuje and the Khumbu Glacier. The face is best approached from Lobuje by crossing moraines west of the lodges and ascending the scree-filled hollow beneath the face and above the small lake south-west of Lobuje. On the first ascent a camp was placed beneath a large boulder near the foot of the face.

At the foot of the face on the left-hand side is a snow cone with two couloirs leading from it. The route takes the left-hand couloir. The couloir gives at least four big ice pitches before exiting on to the South Ridge. This can then be followed to the summit. On the first ascent, the descent was made down the South Ridge and then by scrambling down on the east side back to Lobuje. The ascent to the Far East Peak and down to Lobuje was made in the day. The climb is graded Alpine TD, with sections of Scottish 5.

Lobuje East. The rocky East Face is separated from the mixed terrain of the North East Flank by the Bibbler/Freer Ridge. The skyline ridge is the normal route of ascent.

Mark Twight descending the South-East Ridge of Lobuje.

East Ridge

First ascent was by Todd Bibbler and Catherine Freer in 1985. This is the obvious rock prow that marks the junction of the East Face and the North-East Face. It is easily seen, rising above Lobuje. This ridge had certainly received previous attempts and may even have had a previous ascent.

Other Possibilities

The North-East Face of the mountain rising above the Lobuje Glacier would seem to offer endless, albeit difficult, new route options on steep rock and ice.

One of the most striking lines on Lobuje East is an impressive, very steep line of ice dropping from the summit to the south-west. To appreciate the full scale of this line the mountain is best viewed from the Tso La (5,300m/17,388ft).

6 Pokalde (5,806m/19,049ft) and Kongma Tse (5,820m/19,095ft)

POKALDE

This mountain was first climbed in 1953 by a route from the Kongma La along its North Ridge. Despite its lowly magnitude the mountain's first ascensionists were giants of the mountaineering establishment, a fact that incidentally is true of many of the so-called trekking peaks. This party was made up of John Hunt, Wilfrid Noyce, Tom Bourdillon and Mike Ward, all members of the 1953 Everest expedition. Hunt, who was the leader of the expedition, didn't actually make the summit due to illness.

Pokalde is an insignificant-looking mountain when seen from Pheriche, from where it appears as a crenelated rocky ridge dominated by the vast bulk of Nuptse. Seen from Lobuje or Gorak Shep the peak looks more interesting rising to the south of the Kongma La (5,535m/18,159ft), an infrequently traversed pass that leads into the Chhukhung Valley. The northern side of the mountain has a small hanging glacier that is best reached along the ridge rising from the Kongma La. By and large the rock on the mountain is poor, although it does offer some interesting scrambling on the well-defined ridges. The summit provides a

The rocky southern flank of Pokalde rising above the huge lateral moraine near Pheriche. On the right is the massive South-West Flank of Nuptse.

Pokalde, on the left, seen across the rubble covered Khumbu Glacier from near Lobuje. The left-hand skyline is the route from the Kongma La. In the distance are Kangtega and Tramserku.

good viewpoint and from that perspective is a fine little peak.

As Wilfrid Noyce wrote of it after the first ascent during the acclimatisation phase of the 1953 Everest expedition:

'A jolly ridge, in the alpine sense . . . Everest and Makalu reared above the clouds like two great canine teeth, "fangs excrescent" upon the jaws of the earth, in Mallory's phrase. Gaunt and yellowy-brown, they seemed to have shaken off the winter snow.'

THE TREK

The Everest Base Camp trek is followed as far as the yersa at Bibre between Dingboche and Chhukhung. From there a high camp can be established near the small lakes beneath the Kongma La. From this camp it is a short, steep climb to the col or a traverse south-west avoiding a small glacier to the North-East Flank of Pokalde.

Those interested in the South Face of the mountain should make Pheriche their base. The mountain can then be reached by climbing the huge lateral moraine and traversing over grazing meadows to the scree cone below the face.

The North-West Face of the mountain is best approached from Duglha at the snout of the Khumbu Glacier. From there paths through the lateral moraine lead north-east toward the Lingtren Tso and the grazing meadows below the Kongma La. There are several suitable sites for camp in the cwm beneath the pass. For those that have walked in from Lukhla, a traverse of the col would be a good way to acclimatise.

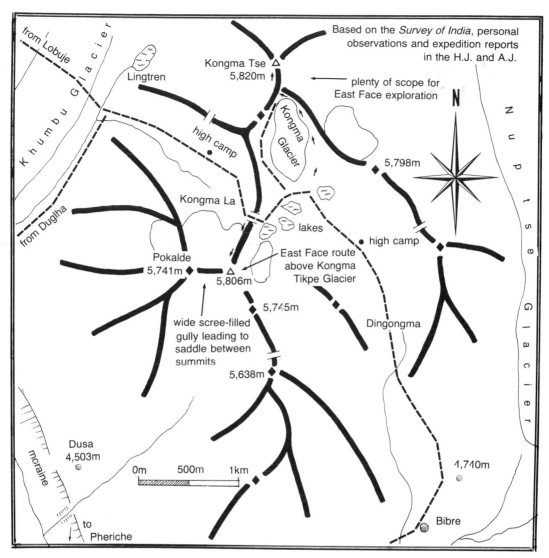

Based on the *Survey of India*, personal observations and expedition reports in the H.J. and A.J.

from Lobuje

Khumbu Glacier

Lingtren

Kongma Tse △
5,820m

plenty of scope for East Face exploration

N

Kongma Glacier

high camp

5,798m

N
u
p
t
s
e

G
l
a
c
i
e
r

from Duglha

Kongma La

lakes

high camp

Pokalde
5,741m ◆

△
5,806m

East Face route above Kongma Tikpe Glacier

wide scree-filled gully leading to saddle between summits

5,745m

Dingongma

5,638m

Dusa
4,503m

0m   500m   1km

4,710m

moraine

to
Pheriche

Bibre

KONGMA TSE AND POKALDE

THE CLIMBS

North Ridge

First ascent was on 15 April 1953 by Noyce, Bourdillon, Ward and Sherpas. A fine route up a snow arête leading to a final rocky section below the summit.

From a base camp placed near the small lakes on the Chhukhung side of the Kongma La, climb to the rugged, bouldery pass that is used as a yak route between pastures of Chhukhung and Khumbu.

Follow the 'jolly ridge', which is a snow crest that leads to two pinnacles of loose rock, which in turn are climbed. The ridge continues to a final strenuous pull over some granite splinters which lead to the narrow rocky summit. The climb is possibly Alpine AD.

Other Possibilities

The summit has also been reached from the Pheriche side by an ascent of the couloir that drops from a snowy col to the west of the main summit. This is reported to be steep and loose although very easy as far as the col, when the climbing on rock becomes quite difficult and out of keeping with the rest of the route.

The North-East Flank of the mountain above the lakes, below the Kongma La on the east side, is perhaps the easiest way to the summit. The route leads up broken rocks, boulders and snow to the summit ridge which is then followed to the top. There is no distinct line; one simply follows the line of least resistance or most interest.

KONGMA TSE

Formerly called Mehra Peak and simply Mehra, this attractive mountain rises to the north of the Kongma La, stands above the Khumbu glacier opposite Lobuje, and is one of several small summits, including Pokalde, that make up the long South-West Ridge of Nuptse carved out between the Khumbu and Nuptse Glaciers. Seen from Gorak Shep, the summit has a diamond-shaped hanging glacier above a steeply inclined rock wall that makes up the mountain's North Face, which is in turn slashed by a diagonal ice ramp leading to the lower edge of the glacier.

From the south the mountain is much more

Kongma Tse, on the right, seen from Gorak Shep. This is one of several peaks that are part of the bony South-West Ridge of Nuptse.

Seen from Kala Pattar, Kongma Tse with its diamond-shaped glacier is dwarfed by the spire of Ama Dablam.

THE TREK

The Everest Base Camp trek should be followed either from Kathmandu or Luklha and left either to gain the Imja Valley and the east side of the Kongma La, or to continue towards the Khumbu Glacier making a way up its east bank for approaches to its Khumbu face.

THE CLIMB

South Face Glacier

This is best approached from Dingboche in the Imja Valley. Follow the main trail to Bibre and ascend towards the kharka on the hillside to the north-east at 4,740 metres (15, 551 feet). A faint trail then leads northward toward the high grazing at Dingongma. A high camp can be placed below the lakes around 5,300 metres (17,388 feet).

Ascend the rocky hillside north-west towards the glacier tumbling down the southern flank of Kongma Tse, and find a way over moraines between the two well-marked lakes below the snout of the glacier. Gain the glacier on its western side, finding the easiest line up its true right bank below the South Ridge of the mountain. It is equally feasible to ascend the true left bank below the South-East Ridge.

At the head of the glacier climb broken rocks and snow to gain the south ridge and follow this to the summit. Descend by the same route.

I have found no other details of routes on this mountain or indeed of who actually made the first ascent. Obviously there is plenty of scope for exploratory climbing here.

approachable. Seen from the lakes east of the Kongma La a small, stepped glacier descends from the summit between long, rocky arms that make up the mountain's South and South-East Ridges. The margins of the glacier provide the normal route of ascent.

As with Pokalde the views from the summit are spectacular, especially so because of the nearness of the massive south face of Nuptse. The views northwards towards Pumori and the Lho La are also outstanding.

7 Imja Tse (6,189m/20,305ft)

The name Island Peak was given to the mountain in 1952 by Eric Shipton's party who were on their way to explore the Barun Gorge. Seen from above Dingboche the mountain does indeed resemble an island in a sea of ice. In 1983 it was renamed Imja Tse, although for most people the descriptive name of Island Peak seems to have been retained.

The mountain was first climbed in 1953 by a very prestigious team in preparation for the ascent of Everest. They were Charles Evans, Alf Gregory, Charles Wylie and Tenzing Norgay, with seven Sherpas who were trying out the newfangled oxygen sets; as practice, of course, for loftier things. Fortunately this didn't set a precedent and most people seem able to climb it without bottled air, although a Sherpa

I once reached the summit with called the cigarette he was smoking, 'Sherpa oxygen!'

Seen from the moraines between Pheriche and Dingboche the mountain doesn't look too impressive, dwarfed as it is by one of the largest mountain faces in the world; the South Face of Lhotse. However, on close inspection it reveals itself to be an interesting and attractive summit with a highly glaciated West Face rising from the Lhotse Glacier. The mountain itself is really an extension of the South Ridge of Lhotse Shar and is separated from it by a small col. Above this gap, rising to the south, is a classically beautiful ridge leading to the summit of Imja Tse. The continuation of this ridge, descending south-west, provides part of the normal route of ascent and leads in turn to the

Approaching Imja Tse from Chhuckhung. To the left of the rocky South-West Face are the tumbling seracs of the West Face, above the Lhotse Glacier.

74

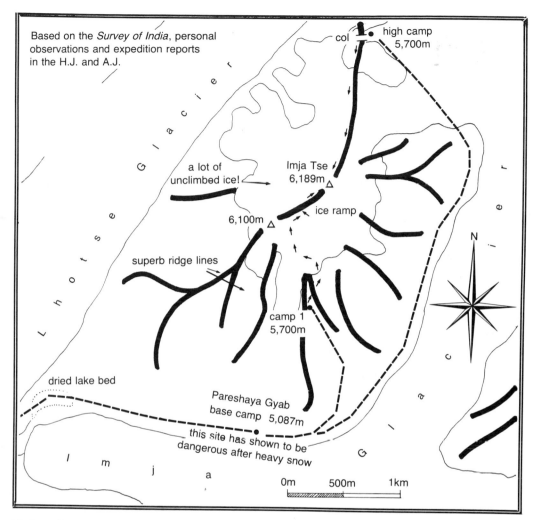

Based on the *Survey of India*, personal observations and expedition reports in the H.J. and A.J.

col — high camp 5,700m

a lot of unclimbed ice!

Imja Tse 6,189m △

ice ramp

6,100m △

superb ridge lines

camp 1 5,700m

dried lake bed

Pareshaya Gyab base camp 5,087m

this site has shown to be dangerous after heavy snow

0m   500m   1km

IMJA TSE

South Summit, seen capping the rocky west facet of the mountain when viewed from near Chhukhung.

As well as providing an enjoyable climb the peak also provides some of the most striking scenery in the Khumbu. If the peak can be likened to an island in a glacial sea, then the mainland forms a semicircle of cliffs that rise in the north to the rugged summits of Nuptse (7,879m/25,850ft), Lhotse (8,501m/27,890ft),

Lhotse Middle Peak (8,410m/27,590ft), as yet still unclimbed and Lhotse Shar (8,383m/ 27,503ft). To the east, rising above the frozen waves of the Lhotse Shar Glacier, is Cho Polu (6,734m/22,093ft), beyond which can be seen the red granite mass of Makalu (8,475m/ 27,805ft). To the south of the Imja Glacier the icy flutings of Baruntse (7,720m/25,328ft) and the Amphu peaks lead the eye to the lofty pinnacle of Ama Dablam (6,856m/22,493ft),

Loaded yaks crossing the dried lake bed beneath *Imja Tse* on the way to base camp.

which is like a giant sea-stack guarding the entrance to the glacial bay in which Island Peak stands.

THE TREK

The Everest Base Camp trek should be followed from either Luklha or Kathmandu as far as Tsuro Og. Where the trail divides, take the right-hand branch leading to Dingboche and Chhukhung.

THE CLIMBS

South-East Flank and South-West Ridge

This was the route of the first ascent. After a little rock scrambling the route involves a small amount of glacier crossing followed by a short, steep snow climb to a ridge which leads to the summit.

The usual site for base camp is at Pareshaya Gyab (5,087m/15,518ft), between Imja Tse and the lateral moraine of the Imja Glacier. This is not a particularly attractive place and in the event of very heavy snowfall it has proved to be exposed to avalanche danger.

To reach base camp from Chhukhung (4,730m/15,518ft), the path at first climbs quite steeply to the south before following the moraine east along the main valley below the southern or true left bank of the Lhotse Glacier. The trail then follows glacial streams to the snout of the Imja Glacier. At this point the path swings north-east and crosses a dried up

Mike Tillett and Jerome Greggory at the high camp on Imja Tse. The route traverses a rocky gully on the right to gain the right-hand skyline ridge.

lake bed between the Lhotse and Imja Glaciers.

From a base camp at Pareshaya Gyab, a well-acclimatised party in good conditions should be able to make the summit and return in a day. However, one of the joys of Himalayan mountaineering is the high camp or alpine-style bivouac and for most parties this will prove essential for a safe ascent.

From base camp the route skirts south-east around the base of Imja Tse between the moraine and the mountain before turning north-east and climbing steep grassy slopes and small rocky steps. Occasional cairns are to be found marking the path. Easy scrambling up an open gully leads between two well-defined ridges and the site of high camp on the left-hand ridge below and to the right of a

Descending the classic North Ridge of Imja Tse during the first ascent in 1958.

small hanging glacier (5,280m/17,323ft). Care should be taken in the placing of a camp or bivouac to avoid possible avalanche danger from ice above.

From a high camp on the left-hand ridge scramble across the broad open gully and gain the right-hand ridge. Follow this, which gives easy scrambling to the snow-covered glacier above. A way needs to be found out leftwards, avoiding seracs and crevasses before turning back northwards over snow-covered scree in the margin between the glacier and the base of the main summit ridge.

After crossing a gully with some stone and icefall danger, a steep snow and ice ramp leads upwards for nearly 100 metres (300 feet), to the summit ridge. The last moves on to the ridge often prove difficult and many parties leave a fixed rope in place to aid descent. The ridge itself is a classic and undulates towards the main summit which is reached by a final tricky snow pitch. Grade: Alpine PD.

The superb South Ridge of Island Peak, with Ama Dablam on the left and the Lumding Himal in the distance on the right.

Ben Holt descending the rocky ridge towards high camp after an ascent of Imja Tse.

On the South Ridge of Island Peak with the Lhotse Glacier and the Imja Valley below and spires of Taweche and Cholatse beyond.

North Ridge

First ascent was in 1958 by Alf Gregory, Dick Cook and two Sherpas. North of the main summit the ridge continues to a col (5,700m/ 18,700ft). The route climbs the ridge from the col, which is reached by following the true right bank of the Imja Glacier and later the moraines on the right bank of the Lhotse Shar Glacier, before climbing north-west over snowy slopes to the col. On the first ascent, a camp was placed on the col. From the col, follow the ridge which is a magnificent snow arête, due south. This steepens for the final summit pyramid. This is a long ridge that would be difficult under soft snow conditions and may under other conditions have a marked cornice. The climb is a little more difficult than the normal route, and is graded Alpine PD+.

Without doubt a complete traverse of both the routes described would make a superb outing, especially so with parties traversing from each end so that there was no need to backtrack to collect camps.

West Face

The West Face of the mountain also offers good routes although none have been recorded. Dr Peter Hackett, when he was resident doctor at Pheriche hospital, did climb on the west side of the mountain but no details of his exploration are available.

8 Rolwaling Himal: Ramdung (5,925m/19,439ft) and Parchamo (6,187m/20,298ft)

In 1951 after the Everest reconnaissance, during which the first western exploration of the Rolwaling was made, Eric Shipton wrote in *The Times*,

'This form of mountaineering, the exploration of unknown peaks, glaciers and valleys, the finding and crossing of new passes to connect one area with another, is the most fascinating occupation I know. The variety of experience, the constantly changing scene, the gradual unfolding of the geography of the range are deeply satisfying, for they yield a very real understanding, almost a sense of personal possession, of the country explored.'

It was during this expedition that Shipton, with Murray, Ward and Bourdillon crossed the Manlung La north of Tesi Lapcha whilst Hillary, Riddiford and Dutt crossed into Rolwaling over Tesi Lapcha, meeting up at Beding before returning, via Barabise, to Kathmandu.

In 1952 Shipton, with Alf Gregory and Charles Evans during the Cho Oyu expedition, ascended the Tesi Lapcha from Thame, made an attempt at and all but climbed to the summit of Parchamo, but were turned back by a steep step above a crevasse on the North-West Ridge. Shipton had decided it would be better sport to climb without crampons and well it might have been, but they lost the summit. They did go on to explore the Drolam Bau Glacier northwards, making the first ascent of a fine peak at the end of the valley.

After the 1951 expedition, W. H. Murray was so enthused by the Rolwaling that he organised another lightweight sortie to the area with Tom McKinnon, George Roger, Douglas Scott and Tom Weir, all members of the Scottish Mountaineering Club. Included in the peaks, passes and glaciers crossed and climbed was the first ascent of Ramdung in the post-monsoon season of 1952.

Perhaps the most successful lightweight expedition to operate in Rolwaling was the Merseyside Himalayan Expedition of 1955 led by Alf Gregory. Greg, as he was affectionately known on the 1953 Everest expedition (and indeed is still known), was also involved elsewhere in the Khumbu on the first ascent of other trekking peaks. During the Merseyside expedition, which included Dennis Davis and Phil Boultbee, nineteen summits were climbed in the course of some extensive exploration, included in which was the first ascent of Parchamo.

Thus the high and remote Rolwaling Valley normally provides access to two of the permitted trekking peaks: Ramdung and Parchamo. However, since 1984 the Rolwaling has been closed to Western trekkers and thus Ramdung has officially been 'out of bounds', although the NMA sometimes still grants a peak permit, despite the fact a trekking permit cannot be had. Although no official reason has been given for the closure, rumours have ranged from changes in regional boundaries, to dangers to porters crossing the Tesi Lapcha, to reports of unofficial

A traditional Nepali swing on the trail to Everest. In the distance are the peaks of the Rolwaling, with the distinctive twin summits of Gauri Shankar on the left and the ice peak of Menglungtse centre.

crossings into Tibet by climbers and trekkers.

Parchamo, on the other hand, isn't totally lost since it can be approached from the Khumbu side by ascending the Tesi Lapcha pass from Thame and climbing the peak from a high camp on the col itself.

In terms of a mountaineering adventure however, the journey through the Rolwaling, climbing a peak and crossing a high glaciated pass, followed by a descent and return through new country, is always to be preferred, capturing as it so closely does the essence of Shipton's sentiments expressed in *The Times*. Perhaps in the near future the valley will again be opened and a small number of expeditions allowed to return to Rolwaling.

THE TREK

Day 1: Kathmandu/ Barabise/Gortali

Take the bus (or hire transport) from Kathmandu to Barabise; the journey is via Dholalghat and Lamasangu and takes about three hours. Cross the Bhote Khosi and walk a short way down the left bank of the river to Sun Khosi Bazaar, once an important centre before the highway came and Barabise superseded it.

Follow the trail up the Sun Khosi River, which in fact is little more than a stream, to Bhudipa at the head of the main valley where the river is now several streams and the terrain rises steeply. A good campsite can be had at Gortali village (1,200m/3,937ft).

Day 2: Gortali to Dhumtali

Take the main trail heading generally north-east, climbing through the village of Dolangsa (2,489m/8,166ft) to the small monastery beyond, which makes a good spot for lunch. The gompa just about marks the limit of cultivation with the terraced hillsides giving way to forests of oak, dominated by rhododendron with numerous clearings (kharka) used for grazing. The kharka, as elsewhere in Nepal, make good campsites; those with buildings (goth) often have water nearby. The kharka at Dhumtali (2,900m/9,514ft) is better than most in that it has water and fine views. This point is about six hours from Gortali.

Day 3: Dhumtali
to Sangawa Khola

Climb quite steeply through forested hillsides, crossing the Magarko Danda by the Tinsang La (3,319m/10,889ft), which has good views of Gauri Shankar (7,145m/23,442ft) and Jobo Bhamare (5,927m/19,445ft). Descend from the pass to the houses of Rupthang, crossing the stream and following the trail along the north bank to Bigu Gompa, a fine and interesting monastery set among juniper on a terraced hillside. The building which houses a nunnery was built around 1933. There are good campsites here; or cross the stream below Bigu and continue down to the river and the bridge over the Samling Khola (1,600m/5,250ft), where there is a good campsite. In all the journey takes 6 hours from Dhumtali Kharka.

Day 4: Sangawa Khola
to Bulung

Contour the ridge and descend down the left bank of the Sangawa Khola, which later joins the Tamba Khola. The trail leads through Lading (1,778m/5,833ft) and continues through forest before crossing the Jorong Khola to Chilangka (1,923m/6,309ft). Continue south-east above the Sangawa Khola, crossing several tributary streams whilst staying below Chayarsa and above Laduk, where the path passes a chautara, well decorated with religious paintings.

Chautara are interesting structures and are found along trails throughout Nepal. They form a platform, often stepped, on which a porter can easily rest a heavy load without having to lower it to the ground. Sometimes they are found in glorious positions, almost in homage to the landscape, and invariably they are built around two trees whose spreading roots cling to the platform, binding the whole together. Wondering who the benefactors were, I once asked a sirdar about them, and he explained that a rich villager or a bahun (priest) would have one built, normally around two trees that may have been planted for the purpose. One of the trees, with large leaves, is called 'Bar'; the other, a smaller leafed fig, is called a 'Pipal'. These are then 'married' as man and wife in a ceremony, bringing shade and rest to all that pass by.

Turn the corner of the Gyalsung Danda above the river that has now become the Bhote Khosi, descending towards Bulung and passing a school above the widely spread village. This is not a long day, but Bulung makes a convenient stop.

Day 5: Bulung to Gongar

Continue north-east along the trail above the Bhote Khosi through the villages of Yarsa and Warang. The latter, situated on a ridge, has a school and is a convenient lunch spot. The trail then descends steeply to Dulang Village (1,897m/6,224ft), near to the river. Continue past Dulang Mandap, an important place of Hindu worship. The trail then leads steeply

Bhanyan and Pipal trees bring welcome shade on the long trek to the mountains.

down to the junction of the Gongar Khola and the Bhote Khosi, and the settlement of Gongar on the wide valley floor. There is good camping either at the river confluence or at the school. In all it is about six hours' trek from Bulung.

Day 6: Gongar to Shakpa

The trail continues along the west bank of the Bhote Khosi, which narrows and later becomes a deep gorge. The trail has an impressive situation and many fine views of Gauri Shankar, and waterfalls cascading down the east bank of the river.

Pass through fields and the nearby settlement of Chhechet descending towards the river which is crossed by a suspension bridge (1,524m/5,000ft). The path now climbs steeply towards Simagaon (2,000m/6,567ft) with a cosmopolitan mix of Sherpa and other Nepali peoples. You may be able to buy a fresh supply of locally grown fruit and vegetables for the journey ahead.

For those that want to press on, continue climbing steeply from the village, through rhododendron forest, cresting the ridge to camp in a kharka at Shakpa (2,460m/8,071ft), where there is a pleasant meadow, a goth (hut) and a good water supply. It should take you about six hours to reach the camp from Gongar.

Day 7: Shakpa to Gyabrug

In this area the change from the lush Bhote Khosi to the mountain girt Rolwaling Valley is very distinct.

Tom Weir, after the Scottish Himalayan Expedition, stated that, 'Nowhere else in the world does the Arctic plunge to tropical with such dramatic force.'

Laughing children are a feature of trekking through the foothills of Nepal.

Near Shakpa a path climbs steeply towards the ridge of the Sambur Danda, crossing the Daldung La (3,976m/13,045ft), before descending again to the Rolwaling Valley. This route can be used in the monsoon when it is a safer alternative.

Continue contouring above the Rolwaling Chhu on the northern flank of the Sambur Danda where the rhododendrons give way to open hillside. The path now begins a long diagonal descent to the river past more huts in an area called Gyalche. Beware of steep or wash-out sections of this path which eventually, after descending a slabby area, meets the valley floor and crosses the Rolwaling river by a covered wooden bridge. The valley at this point is steep sided and enclosed.

Continue heading east on the north bank of the river in the narrow shaded valley. The trail passes through the settlements of Nyimare and Ramding, where the houses are typical Sherpa; stone walls with wood and stone roofs. The last yersa before crossing the river is Gyabrug. There are plenty of good campsites around. If you have made good time during the day you might want to continue to Beding.

Day 8: Beding

The village of Beding (3,693m/12,116ft) is the largest settlement in the Rolwaling, comprising thirty-six houses. Situated in a narrow gorge it is a cold place, enlivened somewhat by its well-positioned Gompa. There is a Hillary school in Beding. It is well worth staying an extra day and either exploring the village or hiking off on an acclimatisation day, perhaps towards the Manlung La to the north where there are fine views of Menlungtse (7,181m/ 23,560ft).

Day 9: Beding to Na

It's a short day from Beding to Na, but with increasing altitude and increasingly impressive scenery to slow you down the time passes quickly enough. Follow the trail on the north side of the river. Na is a scattered village, not a permanent settlement, but rather a summer yersa where animals are grazed and potatoes grown. There is a roughly built monastery here. Ahead, up the valley beyond Na, the splendid summit of Chobutse (6,689m/21,956ft) rises above the Tsho Rolpa at the confluence of the Ripimo Shar and Trakarding glaciers.

Ramdung is to the south of Na. Base camp can be established on the south side of the river near Kyiduk where the path climbs towards the Yalung La (5,310m/17, 421ft).

Those going higher might consider taking a rest day either here or at Tsho Rolpa. This is especially important if no rest day was taken at Beding.

Day 10: Na to Tsho Rolpa

This is a short day and could in fact be done from Beding in the space of a day by a well-acclimatised party.

From Na cross the river to the south bank and follow what is now a shallow stream to a crossing point near the Yersa at Sangma. After the wooden bridge climb up a spur to the settlement. Climbing on moraines, traverse steeply above the main stream until finally you reach the terminal moraine, behind which is the dammed Tsho Rolpa. The lake is sometimes called Cho Pokhari. Camp on sandy level ground under a high cliff near the lake (4,500m/14,763ft) which is reached by following the indistinct trail along the moraine on the north side of the lake. It may be safer in other years to traverse the southern side of the lake. Local advice should be sought in Beding.

A rest day taken at Sangma would allow exploration of the area around Omai Tsho and the Ripimo Shar valley to the north.

Day 11: Rolpa Lake to Glacier Camp

From camp the trail traverses the moraine above the north side of the lake. Leaving it on the right it continues along the moraine, occasionally passing rock overhangs. During the later part of the day, the section along the lake is in danger from constant stonefall and should only be done in the early morning. Generally, the best trail keeps to the north side of the moraine.

The route marked on the Schneider Rolwalling map is no longer in use, as the route climbing the slabby area at Hacha Dubgog is too dangerous.

Near the icefall of the Drolambau Glacier cross the rocks and rubble of the Trakarding Glacier south-east to a point where a rocky spur leads up to a low point of the icefall. Climb this at its lowest and easiest point to gain the Drolambau Glacier. There is some danger of rockfall in the area. The medial moraine provides a route up the glacier. A suitable campsite can be found where the glacier flattens out at around 5,400 metres (17,716ft).

Day 12: Glacier Camp to Tesi Lapcha

Continue up the wide, fairly level glacier, with spectacular views of Tengi Ragi Tau (6,943m/22,779ft), Bigphero-Go Shar (6,729m/20,077ft) and the shapely summit of Dragkar-Go (6,793m/22,287ft). Before a spur descending from Tengi Ragi Tau a narrow glacier enters quite steeply from the right. Ascend this to the summit of the Tesi Lapcha (5,755m/18,881ft), where there are prayer flags and cairns.

For the ascent of Parchamo, which is well

The remote Sherpa settlement of Beding in the upper Rolwaling is now out of bounds to trekkers and expeditions.

seen to the south of the pass, a suitable high camp could be located near the Tesi Lapcha on the broad slopes or indeed below the pass on the Khumbu side where there is a sheltered campsite in a hollow, protected by low stone walls. Care should be taken in this area with regard to stonefall from Tengi Ragi Tau. A trough between the ice and the rock usually allows safe passage to the gentler slopes below the pass to the east. Despite the fact that it might still be early in the day, those wishing to

cross into Khumbu are advised to camp here as there is danger of rockfall from Tengi Ragi Tau in the afternoon. In any case, the pass is a splendid place to camp.

Day 13: Tesi Lapcha to Thengpo

From the camp below the Khumbu side of the pass continue eastwards over snow slopes beneath the southern flank of Tengi Ragi Tau

The moon setting behind the North Ridge of Tengi Rangi Tau. The left-hand ridge falls to the Tesi Lapcha.

before bearing south-east to the edge of the glacier snowfields, where a rocky slope is gained leading across moraine to campsites at Ngole. Below you can see a moraine lake.

The trail from here is better marked and continues its long descent down the upper reaches of the Thame Khola to Thengpo, with good views of Ama Dablam and Makalu as well as of the peaks of the Lumding Himal above the Thame Khola. There are plenty of campsites around the dozen or so buildings that makes up Thengpo. A fit or lightly loaded party on the other hand might press on to Thame, 510 metres lower down (1,600ft). Thame is a large village with a police post and was also the birth place of Tensing Norgay.

Day 14: To Namche Bazaar

At Thame, the old trade route over the Nangpa La into Tibet branches north following the Bhote Khosi, which incidentally is the third river so named on this trek.

Thame to Namche is an easy day after many quite hard ones. It also means a return to trekkers' civilisation; lodges, hot showers and extensive menus. Simply cross the Bhote Khosi and follow the good trail down the valley, climbing gently up to Namche Bazaar.

RAMDUNG

Situated south of Na in the upper Rolwaling, Ramdung, also called Ramdang-Go on the

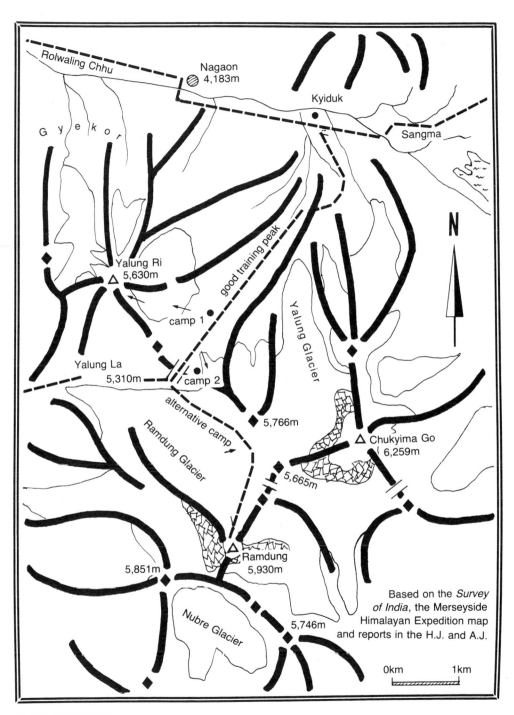

RAMDUNG

The North Face of Hiunchuli, seen from near the base camp used by Bonington's
Annapurna South Face Expedition. The left skyline is the East Ridge, the right
skyline is the West Ridge, which joins with Annapurna South.

Schneider map, is one of a cluster of peaks around the Yalung La (5,310m/17,421ft), a pass giving access to the upper Rolwaling from the south, via the Khare Khola.

The peaks in the area were first explored by the Scottish Himalayan expedition, led by Bill Murray in 1952, when three of the peaks near the pass, Yalung Ri (5,630m/18,471ft), Chhugyima Go (6,259m/20,534ft) and Ramdung were climbed. In 1955 the peak had its second ascent by members of the Merseyside expedition. Before the closure of the Rolwaling, Ramdung had numerous ascents and proved to be an ideal summit for commercial trekking/climbing groups.

Although the mountain by its normal route of ascent, the glaciers of the North-East Flank, is straightforward, its virtues lie in its magnificent position and splendid summit panorama that ranges from Langtang to Everest and provides a splendid view of Gauri Shankar and Menlungtse.

THE CLIMB

North-East Face from the Yalung La

Despite the fact that the peak is not high the approach from Na covers a good distance and most parties have required two high camps for the ascent.

From Na cross to the south bank of the river and follow it east to where the trail near Kyiduk climbs south toward the Yalung La. Suitable campsites can be found at around 4,900 metres (16,000ft). From this camp, Yalung Ri, a viewpoint north-west of the pass, is easily climbable by its eastern glacier and attractive snow ridge. This might prove a useful acclimatisation day for those that need it.

From this camp climb towards the pass, gaining the snow and broad glacier slopes east of the pass. A second camp can be placed here before the glacier (5,500m/18,000ft). Climb

Ramdung seen from high camp on the Yalung Glacier, looking south-west at the route of ascent. This photograph was taken on the second ascent in 1955.

the slopes of the Ramdung Glacier south-west of the subsidary peak (Point 5,766m/18,917ft) and so gain the saddle at its head at its junction with the Yalung Glacier (5,650m/18,537ft).

From the saddle turn right, climbing gradually, at first southwards, to the foot of the summit block of Ramdung, which is climbed more steeply to the summit. This takes about four hours, depending on snow conditions, from Camp II. Descend by the same route.

PARCHAMO

The Nepal Mountaineering Association call this peak Parchemuche, a name by which, as far as I can find out, no one else knows it!

The peak, which lies due south of the Tesi Lapcha, is unnamed on the Schneider Rolwaling Himal map, but is given a spot height of 6,273 metres (20,581ft). The Mandala Lamasangu to Everest map calls the peak Parchoma,

which is quite possibly a spelling mistake. Both Shipton's and Gregory's expedition surveys gave the peak an altitude close to 6,318 metres (20,700ft).

Seen from the pass the mountain is an attractive but straightforward snow peak with a well defined north by north-west ridge rising from the relatively flat, crevassed glacier astride the Tesi Lapcha. To the west of the ridge the face forms a uniform snow slope broken by crevasses and small seracs rising from the rocky lower buttresses above the Drolambau Glacier.

The mountain had an interesting early history, some of which was outlined earlier in this chapter. It was finally climbed in 1955 by Dennis Davis and Phil Boultbee, members of the highly successful Merseyside Himalayan Expedition led by Alf Gregory. As well as climbing nineteen summits in and around the Rolwaling Valley, their explorations took them to the head of the Drolambau, where numerous peaks were climbed, up the Ripimu Glacier

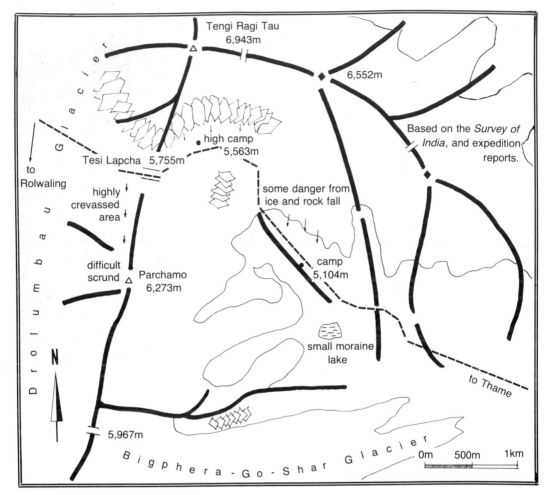

The map shows labels including:

Tengi Ragi Tau 6,943m
6,552m
Based on the *Survey of India*, and expedition reports.
high camp 5,563m
Tesi Lapcha 5,755m
to Rolwaling
highly crevassed area
some danger from ice and rock fall
difficult scrund
Parchamo 6,273m
camp 5,104m
small moraine lake
N
to Thame
5,967m
Bigphera-Go-Shar Glacier
Drolumbau Glacier
0m 500m 1km

PARCHAMO

and into the Menlung Basin via the Ripimu La. This was the most extensive exploration of the area first entered by Shipton that there has been, using a style of expedition, lightweight and free ranging, that alas is no longer possible within the kingdom of Nepal.

THE TREK

The approach to Parchamo from the west through the Rolwaling is no longer officially open to trekkers or mountaineers, with the result that the only practical approach is through the Khumbu via Namche Bazaar and Thame.

The Everest Base Camp trek should be followed from Lukhla or Kathmandu to Namche Bazaar. From Namche follow the trail past the gompa and then north-west around the edge of the spur forming the western side of the basin enclosing the village and contour above the Bhote Khosi to Phurte. Cross the stream and continue through Thomde, descending

Parchamo, seen from the Drolambau Glacier on the approach to the Tesi Lapcha.
The North Ridge follows the left skyline.

to the river which is crossed by a simple bridge. Climb a little to meet the Thame Khola entering from the left. Follow the trail along the stream which climbs through woods to the settlement of Thame amid stone-girt fields set in a broad valley. There are plenty of camping places with scenic views of Kangtega and Tramserku. There is also a checkpost in the village. In all the trek takes about four hours from Namche.

From the village, climb the main trail towards Thamo Teng, leaving that path at the top of the village to follow another trail westwards towards the gompa, passing mani and chorten on the way. Continue on this path west up the valley of the Thame Khola to the yersa at

Thengpo (4320m/14,173ft), which takes about two hours. There are good campsites in and below the settlement.

Leaving the river valley the path bears north-west after Thengpo, ascending around a spur of Tangi Ragi Tau, crossing a rock slide and then climbing grassy moraine below rock overhangs to a rock strewn area where there are possible campsites (4,849m/15,908ft); alternatively continue for a further hour on the moraine to Ngole where there are sheltered campsites beneath overhangs (5,100m/16,732ft). This is the best and most sheltered campsite below the icefall and before the sites below the pass.

Beyond Ngole the climb continues to

91

another possible campsite about one hour on (5440m/17,848ft), although rockfall from Tangi Ragi Tau is often a danger. Continue climbing north-east of the icefall from Tesi Lapcha over scree, often snow covered, to beneath the rock walls of Tengi Ragi Tau. There are possible campsites on rocky terraces with some protection from rockfall from the slopes above. High camp can be placed on these terraces. Other trekkers have forgone the dubious shelter of the rocks for a more exposed site on the open snows above the pass.

THE CLIMB

The north-west ridge was first ascended by Dennis Davis and Phil Boultbee on 18 April 1955.

From a high camp on or near the Tesi Lapcha cross wide, crevassed snow slopes to gain the obvious ridge of Parchamo, rising from the broken glacier of the pass. Some teams have gained the ridge by an obvious snow ramp.

The ridge is followed with little difficulty, although in some conditions crevasses might give problems towards the summit. Several parties have reported a difficult ice step caused by a large undercut crevasse about 300ft from the summit. This is the step that defeated Shipton, Gregory and Evans in 1951 on the first attempt. Descend by the same route. Overall grade Alpine PD+.

Setting out for the North Ridge of Parchamo from a high camp below Tesi Lapcha. The left skyline is the normal route of ascent.

Other Possibilities

The face above the Drolambau Glacier is very attractive and obviously has a great deal of potential, although because of access problems its ascent may not be practicable.

The Khumbu (east) face of the Parchamo is approachable and undoubtedly presents major problems, protected as it is by rock walls low down, and with a fluted icy headwall protected by a band of seracs.

9 Naya Kanga (5,844m/19,180ft) and Langtang Himal

Viewed from the hill above Kyangjin Gompa in the Langtang Valley, Naya Kanga is a shapely mountain rising to the west of the Ganja La (5,122m/16,800ft) which is a popular, although at times difficult, pass giving access to Helambu and the Kathmandu Valley. The normal route of ascent on Naya Kanga is via the North-East Ridge, an aesthetic line on snow and ice, classically alpine in character. Research has not revealed who made the first ascent despite the fact that several romantics would like to credit the ubiquitous Tilman with the feat. Naya Kanga was formerly called Ganji La Chuli.

A recent reclassification of boundaries by Hakur Gurung marks the Jugal Himal as those mountains south of the Langtang Khola, and the Langtang Himal as those mountains north of the river. Traditionally, Jugal Himal was understood to mean those mountains north and east of the Balephi Khola along the border with Tibet. If this new boundary is accepted, then Naya Kanga is in the Jugal rather than in Langtang Himal.

The Langtang valley lies roughly thirty kilometres north of Kathmandu quite close to the border with Tibet. Indeed one of the rewards of gaining the Ganja La or the summit of Naya Kanga is the superb views of peaks close to or in Tibet. The stunning panorama looking north-east over peaks in the Jugal Himal includes Lanshisa Ri (6,370m/20,899ft), Pemthang Ri (6,836m/22,428ft), and Pemthang Karpo Ri, or Dome Blanc (6,830m/22,412ft), to Shishapangma (8,046m/26,398ft) which is the highest peak in Chinese territory and the last of the 8,000 metre summits to be climbed.

The Langtang Valley was declared a national park in 1976 and remains the second largest in Nepal, covering approximately 1,700 square kilometres (660 square miles). Within its boundaries are some 45 villages, home to a people who are thought to have come from Tibet via Kyirong and who in turn have mingled with the Tamangs of Helambu. Despite the fact that they are similar in appearance to the Sherpas of the Solu/Khumbu, both they and their language are quite distinct and are said to resemble, much more closely, the Tibetians of Sikkim.

Whereas the major rivers of Nepal flow south from Tibet, cutting through the Himalayan chain, the Langtang Khola, a major tributary of the Trisuli Ganga, flows east to west, cutting, as it were, across the grain of the country. The Trisuli, or Bhote Khosi as it becomes above Dhunche, forms an important corridor and ancient trade route through the mountains between the Ganesh and Langtang Himal, to Kyirong in Tibet.

The lower Langtang is still heavily wooded with blue pine, oak, birch and bamboo. In the springtime the hillsides are heavy with rhododendron flowers. This abundant tree cover provides a good habitat for Nepal's increasingly rare wildlife. The park is the recorded home of more than 1,000 plants, some 160 bird species and 30 mammals. Included in these are the serow, goral and the rare red panda. Alas, despite having spent a lot of time looking for and photographing the former two, both goat-like antelopes, I've yet to get a glimpse of the panda.

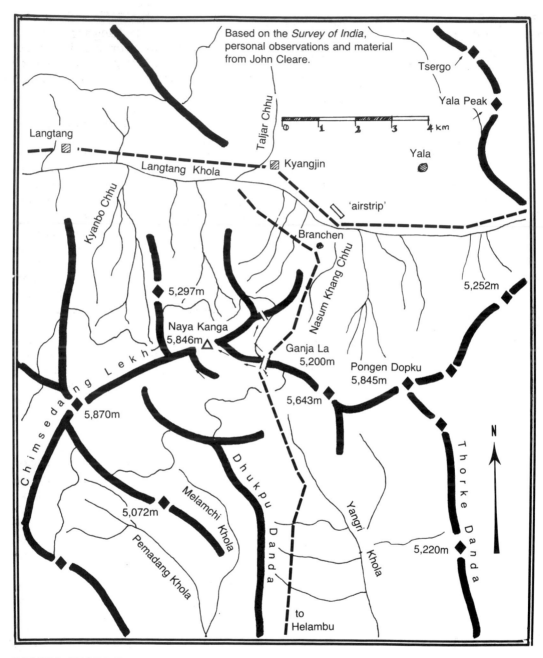

Based on the *Survey of India*, personal observations and material from John Cleare.

Tsergo

Yala Peak

4 km

Langtang

Taljar Chhu

Langtang Khola

Kyangjin

Yala

'airstrip'

Kyanbo Chhu

Branchen

Nasum Khang Chhu

5,297m

5,252m

Naya Kanga
5,846m

Ganja La
5,200m

Chimsedang Lekh

Pongen Dopku
5,845m

5,643m

5,870m

Dhukpu Danda

Thorke Danda

N

Melamchi Khola

5,072m

Yangri Khola

5,220m

Pemadang Khola

to
Helambu

NAYA KANGA

Naya Kanga North Face, seen across the Langtang Valley from near Yala. The North-East Ridge is the obvious line between sunshine and shade in the centre of the picture.

Above the tree line, the valley opens up beyond Gora Tabela, into a classical, glacial 'U' shape, bounded to the north by the impressive Langtang Himal, beyond which lies Tibet. The major peaks include Ghenge Liru (Langtang II 6571m/21,560ft), Langtang Lirung (7,425m/23,765ft), Kimshun (6,745m/22,137ft) and Shalbachum (6,918m/22,699ft). To the south, the Chimsedang Lekh forms a ridge of peaks which includes Naya Kanga and Gangchempo, Tilman's beautiful Fluted Peak. Beyond, it extends to the Jugal Himal, terminating in

Dorje Lakpa (6,980m/22,929ft). To the east the upper meadows of the Langtang end in a massive mountain wall, forming the frontier with Tibet. These are the peaks of Pemthang Karpo Ri, Pemthang Ri and Goldum that look so stunning from the Ganja La.

Langtang remained unknown and mysterious until Bill Tilman's exploration in 1949. That was the year the Himalayan Committee of the Royal Geographic Society and Alpine Club asked the Nepalese Government for permission to send a small expedition to the south side of Everest. They refused, but did allow Bill Tilman and Peter Lloyd into Langtang. Following Tilman came Toni Hagen in 1952, who did extensive geological surveys. Both ventured up the Langtang Glacier, probing for routes into Tibet. Tilman also found a pass beyond Gangchempo leading south to the Belephi Khola through the Jugal Himal to Kathmandu.

This is a difficult and adventurous journey through country rarely visited by trekkers. I returned to Kathmandu this way after a visit to Naya Kanga in 1980. It remains one of the finest journeys I've made in Nepal. The way is difficult, even after crossing Tilman's Pass, since several more passes have to be crossed high above the Belephi Khola on the east flank of the Panch Pokhari Lekh. These are magnificent hillsides of hemlock, oak and pine. During our trip, which was made particularly difficult by fresh snowfall, we saw several large herds of Himalayan tahr and the tracks of what we took to be snow leopard. Eventually the trail meets the highway near where the Belephi joins the Sun Khosi.

Another alternative is to go out via Panch Pokhari and Helambu. This same route also provides a marvellous approach to Langtang.

Despite today's ease of access now that the road goes up the Trisuli Valley as far as Dhunche, the valley still retains a hint of Shangri-La, possibly because of the nearness of Tibet and the untrekked wildness of Jugal.

95

Tilman's glorious Fluted Peak, Gangchempo, seen from the moraines above Kyangjin Gompa. Now out of bounds, the peak is rumoured to have been climbed from the south.

THE TREK

Trekking to Langtang

Most people visiting Langtang take the bus or a taxi from Kathmandu to Trisuli and either walk or bus the new road that goes as far as Dhunche. The route up the Trisuli Ganga has long been a trade route to Tibet as well as a trail for pilgrims visiting the holy lakes at Gosainkund and for trekkers going to Langtang. It certainly provides the quickest approach to the valley, and is well served with tea shops and lodges.

For those with the time who don't need to rely on bhatti (local inns) for food and lodging one of the most scenic and interesting approaches is from the south via the Thare Danda (also called the Turin Danda), Laurebina La and Gosainkund with a return journey over the Ganga La or Tilman's Pass to Kathmandu.

The trek north from Kathmandu via Gosainkund to Langtang follows a spectacular and well-defined ridge line marking the watershed between the Melamchi River and the Tadi Khola. Throughout the trek there are spectacular views of the Himalayan range to the north whilst to the south you look out across endless purple foothills toward and beyond the Kathmandu Valley.

Day 1: Sundarijal to Pati Bhanjyang

The trek begins at Sundarijal (1,379m/4,524ft), north-east of Kathmandu. Since the local bus

Looking toward the North-West Face of Mera Peak from the moraines north of
Dig Kharka.

The wonderful solitude of high camp on Paldor Glacier East.

A woman selling fruit in Durbhar Square, Kathmandu.

Mountain made for dreaming. A full November moon rising over Ama Dablam
at the time of Mani Rimdu.

Looking across the Kali Gandaki to the Dhaulagiri Himal from Poon Hill, truly a
trekker's peak and the most popular viewpoint on the Annapurna circuit.

Enthralled by the unfolding dance/drama of Mani Rimdu, Sherpas and
westerners sit watching in the central courtyard of Thyangboche Gompa.

A very traditionally-dressed old man from Langtang. The yak hide and wool boots are no longer a common sight amongst the Bhote people of Nepal.

Paldor; the South-West Face seen from the moraines above base camp. The left-hand skyline is the South-West Ridge; the right-hand ridge is the Cleare/Howell route.

On the summit ridge of Mera Peak, with the serac-like block of the Central Summit behind.

Ronnie Faux trying not to trip the light fantastic on Paldor.

Crossing the Annapurna South Glacier on the approach to Tent Peak. Beyond is
the spire of Machhapuchhare.

John Ball on the South Ridge of Kwangde Lho. (Photo: Trevor Pilling)

service only goes as far as Baudha you may want to hire a vehicle to transport your expedition to the road head which is three hours or so of walking further on.

At the road head, where leaking pipes from the hydroelectric power station emerge from the hill, assemble your caravan for the walk-in. Cross under the arch and, keeping the pipe on your right, begin the steep climb out of the Kathmandu Valley through damp forest. Pass a small reservoir and the Tamang village of Mulkharka (1,894m/6,214ft). Look out for the waterfalls below the reservoir. The trail tops the Shivapuri ridge soon after Chaubus at Burlang Bhanjyang (2,438m/8,000ft), where there is a good campsite which takes about three hours to reach from the road head.

From the pass, begin the descent via the Chepu Bhanjyang to Chisapani, through oak woods. The views of the Langtang and Jugal Himal to the north are spectacular. The descent continues through farmland to Pati Bhanjyang (1,768m/5, 800ft), astride the saddle that marks the watershed between the headwaters of the Likhu and Sindhu Kholas. You will need to have your trek permit checked at the police post. A very good new path has been built here.

Day 2: Pati Bhanjyang to Panghu Kharka

The route to Helambu descends north-east into the valley of the Melamchi Khola and provides a good alternative in bad weather to the ridge. It's also an alternative route for those wanting to make use of local bhattis or wishing to cross the Gangi La from the south.

Our route continues northward on the ridge to the village of Chipling (2,165m/7,100ft). Continue climbing beyond the settlement to a high point before the trail swings north-east and is followed in descent through forest to the Tamang village of Gul Bhanjyang (2,125m/ 7,025ft) in about 2 hours.

Beyond Gul Bhanjyang the climb starts almost at once, often quite steeply on the new path through forest and clearings, to reach a high point and the crest of the Khodang Dara (2,530m/8,300ft), and the wide new trail comes to an end. From here the trail descends through marvellous forest with open glades. Ahead you can see the Himal and the houses of Kutumsang (2,468m/8,100ft). This is the last place along the ridge where it might be possible to restock with some local provisions; although on my last trip along the ridge an enterprising local was selling tea and glucose biscuits, the staple of many a trekker, from one of the huts at Tharepati.

Beyond Kutumsang the main path stays close to the ridge, passing through numerous forest clearings and a small col with three chorten. Several of the clearings contain goth or shepherds' huts and give an ideal pitch for camp, although water is limited. The views along this section of the ridge are superb. The steep rocky descent from a notch at (3,400m/11,155ft) leads to Panghu Kharka (3,345m/10,974ft) and the site of an abandoned cheese factory where there is good camping.

Day 3: Panghu Kharka to Gopte

If the weather is in your favour stay on the trail closest to the Thare Danda ridge. During springtime the rhododendrons along this section of the route look superb.

A rough trail leads through the forest back to the crest of the Thare Danda and a col (3,337m/10,950ft). Again there are superb views of Jugal and Langtang Himal. The narrow ridge crest leads above the main forest to a high point where you may encounter snow early in the season.

Tharepati is the last group of huts just below the ridge to the west before the trail leaves the Thare Danda. In 1986 a sign pointed to Gosainkund from a notch where there was also a hut just north of a chorten. It took us about six

Sherpini porters load carrying along the Thare Danda on the trek to Gosainkund.
In the distance are the Langtang and Jugal Himals.

hours to go from Kutumsang to Tharepati (3,597m/11,800ft).

From here it is possible to make Gosainkund in a very long day. However, much more enjoyable is a camp an hour or so further on at Gopte. Follow the path north from Tharepati. This soon descends north-west before climbing around the head of the Tadi Khola. It is a good, but at times steep path through rugged country. The trail continues through dense rhododendron over boulders and beneath rock overhangs. After passing through a notch it eventually leads to a rock overhang known as Gopta's Cave (3,566m/11,700ft). In 1986 we actually camped here and were rewarded with distant views southward and a spectacular sunset. The Nepali word for cave is gupha so that Gopta, rather than being the name of a hermit that slept there, is more likely to be local dialect for cave or a cartographer's mistake.

Day 4: Gopta to Gosainkund

A couple of hours from Gopta the trail climbs around the hillside beneath several waterfalls. It crosses numerous large gullies that may be snow-covered. Eventually the trail gains a large hollow below the pass (3,694m/12,120ft) where there is a rocky ravine, a good campsite and water. The trail continues steeply north-west to the pass, the Laurebina La (4,609m/15,100ft).

The trail over the pass will most likely be under snow, with the lakes nearby frozen. Seen from above as you descend to Gosainkund you will understand why the lakes are indeed sacred. On a clear day they reflect the deep azure blue and turquoise of the sky. Be careful if there is a lot of snow about; your porters, wearing basketball boots at best, may have trouble with the descent. Be sure to look after them by kicking the trail and giving them a hand on the steep sections. Snow blindness can also be a problem and you should be

George Fowler looks out over the sparkling lake at Gosainkund below the Laurabina La.

prepared to equip your porters with dark glasses or goggles if you have to cross a lot of snow.

The trail skirts the northern shore of the lakes to reach a cluster of buildings and a lingum shrine (4,381m/14,375ft), that become, during the full moon between mid-July and August, the base for thousands of pilgrims, who come to worship Shiva who they believe created the lakes by thrusting his trident into the mountainside. The streams that gushed forth formed the lakes from which Shiva then quenched a thirst caused by drinking poison. Pilgrims believe that to bathe in the lakes is a way of gaining merit. I'm afraid to say that I gained none when I trekked past them on a crisp November morning after a fresh fall of snow!

Day 5: Gosainkund to Syabru

From the lake the route follows a fine traverse above the lakes of Nagkunda and Bhutkunda below the main lake of Gosainkunda. In under an hour the trail reaches an open ridge with a magnificent panorama to the west that includes Himalchuli, Peak 29, Manaslu and the Ganesh Himal. To the north and east the panorama continues with the Langtang and Jugal peaks. The path continues along the open ridge to a group of huts known as Laurebina (4,450m/14,600ft), just above the forest line on the crest of the ridge. Once again we were so impressed with the spot that we stayed put and made camp there – one of the joys of being self-contained.

Ahead, there are two possibilities for getting

Mother and child near Syabru drying millet on a sun baked terrace.

to Syabru. The most direct route continues down the ridge staying on the north flank where the path descends, quite steeply in places, on the Langtang side of the ridge to Syabru. The other route goes to Sing Gompa (3,254m/10,675ft) and the HMG cheese factory – Chalang Pati. The cheese made here and near Kyangjin Gompa in the Langtang is very good, so are the curds when they have them for sale. The trail to Sing Gompa follows the Syabru path initially on the north side of the ridge. Where the trail bears off right to Syabru there are some goth (3,520m/11,550ft). Continue down the ridge through a forest of fir and rhododendron. The path crosses to the south side of the ridge and before Sing Gompa enters open hillside with the scorched, black

trunks of trees devastated by fire. Beyond can be seen the glistening peaks of Ganesh.

From the gompa, contour the hillside through the forest to a clearing where the path from Dhunche enters. Bear right to the ridge to reach another clearing (3,124m/10,250ft), now in oak forest, where the path from Syabru joins. The left-hand trail continues down through terraces eventually to Bharku or Bhrabal. If you do take the wrong path, don't worry; all paths lead within an hour to a trail junction with a chorten and mani wall. To the left the trail leads to Bharku, whilst the path to the right takes you to Syabru.

Syabru (2,118m/6,950ft) is an attractive village, a mixture of Sherpas and Tamangs. Its houses straddle the ridge, almost part of its physical structure. The shingle rooftops stretched along its crest are like the overlapping scales of a beast. In the early morning when the sun creeps down the hillside across the Langtang Khola, smoke from the fires filters from the houses as the daily ritual of Nepali life begins. To the east of the village, a great amphitheatre of terraces contour the hillside providing a harvest of corn and millet that can be seen drying on the mud flats linking the houses.

Syabru is also the meeting of the ways and for the trekker who for a week or more has remained independent and self-contained hiking along the remote and largely unspoilt Thare Danda, it is something of a culture shock to meet up with other trekkers and to find bhattis selling beer, coke and pancakes.

On the west side of the village, where the path from Dhunche emerges, the ground on my last visit was littered with trekkers' waste; toilet paper and other refuse astride the trail where a source of water also provides the setting for the western preoccupation with washing! The whole thing is a terrible contradiction. It's as if the 'once in a lifetime' idea is taken too literally; 'I'm never coming back, so it doesn't matter'. Problems seem partly to stem from the bhattis. Few have adequate facilities for the increasing

The village of Syabru where the houses are like the overlapping scales of a beast clinging to the ridge.

numbers of trekkers that use them and there is no sewerage system in the hills. Nepalis squat in the corner of a field or use an earth closet or animal byre near their homes. Pink toilet tissue is a western nicety, that, dare I say it, leaves its mark on the mountains of Nepal. I would also say that by and large the organised trekking groups are better in this matter than the independant trekkers. Sherpa sirdars tend to make sure that latrines are dug and filled in and that overnight camps are cleared of rubbish. I don't think it's much to ask or expect for trekkers and expeditions to dig a hole or turn a stone, or perhaps even burn the used toilet tissue; after all a box of matches isn't a lot to carry along the trail.

Day 6: Syabru to Ghora Tabela

Onwards to Langtang; we have a mountain to climb. It is interesting and a little disconcert-

ing that the new (1987) Helambu-Langtang 1:100,000 map in the Schneider series doesn't mark the main trail on the south side of the Langtang Khola. But I can assure you there is one, and it is described below. During the 1987 monsoon the trail from Syabru was badly damaged and trekkers used the Syabrubensi connection on the north side of the river to get into Langtang. The original trail will obviously eventually be repaired and reinstated.

Drop down through the village past a great, lonely tree, contouring north-east across the terraced fields. The trail crosses a stream and climbs before descending to the Langtang Khola in one hour. Several bridges span the river at this point leading to Syabrubensi. Continue upstream on the south bank of the river through a gorge, after which you cross another tributary. The trail leads in a further 45 minutes to a bridge (2,042m/6,700ft). Cross this and climb through forest on the north

101

side of the Langtang Khola, and in an hour you meet the old trail from Syabrubensi. Before you reach the valley floor there are several places selling food and lodging. After a four hour climb from the bridge you reach Ghora Tabela (2,880m/9,450ft), once a Tibetian Refugee Resettlement Project. A lodge has been built and there are good camp sites. Ahead the glacial profile of the valley is evident, not unlike the Lauterbrunnen or Yosemite.

Day 7: Ghora Tabela to Kyangjing Gompa

The trail continues climbing north-east up the valley where there are several settlements and a gompa, which you should visit, on the two hour hike to Langtang village (3,307m/10,850ft). Langtang provides many facilities, and the National Park Headquarters are also here. Many trekkers have complained that the Langtangba are a sour bunch, but I've never had that experience, so I will leave you to make up your own mind.

The base for operations on Naya Kanga is a further two hours onwards and upwards at Kyangjin (3,749m/12,300ft) where there is a gompa and cheese factory, which like the others in Nepal was born of Swiss aid programmes. Kyangjin is in a superb location, and a camp here is dominated by the fluted North-West Face of Gangchempo.

Above Kyangjin to the north there are several hills that provide both spectacular viewpoints and good acclimatisation. The hill behind Kyangjin is called Kyangjin Ri (4,700m/15,420ft). North-east of this there are two glaciated peaks that provide good climbing and require no permit. They are Yala Peak (circa 5,500m/18,045ft) and Tsergo Peak (5,749m/18,861ft). A trail climbs steeply up moraines north-east from Chhongdu to Tharche before traversing to the yersa at Yala. A high camp can be placed in the meadows at the head of the Yala Chhu before the Yala Jhang Glacier.

Between Chhongdu and Marku is a STOL airstrip. Beyond that lies the upper Langtang yak pastures where you often see large herds

North-East Face of Naya Kanga showing the approach to the North-East Ridge.

Looking south to the Ganja La and Naya Kanga from the moraines above Yala.

of tahr grazing on the hillsides to the north. Exploration of the upper valley beyond the lonely hut at Langshisa kharka is well worth the effort. First explored by Tilman it remains little travelled. Those trekking out through the Jugal Himal via Tilman's Pass and the Belephi Khola turn south-east between the flanks of Langshisa Ri and Gangchempo to climb the massive moraines of the Langshisa Glacier towards Urkingmang (6,151m/20,195ft) and the distant col.

THE CLIMB

North-East Face and North Ridge

This is the standard route of ascent and the most obvious when looking at the mountain from the Langtang Valley. It is a classic snow and ice ridge.

From Kyangjin Gompa (3,749m/12,300ft), cross the Langtang Khola to Chhona and ascend the hillside through rhododendron forest towards the Ganja La via Branchen Kharka (4,100m/13,451ft). This provides a good site

103

for an alternative base camp for those that want to be higher.

A fast, well-acclimatised party will be able to climb the mountain and return to this camp in a day. Most parties, however, will find it an advantage to climb from a higher camp or bivouac below the North-East Face.

From base camp continue on the trail to Ganja La and gain the upper cwm filled by a glacier beneath the North-East Face by climbing steeply up moraine. Further adequate campsites are reached within thirty minutes. Continue following the Ganji La track, leaving it to climb steeply up yet more moraine to reach the eastern end of the prominent glacier shelf beneath the North-East Face of Naya Kanga (5,100m/16,732ft). Cross this glacier shelf to the foot of a shallow couloir leading to

North Ridge. Climb the couloir to the notch and the base of the ridge. Above, turn at the prominent ice nose on the left; this is the only technical section on the climb.

The ridge, now broad, leads to a small col on the east-west summit ridge, with the summit itself 30 metres (108 feet) higher on the right. The summit cone may be a bit precarious. This ascent will take between five and seven hours from high camp.

This is a route with little technical climbing, up relatively steep snow and ice slopes. Grade Alpine PD.

Other Possibilities

On the Helambu side of the Ganja La the mountain offers new routes with a variety of

Climbing to the Ganja La from the north in deep and difficult snow conditions.
To safeguard the porter we had to fix ropes to the col.

climbing challenges of increased difficulty and scope for new routes. A camp below the col, on the south side, provides an ideal base from which to explore the many alpine-scale peaks along the main Chimisedang Lekh in the glacier bowl west of the Ganja La and to the south of Pongen Dopku.

The pinnacled ridge rising from the Ganja La has been climbed from the south side by at least one commercial climbing group. Sir George Bishop, who was in the party, reports that it involved no particular technical difficulty.

Both myself and John Cleare have made new routes in this area. We have both also been involved in attempts on the South Face of Naya Kanga and have failed because of technical difficulty and available time.

The whole of the North Face to the right of the climbed ridge as you look at the mountain has immense possibilities, that would obviously be more difficult than the normal route but certainly not extreme.

RETURN TREK

The quickest return to Kathmandu is back to Syabru to pick up the main trail to Dhunche. From Dhunche it is possible to go by vehicle to Kathmandu in around six hours. Far more interesting and adventurous for those that have the time is a trek out from Langtang over Tilman's Pass through Jugal Himal and the Belephi Khola or over Ganja La and out through Helambu. Either will take around one week. After heavy snowfall both of these routes can be very difficult; for several days you will be in remote country and it is essential that all of your porters are well equipped and self-sufficient.

Ganja La and Helambu

From the high camp on Naya Kanga follow the trail towards the Ganja La, traversing steeply from right to left to the cairned summit of the pass (5,121m/16,800ft). There is a small glacier on the far side; descend to a camp by the second of two small lakes on the west side of the glacier below a spiky rognon. This is a rubble covered site.

If time allows a much better camping place for all concerned can be found at Keldrong Kharka (4,298m/14,100ft), a little over two hours further on.

Descend steeply from the glacier through moraines to the Kharka; this provides a first-class and very beautiful campsite just before where the wide, flat valley, below the glacier, plunges steeply down and the trail starts off across the steep east-facing hillsides of the

Climbing in the Langtang Himal with Gangchempo beyond.

Dukpu Danda. There is a cave for porters and the first water and wood is at 4,510 metres (14,800 feet).

Keldrong Kharka to the Kharka Before Dukpu

This is a good day's hike with a great deal of up and down walking through hillsides studded with kharka. There is little water until the last kharka before Dukpu (4,023m/13,200ft). The kharka can be recognised as being in a narrow cwm – facing east of course, from which bearings are 104 degrees to Chaduk Bir and 111 degrees to Numbur, with a big boulder just below the trail and a very smoke-blackened 'rock shelter' on its north flank. There is a steep ascent to a little col just before it, a steep descent into the cwm and a steep ascent to another little col immediately after. Water is five minutes down into the cwm. This is a reasonable site, with wood, water and good views. It is about six hours' walking from Keldrong.

The Kharka Before Dupku to Tarkeghyang

From the kharka it is another twenty minutes to Dupku at 3,993 metres (13,100 feet). There seems to be no water here post-monsoon. A final col is crossed, marked with chortens (4,054m/13,300ft), which is reached after nearly two hours, and then the long descent starts into Helambu. One hour from the final col (3,627m/11,900ft) there is a small clearing

Climbing the stepped glacier of Tsergo peak on the north side of the Langtang Valley. This provides perfect acclimatisation for Naya Kanga.

On the summit of Yala Peak in the Langtang.

on the narrow ridge crest after a long diagonal descent on the western side of the ridge, passing wooden water-troughs on the way. There is water here and an excellent camp site, discovered by John Cleare and Ian Howell in 1976. The small spring is 100 yards beyond the camp on the eastern flank of the ridge.

There have been recent landslips near Tarkeghyang and the final section of the trail past the gompa has been washed away leaving a slightly unpleasant, loose ravine to be crossed before the steep descent can be made to the camp site just above the village. This is quite a long and hard downhill day.

Tarkeghyang to Gyathum

The first leg of this part of the trek is downhill into the valley of the Melamchi Khola through heavily cultivated hillsides. A new wire-and-rope bridge has been built to replace the fragile old chain bridge where the trail crosses from the east to the west bank of the Melamchi, about an hour north of Talamarang. Continue on the main trail through cultivated country to Gyathum or thereabouts. In all it takes about eight hours from Tarkeghyang.

Gyathum to Pati Bhanjyang

The trail ahead is a well-used trade route. Travel through the village of Talamarang and up the river valley to the west and ascend through pretty country to the very scruffy village of Pati Bhanjyang; you are now back on the route already described. Follow that route back to Sundarijal and so back to the capital.

10 Ganesh Himal and Paldor (5,928m/19,450ft)

On a clear day the Ganesh Himal, with the icy fangs of Pabil (7,101m/23,300ft), Lobsang Karpo (7,150m/23,458ft), GI (7,406m/24,298ft) and GV (6,950m/22,802ft) can be seen forming an imposing backdrop to the north-west of Kathmandu. Paldor, which can just be picked out from the mass of shapely summits, was first climbed by Bill Tilman, Peter Lloyd, Tenzing Sherpa and Da Namgyal during the monsoon of 1949 by the North-East Ridge, although it must be said that it is difficult to fit Tilman's description to the actual route.

Paldor lies at the south-east end of the Ganesh Himal marking the junction of the Tiru and Khurpu Dandas at the head of the Mailung Khola, a tributary of the Trisuli Gandaki.

The name Ganesh is taken from the elephant-headed Hindu god of good luck, probably the most popular deity in the Kathmandu valley. As the son of Shiva and his consort Annapurna, or Parvati, his head was severed by his father who then promised to replace it with the first head that came to hand; the first happened to be an elephant's. Images of Ganesh, sitting astride a shrew, can be seen all over the valley. Since he can cast aside obstacles, his help is invoked whenever a difficult task is to be undertaken. Think on!

TREKKING TO GANESH

The quickest route of approach is via the new road as far as Dhunche in the Trisuli Valley, about six hours by truck from Kathmandu. Above Dhunche the trail is followed on the east bank crossing the bridge over the Langtang Khola to Syabrubensi. The main river, now the Bhote Khosi, is crossed by a rickety suspension bridge just north of the village. A path is then followed via Thangjet and Gatlang, crossing the Karpu Danda via a small col. It then heads northward along the ridge before dropping into the forest above the Mailung Khola to pick up the newly built road that leads to an army post. Beyond this the trail climbs, via a big mine at the head of the valley. Above and beyond is base camp in a moraine-filled valley below the South Face of Paldor. This can be covered in less than a week from Kathmandu.

There is a direct route to the mine at Lari, that follows the Mailung Khola, taking about five days from Trisuli. A much more interesting and enjoyable approach is the trek from Sundarijal to Gosainkund and Syabru, described in the chapter on Naya Kanga and the Langtang. Following this trek it takes five days to reach Syabru.

Day 6: Syabru to Thangjet

From Syabru a trail descends north-west above the Langtang Khola to the bridge at Syabrubensi. Follow the path through Syabrubensi (1,462m/4,800ft) toward the Bhote Khosi. Across the river, on the hillside opposite, the desolation left by the building of the new road is well in evidence. When I last trekked through here large boulders regularly avalanched down the hillside following explosions high up on the ridge. For those trekkers that failed to gain

A fine featured Nepali woman selling apples.

merit by bathing in the lakes at Gosainkund and are now in need of a hot bath, just a short way downstream on the west bank there is a hot spring below some old mine buildings. Cross the Bhote Khosi by the suspension bridge just beyond the village – this might still be in need of some new planking. However, the largest holes are capped by larger stones and where these are missing the view of the river, a long way below, is quite moving!

Those having a break from hot baths, believing an oily skin is good protection from the cold, should turn right over the bridge and head upstream by a path that seems to get washed out every monsoon. However, it is an attractive route. Follow it, traversing around the foot of the spur into the valley of the Chilime Khola. Cross the river by a suspen-sion bridge to the north bank and follow a path upstream to another large suspension bridge by which you re-cross to the south-bank, passing through Gholjong Sango, where the valley now widens. The trail follows a well-engineered water channel and leads eventually to Thangjet (1,676m/5,500ft), near the confluence of the Chilime and Brindong Kholas. Surprisingly, this fairly large village is not marked on the recent Schneider map. There is good camping, in terraced fields with some fine chorten, near the village

A trail is said to exist that crosses the Jarsa Danda to Thangjet, but I couldn't find it and in any case the new road may have spoilt that particular way. Local help should be sought with regard to the new road.

Day 7: Thangjet to Yuri Kharka Camp

The people of the Brindong Khola's main village of Gatlang (2,438m/8,000ft), are a colourful and interesting community, although some trekkers have reported an unfriendly welcome; but then they see so few visitors that their caution is understandable. They appear to be a mixture of Tamangs and a more recent Tibetan influence. Despite the nearness of the new road and the relative proximity of Trisuli they seem little influenced by outsiders and are highly individualistic in their style of dress. The valley has extensive terracing and is agriculturally prosperous with rice, millet and corn as well as large herds of buffalo and goats.

The trail climbs steeply through terraced hillsides to Gatlang, passing mani-walls piled with carved stones and lotus flower mandalas. All along the route the glistening mica schist, into which the runnes are cut, shine out the mantra: Om Mani Padme Om. Said softly under the breath it sets a perfect cadence for climbing the hills of Nepal. Out of respect for local custom do remember to pass the mani on their left side. Looking back along the trail the Langtang Himal dominates the skyline.

Gatlang is a crowded village with stone-built houses huddled together. The smoke of cooking fires perpetually filters through the wooden tiled roofs to mingle with the prayer flags that drape from bamboo wands. Man, animals and mountainside are so closely bound that none seem to have an identity separate from the other. It will be interesting to see what changes the new road, built on the ridge above the village, will have on this until now isolated community.

Beyond Gatlang the trail enters into forest; permits may be checked at an army post below Yuri Kharka, a small clearing with running water.

Day 8: Yuri Kharka to Camp Below Lari Mine

Beyond the kharka the trail continues through the forest climbing steeply to a notch, the Kurpadanda Bhanjyang (3,739m/12,267ft), shown as Paldol Bhanjyang on some maps. From the ridge there are fine views from the Annapurnas in the west to the Langtang and beyond in the east. On the far side of the Mailung Khola is the ridge of the Tiru Danda and the pass of Pansing Bhanjyang. These provide the best walk-out from Paldor.

From the Kurpa Danda Bhanjyang follow a path north along the crest at first and then traverse the steep hillside on the west flank. The path is quite spectacular in places but soon descends into the pine forest to meet the new road. Follow the road for a while, which is being extended to the army post at Samathang where there is a radio; we found the soldiers to be a friendly and chatty bunch. Continue up the main valley by the stream. All along the path there are thousands of small garnets and other minerals. Toward the head of the valley the path steepens, climbing on the right side of the stream. Fine waterfalls enter from the right. There are several campsite possibilities close to the trail at this point.

Day 9: Lari Mine Camp to Base Camp

Climb steeply to the mine at Lari which has a variety of buildings and tramways. On our visit they were very secretive about what they were actually taking from the hill; it is rumoured to be manganese. There is a radio at the mine, and a helicopter landed nearby whilst we were on the mountain.

Beyond the mine, climb steeply above the gorge of the river. The path, quite rocky in places, climbs between outcrops and traverses north-eastwards to a small valley bounded by moraines below the glaciers of Paldor. Base

A Gurung mother and child with a traditional swinging baby basket.

camp can be sited here, below the confluence of the Paldor West and Paldor East glaciers just north of a fine rock pinnacle that Cleare called 'Neddy's Thumb', at an altitude of 4,500 metres (14,900 feet). There is a good supply of running water.

CLIMBING IN THE PALDOR AREA

The area around Paldor provides an ideal location for an alpine-style climbing holiday. As well as Paldor, for which a permit is required, there are several lower peaks, both rock and ice, that provide good climbing in a long day from base camp or a high camp. I am grateful to both John Cleare and Dr Hamish Nicol for detailed accounts of their explorations and ascents in the area. Indeed most of the names

now adopted for many of the small peaks around Paldor were given by Cleare and later added to by Nicol. The latter also produced the first interim guide to the Paldor region, which was circulated to a few friends in the Alpine and Climbers Club.

From a high camp the routes on the mountain are not long, although all have some technical interest, usually on snow or ice. Tilman's Ridge is marginally the easiest climb. Both the North-East and South-East Ridges can be climbed from the same high camp on the Paldor Glacier East.

Paldor

North-East Ridge (Tilman's Ridge)

From base camp, follow a path below the conspicuous moraine on its east side as far as

111

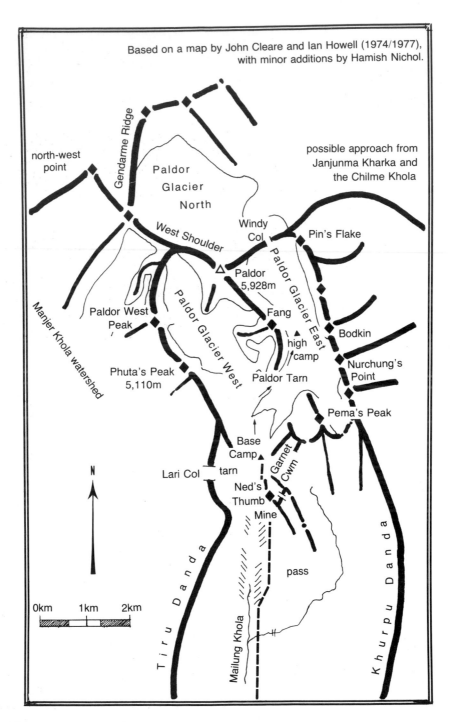

Based on a map by John Cleare and Ian Howell (1974/1977), with minor additions by Hamish Nichol.

north-west point

Gendarme Ridge

Paldor Glacier North

possible approach from Janjunma Kharka and the Chilme Khola

Windy Col

Pin's Flake

West Shoulder

Paldor Glacier East

Paldor 5,928m

Paldor West Peak

Paldor Glacier West

Fang

high camp

Bodkin

Nurchung's Point

Phuta's Peak 5,110m

Manjer Khola watershed

Paldor Tarn

Pema's Peak

Base Camp

Garnet Cwm

Lari Col

tarn

Ned's Thumb

Mine

pass

N

Tiru Danda

Mailung Khola

Khurpu Danda

0km 1km 2km

PALDOR

112

High camp on the Paldor Glacier East.

Paldor Tarn. Here there is a small and inconspicuous lake to the south of the peak called Fang. Cross the stream issuing from the lake and aim for the scree and boulder slope which lies to the east of the East Ridge of Fang. This boulder slope is the true right bank of the lower third of the Paldor Glacier East. High camp can be placed just east of the Fang on the Paldor Glacier East at an altitude of 5,200 metres (17,060 feet), in a magnificent amphitheatre of alpine-scale peaks. Porters on previous expeditions are reported to have reached this camp in gym shoes. On my own expedition (post-monsoon 1985), we were in deep snow at base and crampons and axe were required to reach this camp. The glacier at this point is flat and uncomplicated by crevasses.

From high camp follow the Paldor Glacier East, without difficulty, north towards a col on the North-East Ridge (Windy Col). Cross the bergscrund and climb a steep snow slope to gain the col. This may be very difficult, in which case ascend the slope to the left, climbing diagonally towards a rocky pinnacle. This was hard ice when we climbed it in November 1985 and it felt quite exposed.

Once on the ridge, climb over several pinnacles of loose rock leading to a horizontal snow arête that narrows dramatically. Follow this to the foot of the final 150 metre (492 feet) headwall. Ascend this on steep snow to the junction of the South-East Ridge, which may be corniced. Continue easily to the summit. Descend by the same route. This is Alpine AD climbing and takes five to seven hours from high camp.

South-East Ridge

This was first climbed by John Cleare and Ian Howell in 1974. Between Tilman's ascent in 1949 and Cleare's expedition of 1974 it is possible that Paldor had no other ascents. Since then the mountain has received more attention and many new routes added.

This route climbs the long snow and ice arête that descends to the fine rock peak of Fang. The lowest point of this ridge is best reached, from a high camp on the Paldor Glacier East, by a steep snow and ice slope (55 degrees). Depending on season and conditions, various parties have found it to vary from difficult and dangerous to straightforward!

The ridge has also been reached via a potential avalanche couloir from the Paldor Glacier West. The ridge above is followed, in places quite steeply, but without major difficulty to the summit. Alpine AD+.

A combination of both these routes has been made as a traverse and is highly recommended.

George Fowler and Ronnie Faux traversing Tilman's Ridge on Paldor. Beyond to the left is the peak of Shishapangma, the highest mountain in Tibet and the last 8,000 metre summit to be climbed.

South-West Buttress

The first ascent of the South-West Face via the Central Buttress was made in 1986 by Sandy Allen, although most of the route had been climbed previously by Sherpas.

This is a route of little technical difficulty and poor protection. Serac fall danger is reported to be minimal. From a high camp below the face ascend the right-hand side of the central buttress, avoiding rock steps to reach the spur which connects the buttress to the face. Follow this to join the upper face (45 – 50 degrees) which is then followed to the summit, ascending diagonally rightwards to avoid the bergscrund. This was climbed in under three hours on the first ascent. Alpine D.

West Ridge

First ascent was by Nick Yardley, Gareth Yardley and Dave O'Dowd on 6 November 1986.

From a high camp on the Paldor Glacier West cross the bergscrund to gain the col below the ridge where the Tiru Danda in fact abuts on to the South-West Face of Paldor.

From the col a snow arête is followed until it merges with the face. Above, snow gullies which are steep in places (55 degrees) are followed for 200 metres after which you weave through broken rocky outcrops to reach a final slope leading to the West Shoulder. From the shoulder a ridge is then followed to the summit, which was reached after three hours' climbing from a high camp.

A snow arête leads from the col and merges into the face. Snow gullies are followed for 200 metres until a series of broken rock outcrops leads to the final snow slope. The ridge above is followed to the top. Technically straightforward but poorly protected with some loose rock. Alpine D+.

A view from high on the South-West Ridge of Paldor looking into the valleys of the Ankhu Khola system.

OTHER CLIMBS IN THE PALDOR AREA

The area around the Paldor base camp has numerous small peaks around 5,000 meters in height that have provided some interesting climbing with scope for exploring new lines. The peaks are both unnamed and unmarked on official maps and the names used are those given by the first ascensionists. They are given here to complete the picture of climbing in the area and as climbable viewpoints of relatively low altitude do not require a permit.

Fang, South Ridge

This is the obvious rock peak terminating the South-East Ridge of Paldor and is separated from it by the col which has to be gained when making an ascent of the Cleare/Howell ridge. It is a pleasant climb over mixed ground although there is a certain amount of loose rock.

From a high camp on the Paldor Glacier East cross snow slopes to gain the South Ridge of Fang above the first pinnacle, after which the ridge is followed passing a series of pinnacles both to left and right until the summit is gained.

Descent can be made down the East Face by an awkward 50 metre abseil from the summit into a couloir from which the East Glacier is easily gained. In all it takes about five hours for the round trip. The first ascent was made by Nick Yardley, Gareth Yardley and Dave O'Dowd.

Phuta's Peak (5,110m/16,765ft), South Ridge

Clearly seen from base camp this peak lies on the Tiru Danda Ridge, and is the highest visible point west of Paldor. The mountain can be climbed easily from base camp by its south ridge in about three hours. A good training climb.

Paldor West Peak (5,500m/18,045ft), South Face

First climbed in 1980 by Sir George Bishop, the peak of Paldor West is not visible from base camp. Paldor West lies to the north of and is obscured by Phuta's Peak.

It is probably best to use a high camp on the Paldor Glacier West. This is highly crevassed and should be treated with respect. From this camp the peak can be climbed easily by its South Face, which is a scree and rock slope.

Between Phuta's Peak and Paldor West are numerous rock pinnacles that would provide interesting sport.

Pema's Peak (5,300m/17,388ft)

This is an attractive mountain which lies to the south-east of the ice-fall descending from the Paldor Glacier East. Its southern ridges form the eastern boundary of the cirque in which the high camp for Paldor lies. Fang guards this ice fall to the north-west, Pema's Peak guards it to the south-east.

West Glacier and South Ridge

First ascent was by T. Leggett, H.G. Nicol, A. Wedgwood and Ang Danu in 1984. From base camp climb a wide, easy scree-filled gully to the east of base camp and directly opposite to it. At 4,800 metres (15,748 feet), you reach a small, flattened hump which from below looks

Approaching Paldor Glacier East from base camp.

like a peak (Roger's Peak). At this point turn north and follow the obvious line of scree-filled valley which lies between the Pema's Peak South Ridge on the right, forming the right hand skyline, and the broken ridge on the left, which overlies the base camp. The little valley is unmistakable and leads without incident to Pema's Peak West Glacier. The foot of this glacier could also be reached direct by ascending a steep scree-filled gully which climbs up to it from the boulder fields just to the north of base camp, but this looks unpleasant.

Put on crampons and follow this glacier without incident or difficulty to the col at its summit. Turn north-west and climb the ridge to the summit. Standard Alpine PD, which can be climbed in four hours on the first ascent.

East Flank by the Paldor Glacier East

From the base camp follow the route to Paldor high camp on the Paldor Glacier East. At 5,200 metres (17,060 feet), the glacier is relatively uncrevassed and can be crossed easily. Cross it to the east side below Bodkin Peak. At this point turn south, contour round the easy glacier, climb a short snow slope and so ascend easily to Pema's summit.

Neddy's Thumb (4,900m/16,076ft)

This is the first peak to be seen of the Paldor group as you approach the area from the south up the Mailung Khola. It forms an impressive rock peak rising above and to the south of base camp. Due to the nature of the rock the best climbs are to be found on the South Face.

South Ridge

The route described was first climbed by T. Leggett and A. Wedgwood 1984. This provides a straightforward rock climb (UIAA grade 111).

From base camp walk easily round the west side of the Thumb to a notch on the South Ridge overlooking the Mailung Khola. Climb directly up the South Ridge to the summit. Descent can be made to the col on the east side and then back down scree to base camp.

Sgurr Lhakpa (4,700m/15,420ft), North Ridge

The first ascent was by H.G. Nicol, T. Leggett and Lhakpa Gyalu in 1984. This peak lies on the Tiru Danda due-west of base camp. An attractive, jagged peak, it looks like a piece of the Cuillin Ridge in Skye. However, it is not made of gabbro and the rock gnasty! In spite of this it makes a very pleasant half-day excursion from base camp.

From base camp, contour westwards across moraines. Then strike across the steep hillside above the ruined mine buildings at Lari. Beyond Lari climb to an obvious col to the north of Sgurr Lhakpa, where there are numerous cairns and mani-stones and views into the Ankhu Khola. Turn south and climb the rocky ridge, following its ups and downs, taking the easiest line (UIAA 111) to the summit.

THE RETURN TREK

The new road will obviously provide the quickest return for those that are running out of time; or, indeed, you can retrace your steps to Syabrubensi and continue to Dhunche and try to hire a truck back to Trisuli. But there is a much finer alternative for those that can prolong the journey for another week and want to enjoy some of the finest high ridge rambling in Nepal; the Tiru Danda.

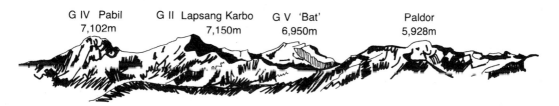

G IV Pabil	G II Lapsang Karbo	G V 'Bat'	Paldor
7,102m	7,150m	6,950m	5,928m

The Ganesh Himal seen from high on the Tiru Danda to the south-south-west, some 23km (14 miles) distant. There are seven major Ganesh peaks, but the others remain hidden from most southern directions. From a drawing by John Cleare.

Ian Evans and George Fowler skywalking on the airy Tiru Danda, north of Pansing Bhangjang.

West of the Mailung Khola the valley is bounded by a high ridge that terminates in the peak of Paldor itself. Traversing this ridge on the walk out to Trisuli is, for several days, delightful, with magnificent and extensive views not only of the main Ganesh Himal to the north, but also of Manaslu (8,156m/ 26,638ft), Peak 29 (7,871m/25,706ft) and Himal Chuli (7,893m/25,895ft) to the north-west. Beyond them, still further to the west, you see the peaks of the Annapurnas. Eastward from the ridge there are yet more views of the Langtang and Jugal Himals.

Day 1: Base Camp to Pansing Bhanjyang

From base camp retrace the ascent route to the army camp in the Mailung Khola. Continue down the west bank of the river and climb through forest to a pass on the Tiru Danda, the Pansing Bhanjyang (3,822m/12,540ft). The trail that leads to the meadow and huts below the pass is spectacular, with stunning views across

the valley over the Khurpa Danda to the Lang-tang beyond. There is a kharka with huts below the pass on the east side, with good camping.

For those with the time it is well worth camping at the huts and spending a day exploring the Tiru Danda north of the Pass. The springy turf makes for ideal tramping and the faint path along the ridge top is superb and barely worn, although you will find the odd prayer flag and mani stone on higher points left by local herders. Whilst we were on this walk a lonely Lamageiyer, riding the ridge thermals, came to see what we were about; few trekkers pass this way. You may well find a lot of snow along the ridge.

Day 2: Pansing Bhanjyang to Wading

Camping places with water along the crest are strictly limited. From the kharka climb to the pass and the trek south along the Tiru Danda, a spectacular trail through rhododendron forest and open meadows and kharka. The thickly forested hillsides are full of rhododendron and the spring show is spectacular. Follow the main crest until a path trending north-west leads toward the Ankhu Khola on the north side of a spur of the main Tiru Danda. Follow this down and across a heavily wooded hillside to some huts and a good water supply in a forest clearing at Wading (3,700m/12,139ft). The path eventually leads into the Ankhu Khola and Tipling village.

The view of the Ganesh Himal rising above the deep, cloud-filled valley of the Ankhu, is awesome; especially so with moonlight reflecting from the cloud, bathing their icy southern flanks in its cold light.

Day 3: Wading to Rupchet Kharka

Regain the Tiru Danda at Singla Bhanjyang. The ridge is followed, often steeply, along its undulating crest until it terminates abruptly at a clearing with spectacular views from the Annapurnas to the Ganesh. From here the path descends very steeply through a marked cleft on the west side of the ridge (circa 4,000m/13,000ft), cutting through a subsidiary spur which leads in turn to a clearing. We camped in the clearing at Rupchet. On a clear day this gives walking second to none. As with many of the high ridges, snow may persist until late in the season.

Day 4: Rupchet Kharka to Bumdang

The trail continues down through forest towards the terraced valley of the Salankhu Khola and the village of Gonga. It was whilst descending from the ridge that myself and a porter were shocked rigid by a Himalayan Black Bear that crashed through the trees and cut across the path a yard in front of us, only to vanish, smashing through the dense forest below the trail.

A path can be followed to Gonga and then south-east to the village of Bhalche in the Salankhu Khola to the trail to Trisuli above the west bank of the Trisuli Khola, or alternatively you can cross the Trisuli to the east bank on a path that joins the new road at Betrawati.

A more interesting route can be hiked, which leads south-west from Bhalche across the Salankhu through interesting terraced farm land via Bumdang.

Day 5: Bumdang to Trisuli

This is a long day and can obviously be split. From the village the trail traverses steep terraced hillsides and a ridge by an impressive notch that had numerous mani stones, prayer flags and chorten above a natural rock arch. The trail then leads to the valley of the Samrie Khola, which is often steep, and in places rocky. Eventually it leads through cultivated fields and continuous settlements to the hubbub and civilization of Trisuli Bazaar which, after weeks in the high mountains, will seem as much a culture shock as your eventual return to the west! The trail along the Samrie Khola is the main trade route west to Ghorka.

ALTERNATIVE RETURN TREK

Should the Tiru Danda prove to have too much snow for safe travel, instead of heading south along the ridge at Pansing Bhanjyang follow the main trail, albeit narrow and in places steep, into the forest, westwards above the Linju Khola. The path goes through several kharka and becomes rocky, although less steep, as it continues through attractive woodland to the edge of the forest (circa 2,529m/8300ft).

Continue descending through terraces to the village of Tiblung (2,118m/6,950ft). Beyond the village the trail steepens and becomes rocky as it drops for over 300 metres through

Moonrise over a peak in the Ganesh seen from base camp on Himalchuli.

an impressive gorge; the hearties in the party might be interested in a swim in pools at the bottom. Beyond, the trail makes a steep and sometimes dusty climb to the village of Serthung (1,981m/6,500ft), where there is good camping.

The route now continues through terraced hillsides. The trail is often impressive both in its steepness and for the views back to the main Ganesh range. Below are the gorges of the Anku and Manjar rivers that meet near the settlement of Barang (Burang on some maps, 1,646m/5400ft). The trail continues along the true left bank of the Anku through terraces and numerous houses. The trail crosses two major landslides where care should be taken as the footing is loose. Campsites along this section of the trail are limited.

Soon, the trail descends into the precipitous gorge of the Churing Khola (1,146m/3,760ft), where the dust of the last days' hiking can be washed away, followed by a sweaty climb out of the valley! Continue traversing around hillsides to the village of Khuri (1,645m/5,400ft). The way ahead undulates through cultivated

terraced farmland before turning eastwards at Darkha (1,707m/5,600ft). The route now continues in the Chimtang valley, a tributary of the Anku, through numerous small villages and settlements before it eventually descends into the gorge of the Chimtang Khola. Numerous possible campsites can be found after the steep climb out of the gorge.

Continue climbing steeply up the hillside, which is still terraced, to the linear village of Chimtang (1,706m/5,600ft). The way beyond now crosses scrubby hillside into an attractive small valley forested but with open glades. The river is crossed by a bridge, after which a steep trail ascends through forest to Mergang Bhanjyang (2,081m/6,830ft).

Continue along the hillside on the southwestern flank of the ridge, which in spring is a mass of flowering rhododendron, until you reach the village of Dhurale (1,640m/5,380ft). Just below the village the path from Bumdang is joined and is followed in descent to the Samrie Valley and the main Trisuli/Ghorka trail. Turn east to the 'fleshpots' of Trisuli.

11 Mardi Himal (5,555m/18,225ft)

Less than fifteen miles north of Pokhara, as the crow flies, this mountain is the most southerly of the Annapurna range. From some viewpoints it seems little more than an outlier on the south-west flank of Machhapuchhare. Mardi Himal is the lowest and perhaps least climbed or visited of the trekking peaks.

The attention of western mountaineers was first drawn to Mardi Himal by the photographs of Basil Goodfellow, taken in 1953. However, it was not until 1961 that the mountain received its first ascent. Once again it was Jimmy Roberts who, with two Sherpas, climbed to the summit by a route on its East Flank. Although there are rumours that another route has been made on the South-West Face, Roberts' route is the only recorded line and the one used on subsequent, known ascents.

Best seen from the south, the mountain terminates the South-West ridge of Machhapuchhare as a distinct and separate mass, at right-angles to that ridge. On Mardi Himal's South-West Face are three well-defined ridges rising from rock buttresses and separated by hanging glaciers. It is the most southerly of these that is said to have been climbed, but no details are available.

Mardi Himal's East Face is separated from Machhapuchhare ridge by a col (circa 5,200m/17,060ft). The normal route of ascent reaches this col from a glaciated amphitheatre that rises above a hidden plateau; the 'Other Sanctuary', as Roberts calls it.

Obviously, the peak has a commanding view of the Annapurna Range and undoubtedly a spectacular one of the Himalayan Matterhorn, Machhapurchhare. Few westerners visit the valleys and ridges south of Mardi Himal. They are steep sided and heavily wooded with bamboo and rhododendron. Above the forest, high alpine pastures provide good grazing and a habitat for undisturbed wildlife. Despite its lowly altitude the mountain obviously has a great deal of potential for those interested in small-scale exploratory mountaineering and the ridges already mentioned present obvious climbing challenges at a reasonable standard.

MARDI HIMAL TREK AND THE OTHER SANCTUARY

This rarely visited area provides a tough trek removed from the tea houses and lodges which dominate most of the trekking in and around the Annapurna Range. The trail to base camp is short and sharp on ill-defined trails that would be particularly difficult in wet and snowy conditions. I'm grateful to Robin Marston for supplying details of this approach.

Day 1: Pokhara to Mardi Pul

The trek begins in Pokhara. Whatever way you choose to get there from Kathmandu, the road leads north through the town to the Shining Hospital. Porters and equipment are usually massed here in the dusty field and whether you have driven or flown from Kathmandu there should be time the same day to get to Mardi Pul ('the bridge'), 1,050 metres/3,444ft, which is about three hours' walking from Pokhara.

Start up the busy trail to Hyenja, past the ribbon development of the ever-growing suburbs of Pokhara and the new water irrig-

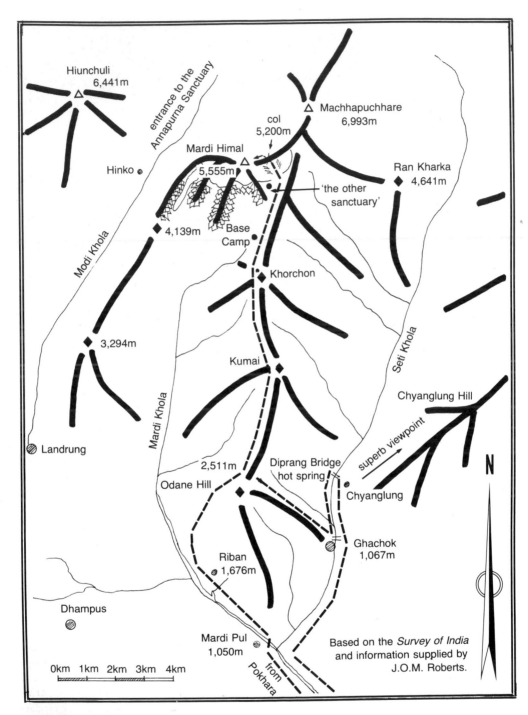

Hiunchuli
6,441m

entrance to the Annapurna Sanctuary

col
5,200m

Machhapuchhare
6,993m

Mardi Himal
5,555m

Hinko

Ran Kharka
4,641m

'the other sanctuary'

4,139m

Base Camp

Modi Khola

Khorchon

Seti Khola

3,294m

Kumai

Chyanglung Hill

Mardi Khola

Landrung

2,511m

Odane Hill

Diprang Bridge
hot spring

superb viewpoint

Chyanglung

Ghachok
1,067m

Riban
1,676m

Dhampus

Mardi Pul
1,050m

from Pokhara

Based on the *Survey of India*
and information supplied by
J.O.M. Roberts.

N

0km 1km 2km 3km 4km

MARDI HIMAL

122

Mardi Himal, showing the triple ridges of the South and South-West Face rising above the cloud-filled Other Sanctuary. The route gains the right-hand ridge and follows snow slopes to the summit.

ation project. This is a major trade route and is usually bustling with trekkers; the pale pink variety, just starting on their journey and the serious-faced striding kind, returning from their Annapurna pilgrimage. As well as the westerners, the road carries a multitude of locals travelling to and from Pohkara with strings of ponies trading as far as Mustang and an assortment of Indian and Russian vehicles churning up the dust en route to Suikhet near the head of the Yamdi Khola.

Shortly after passing the original Tibetian Refugee Camp the trail divides. Take the right-hand branch which leads north across paddy fields and then follows the west bank of the Seti Khola. Follow the trail to where it drops down to the river just after the confluence of the Seti and Mardi Kholas and cross the small bridge which leads to the village of Mardi Pul. There is an excellent camp site on the west bank of the river just above the bridge.

Day 2: Mardi Pul to Odane Hill

The trail then follows the east bank of the Mardi upstream before turning right up the hill to the Gurung village of Riban (1,676m/ 5,500ft). This is a good place to stop for lunch as water is in short supply higher on the trail.

Ahead the route becomes much steeper as it climbs uphill from the village, past a chautaara, shortly after which the trail divides. Take the right-hand fork which leads past some cow sheds. Until now the trail has been steep, now it becomes even steeper! Climb through bamboo forest towards a massive slab of grey rock. The path bears round to the left on to the rhododendron-covered ridge.

Despite the steepness of the route the ridge-line path offers ever-increasing views of the surrounding country. The path passes through a small clearing, Lalghar Kharka, and continues along a faint track to another clearing marking

A woman in the Pokhara Valley harvesting rice, the staple food of lowland Nepal.

a high point on the ridge. This is Odane Hill (2,510m/8,232ft); in all this is a climb of 1,500 metres (4,921ft) and Odane Hill provides a good campsite with water. This is a full hard day of mostly uphill walking.

Day 3: Odane Hill to Kumai

The route continues along the ridgeline, but beware false trails that can lead you astray! The reward of the previous day's hard work is cool mountain air and a stunning panorama, with Machhapuchhare (6,997m/22,950ft) straight ahead. To the west is Annapurna I (8,078m/ 26,495ft), towering above Annapurna South (7,273m/23,527ft) and Hiunchuli (6,336m/ 20,782ft), the western bastion guarding the entrance to the Annapurna Sanctuary. To the east are views of the granite mass of Annapurna

II (7,937m/26,033ft), Annapurna IV (7,525m/ 24,682ft) and Lamjung Himal (6,986m/22,914ft), like the bulk of a sleeping elephant. Further east beyond the Marsyangdi are the triple giants of Manaslu (8,156m/26,751ft), Peak 29 (7,835m/25,706ft) and Himalchuli (7,540m/ 24,731ft). Given that the distant summit snows of Dhaulagiri (8,167m/26,787ft) can also be seen, three of the world's highest mountains are on view along this trek.

Water shortage presents a bit of a problem on this section of the route, so water-bottles should be full and re-filled where possible.

Eventually a short, sharp climb leaves the main forest behind and leads to a fine camping area amid alpine grass land. This is another tough day, taking about seven hours from Odane Hill.

The sacred summit of Machhapuchhare dwarfing the Mardi Himal, which rises in front of and slightly to the left of its summit. The walk-in follows the ridges running diagonally to the right.

Day 4: Kumai to Khorchon

Continue climbing steeply along the ridgeline to grazing pastures called Khorchon at around 3,568 metres (12,000ft). A relatively short, although once again, steep day.

Day 5: Khorchon to Base Camp

The trail now leads steeply across a ridgeline to a hidden plateau beneath the south face of Mardi Himal and the South-West Ridge of Machhupuchhare; this is the 'Other Sanctuary', so called by Jimmy Roberts. Base camp can be sited around 4,100m/13,451ft.

THE CLIMB

This is a climb of little technical difficulty, where route finding and effort are the major problems. What difficulties there are can be found in the couloir leading to the col below the East Face. Late in the day this might present avalanche danger under fresh snow conditions.

From base camp ascend steeply towards the col between the East Face of Mardi Himal and the connecting ridge of Machhapuchhare. A high camp can be placed at 4,650 metres (15,256ft). From camp reach a snow couloir leading to the col with a steep section of perhaps 45 degrees. At the col further steep snow slopes lead to the summit of Mardi Himal. Grade: Alpine F. Descend by the same route.

On the first ascent a pair of pyjama trousers tied to a bamboo wand were left on the summit as a marker pennant. The flapping legs, it was felt, would resemble the unusual twin points of the Nepali flag!

RETURN TREK

Base Camp to Kumai

Return from base camp through the high grazing country called Khorchon and follow the same trails back to Kumai.

Kumai to Ghachok

This descent from Kumai (3,049m/10,000ft) is a hard day for weary knees, as much of the altitude gained is lost on the return to the valley. Descend on the ascent route almost as far as Odane Hill. Just before the high point a small track goes left down the east flank of the ridge, dropping steeply to grazing country and a good lunch spot at Hile. Afterwards, the trail descends ever more steeply to the pros-perous farming village of Ghachok (1,067m/ 3,500ft), in the valley of the Seti River. A day of descent taking nearly eight hours.

Ghachok to Pokhara

The direct route is to cross the Seti to the east bank and follow the main trail south. An increasing number of people, buildings and eventually vehicles bring about the transition to normality after the wild remoteness of the ridges south of Mardi Himal.

For those that have a day to spare and want to put off getting back to civilisation there is a good day's hiking to be had from Ghachok to Changlung Hill, east of the Seti. The river has carved out a profound gorge which can be followed north on the west bank, high above the river. After the long, hard descent this is a delightful contrast and it leads in a couple of hours to the little bridge at Diprang where there are nearby hot springs, which might just take the aches out of wobbly knees. Cross the river and climb Changlung hill opposite which gives yet more marvellous views of the Annapurna Himal and good campsites. It is possible to return down the east bank of the Seti to Pokhara in about five hours.

12 The Annapurna Sanctuary

North of Pokhara the skyline is dominated by the peaks of the Annapurna Himal which form a massive mountain barrier between the deep valleys of the Kali Gandaki to the west and the Marsyangdi Khola in the east. Between these giant waterways, numerous lesser rivers have cut impressive gorges on their journey south from the glaciers of this great range.

For the mountaineer, the most important and impressive of these gorges is that of the Modi Khola which has its origin in the glaciers that tumble from a semi-circle of peaks, forming an amphitheatre that has come to be known as the Annapurna Sanctuary.

The Annapurna Sanctuary was unknown to western explorers until Jimmy Roberts, in 1956, followed the Modi Khola between the portals of Hiunchuli and Machhapuchhare during a reconnaissance for the British Machhapuchare Expedition the following year. This was an expedition which, incidentally, climbed to within fifty metres of the summit, before Wilfrid Noyce and David Cox turned back. Since that time, no official permission has been given for an attempt on the mountain, which has been deemed sacred and out of bounds.

When Roberts entered the amphitheatre there was a local custom that no buffalo, pork, chicken or women could go beyond Hinku for fear of angering the female deities of Annapurna and Gangapurna, hence he coined the name Sanctuary, a place recognised as holy, a private retreat and innermost recess.

Once beyond the confines of the gorge above Hinku there is a breathtaking panorama as the Sanctuary opens up into a giant, glacier-filled bowl, narrowly breached by the Modi Khola.

The western half of the bowl is a semicircle of peaks, beginning with Hiunchuli (6,331m/20,771ft), to the south, one of the most difficult of the 'trekking peaks', which is connected by a horizontal ice ridge to the East Face of Annapurna South (7,219m/23,693ft). The circle then swings north through Fang (7,647m/25,089ft), now called Baraha Shikar, to Annapurna I (8,091m/26,545ft), the ascent of the South Face of which marked a breakthrough into Himalayan 'big-wall' climbing when Chris Bonington's expedition climbed it in 1970. The ridge then circles north-east through Khangshar Kang (7,485m/24,560ft), formerly Roc Noir, to the final peak in the half-circle Tarke Kang (7,193m/23,191ft), once descriptively called Glacier Dome.

Continuing the other half of the circle to the east, the high ridge goes on to Gangapurna (7,455m/24,457ft), before turning south-east to Annapurna III (7,555m/24,787ft). The circle then begins to close when the icy ridge turns south-west to the pinnacle of Gandharba Chuli (6,248m/20,402ft) before it rises to the fantastic spire of Machhapuchhare (6,993m/22,942ft), dominating the entrance to the Sanctuary and indeed the whole skyline north of Pokhara. It goes without saying that the Sanctuary offers one of the most impressive, close-up mountain vistas in Nepal, making it a popular venue for trekkers.

But what of the trekking peaks in the Sanctuary? Hiunchuli has already been mentioned,

127

The massive south walls of Annapurna South on the left and Hiunchuli on the right rise above the Modi Khola and traditional Gurung hipped-thatch circular houses near Landrung.

its lofty and formidable east face forming the western portal to the Sanctuary. Once through the gate, as it were, the circle of peaks is naturally divided by a ridge that stretches south from Tarke Kang into the centre of the amphitheatre, separating the South Annapurna Glacier from the West Annapurna Glacier. It is this ridge that rises first to form Singu Chuli (6,390m/20,965ft), called Fluted Peak by Jimmy Roberts for obvious reasons, which in turn falls to a ridge connecting it to Tharpu Chuli (5,500m/18,045ft), or Tent Peak, as it is generally known.

For many, the trip to the Sanctuary comes at the end of an extended trek around what has become known as the Annapurna Circuit; a superb, although very popular walk around the Annapurna Himal, linking the valleys of the Marsyangdi Khola and Kali Gandaki by crossing the Thorong La. This trek is described in the approach to Pisang Peak and the Chulus (page 166).

There are many routes of approach to the Sanctuary; however, they all come together at Chomrong. They do have one other thing in common – an abundant supply of tea houses and lodges, both simple and sophisticated. Food and lodging can also be had in the Sanctuary but it's not always reliable, especially in the off-peak period, when it is best to inquire at Chomrong as to whether the lodges are open. At busy times it may also be difficult to guarantee food and accommodation at some of them.

The South-West Face of Tharpu Chuli viewed from the moraines west of Annapurna South base camp. The South-East Ridge forms the right-hand skyline with its obvious rock pinnacle near the summit.

The trek to the Sanctuary falls wholly within the Annapurna Conservation Area which was set up by the King Mahendra Trust for Nature Conservation. The trust is a new approach to an increasingly common problem, the need to conserve landscape and still balance the needs and demands of local people, trekkers and the environment. The Sierra Club motto of 'take only memories, leave only footprints' should hold true for everyone who enjoys and is privileged enough to travel the world's high and wild places. The 'minimum impact code' laid down by the trust, if adhered to by trekkers and expeditions, will go a long way to maintaining Nepal's mountains for future generations.

Treks to the Sanctuary usually begin and end in Pokhara. Getting there from Kathmandu presents no real problem. There are daily flights to and from the capital and buses ply the 200 bumpy kilometres that separate them daily. A large group will want to hire a private vehicle for the journey. It can be hard on both the nerves and the bones, but for one reason or another I always enjoy it. It gives one a chance to glimpse a great transect of Nepali life.

If you leave Kathmandu early, before dawn, you will see the roadside settlements come to life. Porters and villagers, wrapped in their thin cotton shawls against the morning cold, squat in doorways or beneath pipal trees, to emerge, like spectres from the morning mist, as you rattle by.

129

But it is much more than distance that separates Pokhara from Kathmandu. Pokhara, fast growing with more than 50,000 inhabitants, shows signs of its hasty development. Its houses and shops are strung out along the road leading north to the Seti Khola, seemingly without plan or order. Its original inhabitants, mainly Newar and Gurung, have been outnumbered, or so it seems, by Tibetian settlers and Manang traders whose horses still ply the trade route up the Kali Gandaki. Overall there is a sense of hustle and bustle around the multi-storey brick buildings that form the commercial centre of the town. But Pokhara is also a place of contrasts. Much lower than Kathmandu, it has a sub-tropical climate and the peaks are more impressive; the Annapurnas are less than 40 kilometers to the north.

Within walking distance, west of the airport, is a lake, Phewi Tal, a place of peace and tranquillity despite the lodges, campsites and shops that have sprung up along the north shore. Spend an evening by the lake or get up before sunrise and go to the southern shore to watch the sunrise on the peaks seen perfectly reflected in the lake, and you will understand what I mean.

THE TREK

This route provides the walk-in to several of the permitted peaks. These are Tent Peak, Fluted Peak and Hiunchuli. The route described gets you quickly into the Sanctuary, even without rushing. However, whatever route you choose it is difficult to go high and thus to acclimatise. My own feeling is that acclimatising is best done in the Sanctuary.

I recommend that most people spend some

Early morning mist on Phewa Tal with the peaks of Annapurna II, Annapurna IV and Lamjung Himal beyond.

time above base camp before making their climb. Arriving on top feeling and looking like death warmed up and wanting only to get down is no way to enjoy a Himalayan summit. Ascending Raksi Peak or exploring the moraines beyond Annapurna South base camp is helpful.

Day 1: Pokhara to Sarankot

There is usually enough time to combine this day with the journey from Kathmandu. From Pokhara there is a road, of sorts, that now goes all the way up the Yamdi Khola to Phedi ('foot of the hill'), where there is a cluster of houses and tea shops. The route then climbs the hill behind to Naudanda (or Nagdanda, 1,425m/4,675ft), a large settlement including shops and inns on the Kaski Danda where you may have your trek permit checked. If you have your own transport you might be able to talk/pay them to take you all the way. If you arrive by bus or air you will need to get to Mahendra Pul, from where you can hire a jeep to Phedi. On the other hand you could follow the road all the way through villages including the Tibetian Refugee Settlement. Often a hot, dusty walk, it does give you a chance to come into contact with Nepalis. However, there is another route that avoids most of the crowd and at the same time gives glorious views.

From Mahendra Pul, where the bus stops, or if you arrive by air, get a taxi to Bindeswari Temple, which is worth a visit. If you have hired a vehicle from Kathmandu, get dropped off at the temple. From near the temple a long, steep climb gains the ridge west of the Yamdi Khola known as the Kaski Danda. It climbs for over 900 metres to the site of the old fort at Sarankot (1,583m/5,200ft). This provides wonderful views and a good campsite on the ridge beyond the lookout tower. Most westerners find the first couple of days walking out from Pokahara very hot and an umbrella is a worthwhile purchase from the bazaar.

Day 2: Sarankot to Tanchok Potana

The magnificent panorama of peaks is soon lost as you traverse the ridge on its southern flank. The main trail is wide and passes through attractive, highly terraced farmland dotted with hipped thatch Chettri houses and small stands of bamboo. There are plenty of tea shops along the way. The trail passes a small reservoir and shrine at Sanri Pokarhi and shortly after Deorali Kashikot it descends towards Naudanda.

This active village has a host of lodges, shops and tea houses. There is a bank and a police post where your trek permit will be checked. Through the town, past the stud farm, take the right-hand path up stone steps. There is almost continuous development along this section of the trail.

Traverse on the left side of the ridge past the spreading bhanyan tree, houses and tea shop. The trail turns a sharp right and continues past neat houses, and ahead you can see Khare on the col.

From Khare our route now turns right rather than descending on the far side of the col to Chandrakot. At Prem Lodge turn right, go behind the lodge and climb up steps through the village. The trail continues to a chautaara where it divides; take the right-hand path and climb steeply past a thatched house.

Continue climbing through forest, and after 200 metres (650ft), take the left-hand trail which at first contours and then continues climbing through the forest. The trail eventually clears the trees, giving good views back toward Pokhara.

The trail continues to climb at first through scrubby woodland and then back into dense forest, past a chautaara (1,860m/6,102ft), and then follows the main trail along the ridge crest, climbing steeply through rhododendrons, heavily draped with epiphitic orchids. The way now contours around the head of the valley through terraces, past a farm house, and emerges at a notch on the ridge where there are lovely grazing meadows and magnificent views of Annapurna South. This is Beri Kharka (2,050m/6,726ft). For those that want a quiet campsite this is the spot and there are rock overhangs for porters to sleep and cook under.

Tanchok Potana isn't far away. Bear right across the kharka and descend slightly through rhododendron forest. Ahead is a building. After 200 metres (650 feet) the path levels out and leads to the house. A larger trail now joins from the right and the path leads horizontally for a while and then up steps to the settlement of Tanchok Potana, with its gaggle of lodges and tea shops.

Day 3: Tanchok Potana to New Bridge

Continue through the village, past the water pipe and down on a well-made paved path to a clearing. Take the right-hand path, marked by red paint marks. Continue on this trail past a demolished building and through the woods, with lovely glimpses of Annapurna South.

Continue along the path, with a slope that drops away abruptly to the right. The trail climbs a little and then levels and continues along a ridge crest to a clearing. In about one hour it leads to a tea shop at Bhichock Deorali (2,113m/6,932ft).

From the deorali ('pass') continue to the chautaara taking the trail to the left, and descend steeply through the forest, getting good views of Ghandrung, across the deep Modi Khola. The way through the woods leads past several lodges. The first, Sanjana Hotel (1,876m/5,150ft), has an extensive menu. Pass a second lodge and then cross a stream and climb to the Tolka Hotel. The path here is well made, hewn from the hillside as it climbs steeply toward a notch and the Tolka Lodge.

A well-made wide path continues high above the Modi Khola, providing fine views of Annapurna South and Hiunchuli. The lodge at Tolka Naga makes good tea, has a well-situated terrace, with an outlook that makes it highly recommendable. The path passes a large meadow just after a school, where you may be asked to contribute to school funds for the Shri Lower Secondary School and write your contribution in a book; this is all above board and not simply a good scam.

Descend steeply from the kharka down stone steps, cross a bridge, taking the right-hand of the path up yet more steps, past a chautaara and on under steep cliffs hung with orchids and delicate bamboo. The hillside below is totally deforested and terraced. Cross a stream with good pools and falls to arrive at Landrung. Be careful not to descend to the suspension bridge over the Modi Khola, but take the right-hand path leading towards New Bridge. Stay on the east bank of the river. Descend through terraces and then through scrubby woodland and boulders where ahead you can see the deep gorge of the Modi Khola. Soon there is a bhatti, opposite a tributary on the west bank. This is Ram Lodge; there are good campsites nearby, but beware the leeches!

New Bridge is a little further on. It is a new suspension bridge over the Modi Khola with a group of lodges and camping places.

Day 4: New Bridge to Chomrong

The way now climbs steeply up the west bank through bamboo woodland, high above the river, entering a side valley where it crosses a recent avalanche chute. This is a good section of the trail with some impressive views.

Crossing another re-entrant it leads in less than an hour past a small house on a spur which illustrates well the demand for marginal land that has arisen in Nepal.

Pass through Chamru, which gets the early morning sun. Follow the trail to the Happy

Tea Shop at the end of the village. Cross the log bridge and ascend steeply to two lodges, the Green Lodge and Tinimini Lodge (1,700m/5,577ft).

From the lodges the trail climbs steeply up the Gimnu Danda with good views of Gangapurna at the back of the Sanctuary. Pass a chautaara and in less than an hour reach a tea shop that provides a welcome break on this tough climb. Ahead the path continues steep and dusty and then on good stone stairs to a crest which leads to Taulu, where paths to the Sanctuary converge. Turn right past the water tap, between the lodges, and head north towards Chomrong. In another ten minutes the route leads past Himalayan View Lodge which is large and offers sophisticated services including solar-heated water.

About 200 metres (650 feet) past the lodge, take the right-hand path, which traverses to a notch (2,168m/7,113ft). Turn the corner and at last you see Chomrong strung out through a terraced hillside above the Chomrong Khola. There is a lot to choose from – lodges large and small, invariably with camping nearby. There have been several instances of theft in the lodges so a great deal of care needs to be taken.

In Chomrong you will need to have your trek and peak permit checked at the police post which is also the ACAP (Annapurna Conservation Area Project) office. This is also a fuel depot, for those needing a re-supply for the time at base. A short way past the office are the Annapurna Hotel and below that Captain's Lodge; both are excellent and have camping space.

From Chomrong the dominant view is that of the massive south flank of Annapurna South and the as yet unclimbed face of Hiunchulu. The deep Chomrong Khola may provide interesting access to this major climbing objective.

Day 5: Chomrong to Deorali

From the Annapurna Lodge the trail descends stone steps and after fifty metres, at a large boulder, it divides. Take the left-hand path, crossing a stream to follow a water channel past a mill. Keep descending, always on steep stone steps, past a small stupa and chautaara to arrive at the river, which is crossed by a suspension bridge.

On the far side climb through terraced fields and then through bamboo, contouring the northern flank of the Chomrong Khola. It's worthwhile looking back, not only to the setting of Chomrong but also to see the height gained and lost with the descent to the river and to think how much good it is doing your acclimatisation. The route leads past a small tea shop and then steeply up more steps past mani-stones and a chautaara. Continuing more gently it leads through a forest of bamboo and rhododendron to a tea shop and Senwa Lodge (2,306m/7,566ft), from where there are good views up the Modi Khola.

A rough descent leads through rhododendron and boulders, but the walking is good. On the crest of the ridge, which is terraced, there is another lodge. After crossing a stream, descend steep rock slabs covered in a velvet of vegetation. Continue to Kuldi Ghar and the Machhapuchhare Lodge. From the lodge, descend at first, then climb up steps past a guest house and helipad. The usual trail bypasses this lodge on the right and then descends steeply crossing below another band of steep rock slabs on a path hewn from ledges.

The route continues through dense bamboo forest, a real feature of this section of the walk-in, and leads to the appropriately named Bamboo Lodge (2,260m/7,414ft). In snow or wet weather the route through this forest of bamboo can be difficult and slippery. It leads past Tip Top Lodge (2,457m/8,061ft), which has an impressive waterfall cascading down

133

the valley wall behind. The way continues through dense bamboo and rhododendron, crossing several streams before the Annapurna Approach Lodge.

The valley is quite narrow now and the path, not far above the river, hemmed in between Machhapuchhare and Hiunchuli. The Hotel Himal is soon reached (2,866m/ 9,403ft), after which the path climbs more steeply through bamboo and then up steps past boulders below a cliff. Crossing a stream the route climbs more steeply to a huge, smoke-blackened, overhanging boulder, under which a small lodge has been built; this is Hinko Cave.

Continue past this, crossing two large avalanche cones, the second of which is the most active. The trail climbs again, soon reaching Kot Deorali where, climbing past a large boulder, there is yet another lodge, the Hotel Panorama, where there is space for camping.

Bhaga, just beyond Deorali, is also a good site, but care should be taken if there has been recent snowfall, for between Deorali and Bhaga there is a potentially dangerous avalanche chute that frequently wipes out the trail. By stopping at Deorali it is possible to cross the danger zone early in the morning, hopefully, before the sun has got to work on the slopes of Hiunchuli.

Day 6: Deorali to Annapurna South Base Camp

Continue along the west bank, crossing a large avalanche cone and arrive at Bhaga where there is a lodge.

Hiunchuli's East Face:
As unlikely as it may seem, the approach to this route is

A view across the Annapurna Glacier South to Singu Chuli on the left and Tharpu Chuli on the right, the approach to which goes up the gully in the centre of the picture.

up the steep flank of the valley behind Baga, details of which can be found in the chapter dealing with Hiunchuli.

To gain the Sanctuary, continue climbing steadily along a lateral moraine, crossing two more avalanche cones. Follow the trough between the moraine and the valley wall (what geomorphologists call a mulde), and arrive shortly at Machhapuchhare base camp and the lodge (3,658m/12,000ft). In the spring of 1988 this was completely buried beneath snow.

Singu Chuli and Tharpu Chuli East Faces are best approached by continuing north up the West Annapurna Glacier from Machhapuchhare base camp.

From this lodge it is less than two hours to Annapurna South base camp, following a well-defined path along the trough on the south side of the moraine bordering the Annapurna South Glacier. The actual crest of the moraine also provides a good walk in a more spectacular position. The base camp site has several lodges and is situated beneath the north-east flank of Hiunchuli. Tent Peak base camp is on the opposite side of the glacier, on a flat shelf above the lateral moraine.

The lodges at Annapurna South base camp provide an ideal base for those interested in the northern flank of Hiunchuli.

13 Hiunchuli (6,331m/20,771ft)

Hiunchuli, with Annapurna South, forms the massive south-facing wall, well seen when trekking north from Pokhara. Hiunchuli is the eastern bastion of this rampart, with its East Face overlooking the Modi Khola, guarding the entrance to the Annapurna Sanctuary. An impressive mountain in its own right, and not, as it was at one time dubbed, 'the eastern outlier of Annapurna South'. Despite the relative ease of access to the mountain and the popularity, rightly so, of the Sanctuary as a trekking destination, it has, like Fluted Peak, received little attention from mountaineers although it obviously offers major new route potential.

From the south, Hiunchuli has few weaknesses in its defences. A precipitous south wall rises above the untracked Chomrong Khola, seemingly menaced by snow avalanches from the slabby, ice-veined buttresses above.

The eastern flank from afar appears the most approachable; however, once beyond Kuldi Ghar, it seems far less so. Out of sight, the mountain remains an unknown quantity approached by only a few, through steep and dense bamboo forest, menaced by unseen avalanche danger from hanging glaciers above.

From the north the mountain rises steeply above the moraines of the Annapurna South Glacier in a series of slabby buttresses and an

Part of the North Face of Hiunchuli seen from the moraines beyond the Annapurna South base camp.

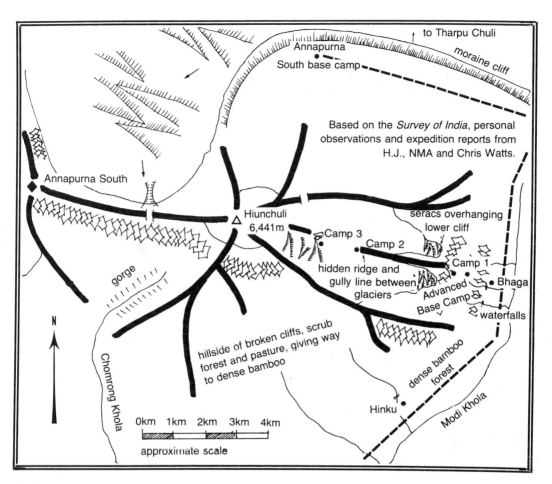

Based on the *Survey of India*, personal observations and expedition reports from H.J., NMA and Chris Watts.

to Tharpu Chuli

Annapurna
South base camp

moraine cliff

Annapurna South

Hiunchuli
6,441m

seracs overhanging
lower cliff

Camp 3

Camp 2

Camp 1

Bhaga

hidden ridge and
gully line between
glaciers

Advanced
Base Camp

waterfalls

gorge

hillside of broken cliffs, scrub
forest and pasture, giving way
to dense bamboo

dense bamboo
forest

N

Chomrong Khola

0km 1km 2km 3km 4km

approximate scale

Hinku

Modi Khola

HIUNCHULI

ill-defined and complicated North Ridge. These in turn lead to a final triangle of fluted ice that form the summit.

The summit is bounded on the east by a ridge that rises in an icy parabola from a small col, from which a steep couloir descends towards the moraines above the lodges at base camp. This is a feasible looking route, and is as yet unclimbed.

The mountain's western arm is the ridge connecting it with Annapurna South, and forming from the north an icy wall. It is this wall that has provided the key to new things.

CLIMBING ROUTES

First ascent was via the South-East Face in October 1971, by an American Peace Corps Expedition led by Craig Anderson. The members were: L. Smith, J. Skow, P. Cross and J. Richards.

Although not a technically extreme climb, it is exposed to rockfall and serac dangers and is a complicated route-finding experience. The first ascent was a fine effort and, like the mountain, is rarely climbed.

From Hinko Cave (3,014m/9,900ft), climb the hillside which is very steep to a base camp

Looking up at the slabs, lower rock wall and hanging glacier on the South-East Face of Hiunchuli.

During the winter ascent a camp was placed at the foot of the rock wall. The start of the diagonal gully can be seen on the right.

in grassy meadows (4,115m/13,500ft), below the South-East Face of the mountain. From base camp cross below two glaciers in sight of the East face. There is potential icefall danger from these glaciers. Climb a rock wall and sight Camp 1 on the glacier above (circa 4,724m/15,500ft).

From Camp 1 cross the glacier running due-east to a rock wall and climb this at its lowest point on good rock. In fact, it is possible to climb the rock wall by a couloir line (600ft) that splits it, running diagonally left to right. Near the top of the couloir, traverse left into shorter couloirs that are followed to the upper snow slope and the site of Camp 2. From Camp 2 cross a large snow basin that leads to the foot of a hanging glacier and Camp 3.

From Camp 3 climb up a narrow avalanche chute (be aware of danger) to the base of a hanging glacier. Traverse left under the hanging glacier to easier slopes on its left-hand side. Snow slopes above are climbed to the site of Camp 4 (6,096m/20,000ft), beneath a large crevasse. Cross the bergschrund to easier snow slopes which in turn lead to the final ridge. Follow this to the top.

This route description and the camp placings are taken from the account of the first ascent.

In 1982 the route and the mountain had a second ascent that followed a variant from Camp 2. This was climbed by Eric Simonson, Bob Wilson, Pete Cummings, Bonnie Nabori, LaVerne Woods, Curt Hewitt, Gary Doyle, Tim Byrnes and Tony Townsend.

138

Between Camp 1 and Camp 2 they fixed approximately 820 metres (900 feet) of rope. Camp 2 was on the hanging glacier (5,334m/ 17,500ft). From this camp they followed a prominent ice ridge east of the avalanche chute, climbed on the first ascent. This gives a safer alternative and better climbing. This leads to the top of the ridge (5,700m/18,700ft), and Camp 3. Above Camp 3 climb steep ice steps to the summit.

In December 1986 the East Face route with several variations received its first winter and lightweight-style ascent by Chris Watts and Lindsay Abbots.

During this ascent the Dream Hotel at Bhagar was used as a base camp. The mountain above is unseen at this point, the view is blocked by the gorge-like walls of the mountain that effectively help to form the 'gate to the sanctuary'.

About one mile beyond Hinko Cave en route to Bhaga, next to an obvious waterfall, you leave the trekking path to climb diagonally leftwards up the hillside through bamboo and crags on a path made by hunters (blaze marks and cut bamboo), leading to the upper meadows below the South-East Face of Hiunchuli. This path is very steep and the way most unlikely, zig -zagging through the lower rock slabs! An advanced base camp was established

Climbing the diagonal gully through the lower rock wall which gave Grade III climbing with one pitch of Scottish Grade IV.

After making an abseil from the top of the diagonal gully a second couloir is followed to a notch in the skyline.

139

at 4,267 metres (14,000 feet). The climb takes about five hours from Bhaga.

From advanced base camp a further five hours carry you beneath the icefall of the North Glacier, mainly through deep snow on the South Glacier, which leads to the bottom of a gully system leading through a rock wall (the same system as was mentioned on the first ascent). A ledge was hacked out left of the gully at the base of the wall for a tent (4,725m/ 15,500ft).

From the ledge, gain the gully and climb this for 200 metres (650 feet); this is fairly straightforward, although there is a difficult pitch near the top (Scottish IV) and some poor rock. This narrow gully is exposed to stonefall danger.

At the top of the gully descend for one rope length into a hollow and climb a second icy gully for three rope lengths and gain a notch in the skyline ridge.

Follow the narrow ridge to the left which in turn leads into a third and final gully, climbed for four rope lengths to another ridge. Climb along this narrow ridge for five rope lengths until you are able to climb on to the North Glacier above the icefall and establish a camp (5,330m/17,487ft). This is a hidden and devious section of the route, and is full of interest.

Continue up the North Glacier, over avalanche debris, all the time threatened by serac danger from above. A further camp can be made on a ledge in a crevasse at 5,700m (18,700ft). There was a great deal of deep snow on this section when first climbed, which meant little height was gained.

From the crevasse a steep climb diagonally leftwards, traversing under the seracs, leads

Lindsay Abbotts in the middle of the ridge and gully section before gaining the ridge leading to the upper glacier.

Lindsay Abbotts on the final ridge section before the upper glacier plateau.

to a long ice runnel, which is climbed (the normal route goes further to the left), to an ice column. Climb the ice column which leads to a serac about 20 metres (65 feet) high. The serac was climbed by traversing leftwards on 90 degree and overhanging ice. A very serious pitch.

Above the serac, climb the summit ridge with one steep pitch which leads to a large crevasse, which is the final obstacle before the large flat summit. Descent was made by the same route, although the serac was avoided.

With the conditions prevailing during our ascent both climbers felt that in the light of objective dangers and technical difficulties the route was Alpine TD.

North-West Face

An ascent was made by a steep ice couloir and ice buttress leading to the East Ridge and by connecting to the South Ridge it led to the summit. It was climbed solo by Japanese climber Masayuki Ando in 1984. No detailed description is available of the route but general details are given below.

From a base camp at or around the lodges at Annapurna South base camp follow the moraines and gain the glacier below the east–west ridge connecting Annapurna South and Hiunchuli. Ascend the glacier to below the North-West Face of Hiunchuli and the foot of a steep couloir leading toward the West Ridge. A camp was placed here on the first ascent.

The couloir is climbed via a steep ice cliff to where the West Ridge can be gained. From

Rene Ghilini finding a way through the difficult icefall on the approach to the North Couloir of Hiunchuli.

On the summit of Hiunchuli with the West Face of Machhapuchhare behind.

the ridge, rappel (250m/820ft) to a point where the South Ridge can be gained. This is followed to the summit. Descent appears to have been made direct to the West Ridge and down the route of ascent. It would appear, however, that the lower section of the route, as far as the connecting east–west ridge, had been climbed before.

In September 1982 Alex McIntyre, Rene Ghilini and John Porter, climbing from a base at the Annapurna South base camp went directly on to the glacier falling steeply from the col between Hiunchuli and Annapurna South, climbing through a dangerous ice fall to gain the route that leads to an upper glacier basin where there was a good bivouac site beneath an ice cliff.

Above is a couloir leading to the right side of the col, which is climbed easily at first but which steepens at the top to give a difficult ice pitch (Scottish 4/5), after which it gains the col, astride a knife-edged ridge. This is the same point reached by the Japanese ascent in 1984 from which the South Ridge is then reached by abseil. The route as far as the col was graded Alpine D+.

It would appear that a French expedition was attempting to climb Hiunchuli by the same route and also reached the col, although taking three days to cover the same ground. It seems they were unable to climb the very precarious West Ridge of Hiunchuli from the col, the solution to which was the abseil to the South Ridge taken by Masayuki Ando.

14 Tharpu Chuli (5,500m/18,045ft)

In 1956 the mountain first received attention from Jimmy Roberts who was exploring the Sanctuary during a reconnaissance for the 1957 British Machhapuchhare Expedition. It was Roberts that gave it the descriptive name Tent Peak; he was also responsible for its nearby neighbour's name, again most descriptive, of Fluted Peak. His attempt to climb the mountain ended high on the North-West Ridge; a route later climbed by the Germans. In fact the mountain was first climbed via the South-East Ridge by members of the Japanese Annapurna South Expedition from Kyoto University in 1964, led by Dr Haruo Higuchi.

Situated in the heart of the Annapurna Sanctuary, Tharpu Chuli is an attractive mountain; part of the ridge line, thrown south from Glacier Dome, that includes Singu Chuli and acts as a central divider between the semicircle of peaks enclosing the Sanctuary. The mountain is sometimes confused with Rakshi Peak, a small summit and viewpoint to the west of Tharpu Chuli, that stands above the normal high camp, said to have been named after Roberts' dog!

As well as enjoyable climbing the mountains offers one of the outstanding viewpoints of the Annapurna massive. From its summit you have a superb panorama of Hiunchuli (6,331m/20,771ft), Annapurna South (7,219m/

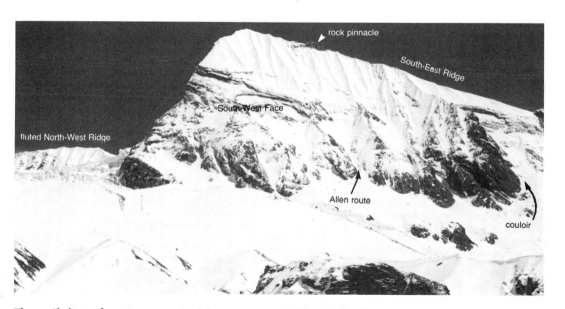

Tharpu Chuli seen from Annapurna South base camp. On the left is the fluted wall leading to the North-West Ridge, whilst the right-hand skyline is the South-East Ridge, approached by the obvious gully on the right.

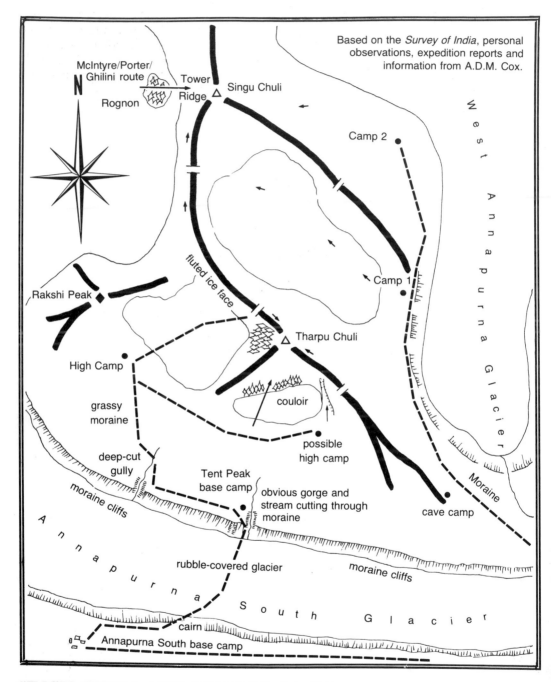

SINGU CHULI AND THARPU CHULI

23,684ft), Fang (7,647m/25,089ft), Annapurna 1 (8,091m/26,545ft), Gangapurna (7,455m/24,459ft), Annapurna III (7,555m/24,787ft), Annapurna V (7,525m/24,688ft), Machapuchhare (6,993m/22,943ft) and of course Singu Chuli or Fluted Peak (6,501m/21,329ft).

Seen from the moraines above the huts at the Annapurna South base camp, the mountain takes on a shape, aptly described by its former name Tent Peak, with its long South-East Ridge forming the sloping ridge pole. The lower half of the South-West Face is a series of rocky

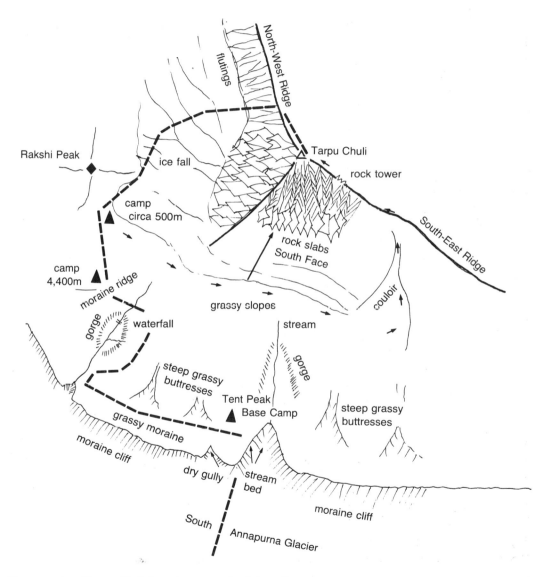

The approach to Tharpu Chuli from Annapurna South Base Camp.

gullies and buttresses giving way to strongly etched snow flutes. Under a lot of snow this becomes a very attractive aspect indeed with a good number of lines. The North-West Face, on the other hand, forms a black rocky triangle, bounded on the left by the North-West Ridge, itself the normal line of ascent, which is gained by the flat glacier to the west.

Tharpu Chuli's relatively low altitude and reasonable approach, without serious objective danger, make this an attractive mountain, especially when combined with its position and ease of access. At present three routes have been recorded and many more are obviously possible. Because of the large number of climbing expeditions that enter the Sanctuary it might well be that the peak has received a lot of unnoticed attention.

CLIMBS

North-West Ridge

First ascent was by Gunter Hauser and party on 24 May 1965 during the German Glacier Dome Expedition. Their report mentions that the peak's central position makes it an ideal point for survey observations. This was also the route by which Roberts almost reached the summit in 1956 and has now become the mountain's standard route.

From the huts at the Annapurna South base camp follow the trail east along the moraine ridge for 200 metres to a well-made cairn. This marks the descent path on to the South Annapurna Glacier. This is quite steep and often snow covered. The path across the glacier is marked by cairns and leads directly to the moraines on the north side of the glacier.

These moraines look loose and formidable. Several ways seem possible. The two described have proven reliable:

1   From the relatively flat boulder-strewn area

Martin Whitaker emerging from the top of the couloir at the start of the South-East Ridge of Tharpu Chuli.

below the moraine there is an obvious stream bed. A faint path leads over loose terrain to the crest of the moraine.

2   To the left of the stream bed is an obvious dry gully, quite narrow in its middle section, that leads steeply to the moraine crest. It would be difficult to avoid rockfall in this gully. The flat, grassy area above the moraine (4,115m/ 13,500ft), is a good campsite and is generally referred to as Tent Peak base camp.

A high camp is necessary. From base camp follow the moraine north-west for about ten minutes to an obvious deep-cut gully. A stream emerges from the gully. A faint path climbs to the top of the east bank up a grassy buttress. In the spring of 1988 I was able to climb directly up the bed of the gully which was snow filled and exit on the left. The other path leads from

146

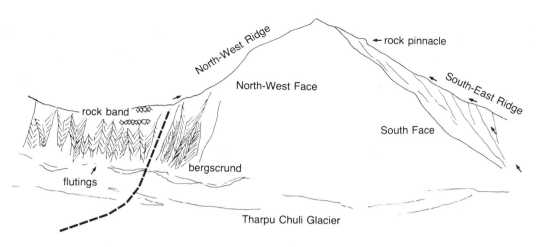

The approach to the North-West Ridge of Tharpu Chuli from high camp.

the top of the grassy buttress to flatter grass slopes. It then crosses the stream above the gully and contours the hillside to reach the flat summit of a buttress (4,420m/14,500ft). This site would also make a suitable base camp.

A ridge above this campsite is followed to a level area which may be snow covered (4,877m/16,000ft). This is a suitable site for high camp. There is a further suitable campsite at 5,030 metres (16,500 feet).

From high camp (4,877m/16,000ft), the level glacier below the west flank of Tharpu Chuli can be reached without difficulty in one hour by following easy slopes towards Raksi Peak and the left-hand side of the glacier, avoiding all crevasses. This leads to the level glacier at 5,334 metres (17,500 feet).

Cross the glacier easily to the foot of the fluted wall separating Tharpu Chuli and Singu Chuli. The wall is approximately 120 metres (400 feet) high at its lowest point, rising to 180 metres (600 feet) on either side.

Several lines are possible, but at the right-hand end the angle is easiest and snow conditions will dictate the best route. At the right-hand end an easy snow slope leads to the foot of a gully. Cross an easy bergschrund and climb the gully between flutings for 60 metres (200 feet) at an angle of 45 degrees, taking the left fork, where the angle steepens to 55 degrees for the final 90 metres (300 feet) to the ridge.

At this point the ridge is broad and easy but soon steepens as you climb towards the summit into a knife-edged ridge of approximately 50 degrees. This is followed for 45 metres (150 feet), after which the angle eases and the ridge leads quickly to the summit.

The overall grade is Alpine PD. Some parties have used fixed rope on the steep section of the flutings.

South-East Ridge

This is the ridge climbed by the first ascensionists in 1964, however, no detailed description of the route was made available. The climb has had numerous ascents since, details of which were given after an ascent by Richard Haszko and Tom Richardson in 1985.

Looking at the mountain from Annapurna South base camp the route takes the obvious wide couloir that joins the South-East Ridge about half-way along its length.

Follow the approach to Tent Peak base camp described for the North-West Ridge. Follow the same route to high camp. From the high camp follow easy ground east under Tharpu Chuli towards the couloir and then cross a small glacier to the foot of the couloir.

Climb the right-hand side of the couloir on snow/ice for 120 metres (400 feet), before traversing left across steep snowfields to the other side of the couloir. Continue climbing the left-hand side of the couloir through a steep, narrow section to gain an open snow-field and finally the ridge. This takes about four hours from high camp.

Follow the 'airy' crest of the ridge to a rock tower which can be passed on the left side by a snow shelf and so regain the ridge on the far side. Continue following this classic ridge, without further difficulties, to the summit. In descent it was quicker to abseil from the top of the rock pinnacle on the ridge rather than make the traverse around its side. The ascent took about six hours from camp. It might be advantageous to make a camp nearer the base of the couloir. The overall grade is Alpine AD.

South-West Face

In 1980 Rick Allen, with a Sherpa, made a direct ascent of the fluted South Face of Tharpu Chuli in one day from Annapurna South base camp, albeit a very long day. The climb was technically straightforward, following a shallow snow gully after scrambling the lower rocky section above the glacier.

15 Singu Chuli (6,501m/21,328ft)

'From Camp-II we enjoyed a fine evening straight across the basin of which our mountain (Machhapuchhare) formed one side. The colossal rampart of Annapurna 1 rose into a golden evening; but it was a smaller peak we examined, a peak of some 22,000 feet which projected into the basin rather as Nanda Devi rises in the middle of its cirque. It was already known to us as Fluted Peak, or more commonly Fluters.'

Wilfrid Noyce.

Singu Chuli is the mountain formerly known as Fluted Peak. A few days after enjoying that view of 'Fluters', Wilf Noyce and David Cox went on to make the first ascent of this attractive and difficult mountain by its North-East Face and the top section of the East Ridge. Despite the relative ease of access to the Sanctuary this mountain has proven too difficult for most commercial climbing groups who have tended to concentrate their efforts on Tent Peak.

Singu Chuli seen from Annapurna South base camp. The West Face is on the left with the obvious rock rib climbed by the McIntyre/Ghilini/Porter route. The narrow arête of the South Ridge falls directly towards the camera, with the fluted South Face bounded on the right, by the East Ridge.

Camcp on the approach to the South and North-East Faces of 'Fluted'.

As you approach the Sanctuary and reach the simple lodges at Machhapuchhare base camp little can be seen of the mountain, which is toward the head of the valley, cradling the West Annapurna Glacier. It is the first summit on the long ridge thrown down from Tarke Kang (Glacier Dome), which separates the South and West Annapurna Glaciers.

The approach to the first ascent route follows a shelf and a trough above the west bank of the West Annapurna Glacier, skirting round the base of the mountain's rocky east ridge to gain the foot of the North-East Face, which is unseen, even from the moraines above the lodges.

Perhaps the best distant view of the mountain is from Annapurna South base camp. From the moraines above the lodges the fluted South Face presents a 'beautiful shape, buttressed by pencil-shadowy ridges of snow and ice', well seen, rising above the ridge connecting it with Tharpu Chuli.

To date, apart from the original route, most efforts to climb the mountain have concen-trated on the face and ridges seen from this viewpoint. The South-West Ridge, the one that ultimately connects to Tent Peak, is an obvious, albeit corniced, line although a far more complicated connecting ridge than at first it appears. The terrain between the two peaks is quite·confused and not at all a straightforward ridge. The fluted face to the right of the ridge, although menaced in places by ice bulges and seracs is set at a reasonable angle and appears an attractive proposition. However, despite rumours that routes have been made on these, no route descriptions have been made available and the NMA have no record of ascents.

THE CLIMBS

North-East Face

First ascent was on 13 June 1957 by C. W. F. Noyce and A. D. M. Cox.

From Machhapuchhare base camp cross the

rubble-strewn snout of the South Annapurna Glacier and follow the Modi Khola on its true right bank until it is joined by a tributary stream from the West Annapurna Glacier. Follow this north-west over moraines and grassy meadows to a rock overhang before the snout of the West Annapurna Glacier. On the first ascent a camp was placed here. Noyce noted that the cave had obviously been used by herders. This would make a good base camp.

Above and beyond the cave, the hillside above the glacier to the north flattens out, forming a grassy shelf. Continue along this shelf to a point where Fluted Peak projects a long, low rock ridge, south-east towards the West Annapurna Glacier. Camp 2 was placed at circa 4,900m/16,000ft under this ridge.

A trough continues between the glacier and the flank of the mountain. This is followed with awkward steps and traverses round the right-hand (east) skyline ridge, and in turn leads to a plateau beneath the North-East Face. A camp can be placed here or several hundred feet higher on a shelf beneath two rock gullies in the centre of the face (circa 5,500m/18,000ft).

From the shelf gain the right hand of the two rocky, snow-filled gullies. This leads to beneath a vertical wall some 122m/400ft high. To the left of this wall, in the centre of the face, is another gully. Follow this and so skirt a serac barrier and afterwards a steep step and a ramp gives access to a shelf which is climbed easily to beneath the gently fluted top section of the face and the upper portion of the East Ridge. Gain the ridge and follow this without difficulty to the summit block, of which Noyce wrote:

'It was one of the strangest summits I have approached. Some capricious giant – there are many round here – must have picked up a serac from the glacier and dumped it on the very top of the mountain. About 100 feet high it had acquired a flat cushiony snow top and snow sides. But the ice of which it was composed remained very steep.'

In the end the summit block fell to a bout of step cutting and was climbed direct. Descent was made by the same route.

South Ridge

This has apparently been climbed using the same approach as for the North Ridge of Tharpu Chuli, with another camp at 5,200 metres (17,060 feet). It obviously provides a reasonably technical ridge climb. This same ridge has also been approached via the West Annapurna Glacier. The route followed the Noyce/Cox route until it was possible to enter the glacier bay beneath the South Face. A camp was placed under obvious sheltered rock

High on the South Ridge of Singu Chuli with Annapurna South beyond.

151

buttresses that are part of the ridge, forming the right-hand side of the face, thrown down from Singu Chuli's summit. The glacier beneath the face is quite broken and awkward and is crossed to the base of the South Ridge. Steep slopes then lead to the crest of the ridge, which is both narrow and difficult.

South Face

This delightful, fluted ice face has apparently been climbed also. It is bounded on the right by the South-East Ridge. The route is said to have followed a couloir line, climbing between two obvious seracs on the right-hand side of the face, leading to the South-East Ridge, which is then followed to the summit.

This face is best approached by the West Annapurna Glacier and is well seen from the grassy moraine shelf above the large rock overhang described in the approach to the North-East Face.

West Face

The first ascent was made by Alex McIntyre, Rene Ghilini and John Porter in September 1982 over three days. This face, opposite the huge South Face of Annapurna I is best approached by continuing up the South Annapurna Glacier so as to reach the face at its lowest point. This steep face provided a difficult route graded ED−.

From the glacier climb out below the West

Descending below the South Face of Fluted Peak under the protection of a rocky spur of the South-East Ridge.

Steep mixed climbing on the second day on the first ascent of the West Face of Singu Chuli.

At the top of the tower ridge, just below the summit plateau on Singu Chuli's West Face.

Face of Singu Chuli with difficulty, up the only obvious break in the moraine to gain a rognon above the glacier from which a distinct spur runs directly to the summit plateau.

From the rognon climb a rock buttress directly to a prominent buttressed spur (similar to Tower Ridge) with good bivouac sites. Continue up the ridge, picking a route around pinnacles linked with steep ice pitches (bivouac places). Continue up steep ice until it is possible to break out on to a peculiar summit plateau. The cone summit of the mountain 'rises like

an Antarctic peak from the plateau' (the same strange summit noted by Noyce). From the plateau an awkward corniced ridge, requiring care, was climbed to the summit.

Both this route and another on Hiunchuli were done in preparation for a new route on Annapurna's South Face and were, in Alex's words, 'heavy duty acclimatisation'.

Descent from this route was made by traversing the connecting ridge to Glacier Dome and then by steep ice and abseil to the glacier.

16 Manang Himal and the Marsyangdi Khola

The Chulus and Pisang Peak rise north of the Marsyangdi Khola in the Manang region of Nepal. This remote upland area lies to the north of and in a rain shadow formed by the main Annapurna Himal. The result is an arid landscape supporting little in the way of forest apart from scanty pine, juniper and scrub rhododendron. Huge glacial moraines abound, etched deeply by wind erosion into fantastic pillars. These winds seem a constant feature of the region and can prove significant on climbs.

Despite the popularity of the area it is poorly served by present maps. The Survey of India,

the US and trekking maps are poor to the extent of being misleading. The most readily available, and most useful, is the Mandala Trekking Map, 1:125,000 Pokhara to Jomosom and Manang.

Manang, closed to foreigners soon after the Chinese invasion of Tibet, was not fully opened again until 1977. Its reopening, along with the opening of the Thorong La, meant that trekkers could enjoy a hiking circuit 'around Annapurna'.

The way to the Chulus and Pisang Peak lies up the valley of the Marsyangdi Khola whose

Sallie O'Connor looking out over the arid landscape of the upper Kali Gandaki and the valley of the Lungpo Khola.

waters flow from the glaciers on the northern slopes of the Annapurnas, the southern flanks of the Chulus and the western glaciers of Manaslu, Peak 29 and Himalchuli. Along its course this already deep glaciated valley has been overdeepened by a river-cut gorge. The Marsyangdi eventually flows south to join the waters of the Trisuli River.

Although the approach up the Marsyangdi is relatively quick and involves no great altitude gain (circa 2,987m/9,800ft at Brathang), the trek takes you through a wonderful variety of landscape and culture; from the subtropical lower reaches of the valley where Gurung and Thakali peoples dominate, to the ethnically as well as socially interesting Manangba people of the upper valley, who live within the rain-shadow of the Annapurnas in an environment that has a distinctly Tibetian feel. They, contrary to appearance and many trekkers' misconceptions, are not simply an isolated, subsistance mountain people. Instead they have for a long time been trans-Himalayan traders who in more recent years have carried on normal and reputedly more illicit trade with the Far East and beyond. Certainly many Manangba leave this high cold valley in the winter months for the warmer confines of Kathmandu and Pokhara where they run lodges and have more comfortable homes. In any case, with the building of the airstrip at Ongre, Kathmandu and Pokhara are but a short flight away.

The actual trek into Manang via the Marsyangdi is in itself interesting and for those with an eye on the Chulus or Pisang, time might dictate that you return down the same valley. But it is not, and this goes for most of the treks in Nepal, a wilderness experience. The middle hills are for the most part, especially along the main valleys, well populated and the trails along which we walk are the highways and trade routes of the country.

A climbing party on the Thorong La looking south-east to the Chulu peaks. The highest summit is Chulu Central and on the right is Chulu East.

THE TREK

From Kathmandu it is possible to drive to Dumre and then continue up the Marsyangdi by a dusty road as far as Bensisahar.

Day 1: Kathmandu to Hile Chaur

A more interesting route, that adds a couple of days to the trek-in, begins in Ghorka. The road journey from Kathmandu takes about four hours. It was from this town that King Prithi Narayan Shah laid siege to and conquered Kathmandu on the festival of Indra in 1768 and so brought to an end the age of the Mallas. It's worth having a wander around Ghorka and making the hour-long, steep climb, up to the Durbar Hall and temple.

From town, descend westwards along a pleasant wooded ridge through Satipipal (1,219m/4,000ft) in less than two hours. For those wanting a short day after exploring Gorkha there is a campsite at Hile Chaur (1,158m/3,800ft).

Day 2: Hile Chaur to Thanti Pokhari

Continue steeply downhill to the Darondi Khola which takes less than two hours; in springtime the walking can be very hot. This is good country for the ubiquitous Nepali umbrella 'cool when it's hot – dry when it's not'. West of the river the trail climbs steeply for nearly three hours to Luitel Bhanjyang (700m/2,300ft).

From the pass you begin your descent to the main valley of the Marsyangdi, although before you meet the river you pass the disused airstrip at Palungtar to your left en route to Thanti Pokhari and the suspension bridge crossing the Chepa Khola, a tributary of the Marsyangdi. In all this is about six hours from Hile Chaur. Along this and all of the major

routes in Nepal you will often come across massive pipal and bhanyan trees growing from a platform, offering both shade and rest. The platform, a chautaara, is built at the right level for a porter to rest his basket on, and is a meeting place in village and bazaar.

Day 3: Thanti to Phalenksangu

After Thanti you enter the main valley of the Marsyangdi where the walking is level as you pass through mango trees on a trail that leads to Tarkughat in about three hours. Across the river you meet the dusty new road from Dumre. Follow this, now on the west bank of the river, to Bhote Odar. The stream before the village is a good repository for sweaty bodies, although our little expedition was joined by a herd of buffalo. Stay on the main trail to Phalenksangu (716m/2,350ft). There are several campsites on the far side of the river. This takes about six hours' walking from Thanti.

Those wanting to make use of the numerous bhattis along the main trail should stay on the west bank of the river and head for Bensisahar.

Day 4: Phalenksangu to Bhulebule

Cross the bridge at Phalenksangu (which means plank bridge!) and climb through paddy fields to join the new trail that climbs high above the river and offers good views of the Namun Bhanjyang (5,174m/16,976ft), a high pass that leads into Manang, east of Lamjung Himal. The crossing of this pass into Manang is both steep and demanding, although not technically difficult. Camping is limited and in good conditions (by that I mean dry under foot), it offers a great route into Manang. The Namun certainly provides the right kind of acclimatisation before a technical climb. For those intending to come out down the Marsyangdi it does make the route into a good circuit.

Near Bhote Odar we bathed in a stream and were joined by water-buffalos and a woman washing clothes.

The trail from Phalenksangu to Bhulebule passes through numerous Gurung villages whilst the Marsyangdi below becomes more impressive as the valley steepens. You pass the village of Ampchaur in two hours, and Simalchaur one hour further on. There are numerous possible campsites along the route for those breaking the day. Across the valley at the confluence of the Kudi Khola and the Marsyangdi is Kudi Bazaar. The route to the Namun Pass can be joined here.

The east bank trail ascends high above the river where it rounds the corner, offering views of Himalchuli (7,893m/25,895ft), which incidentally was the first mountain I came to Nepal to climb, although our approach was from the Buri Gandaki, an equally impressive valley. From its high point the trail descends to Bhulebule (853m/2,800ft). In all this takes about seven hours, perhaps a little less from Phalenksangu. There are lodges and shops in the village.

Day 5: Bhulebule to Syange

Syange (1,067m/3,500ft), or thereabouts, should be your objective for the following day. The river valley heads northward and is much more dramatic. Shortly after Bhulebule on the east bank path you pass the first of the many impressive waterfalls for which this valley is famed. I find it difficult not to stop and take a dip in the pools beneath their ribboned spray. In less than two hours, cross the Musi Khola by a bridge beyond Ngadi (930m/3,050ft).

As you will soon realise, in the Marsyangdi you gain little altitude, which increases the need later on for good acclimatisation. This is especially true for those on a tight schedule.

Pass the old bridge and continue climbing out of the valley and once again enter the Marsyangdi. The path climbs through terraces and forest to Brahman Hill, or the settlement of Bhawandanda, at a saddle. There are plenty of lodges selling refreshment, much needed

Sallie O'Connor crossing a traditional but precarious rope and twig bridge in the Marsyangdi Valley. Most of these have now been replaced with sturdier structures.

after the climb to the village. There are also hot springs by the Marsyangdi. The trail ahead is enjoyable and begins in descent from the village into the valley of yet another tributary of the main river. Cross by a bridge and ascend on a well-engineered trail via Khanegaon to Ghermu fron where the path descends to a suspension bridge. Cross the Marsyangdi and follow the trail to Syange which is about six hours from Bhulbhule. This is the northern limit of rice cultivation in the valley and from here there is a marked change in the valley's character.

Day 6: Syange to Tal

Follow the trail, now on the west bank, through the narrowing canyon of the main river. This section of the route is impressive, with many rock overhangs. Within an hour you pass through Gadi Jagat at a clearing in the forest. This settlement was once important in the salt trade with Tibet.

Waterfalls are very much a feature of this section of the valley and certainly our expedition fantasised about the 'mega' ice routes that would result in a big freeze.

From Jagat continue through the woods to Chamje (1,433m/4,700ft). Cross the suspension bridge to the east bank and ascend high above the river, passing through the now gorge-like section of the valley, formed between the flanks of Peak 29 and Lamjung Himal. In less than two hours the trail enters a section of the valley that was once a great lake bed, indeed the village in the centre of this flat is Tal (1,707m/5,600ft) which means lake. Alas the lake long ago silted up but what remains is also impressive and the sandy flat with its small herds of Tibetian horses grazing the meadows stand in stark contrast to the narrow 'U' shaped profile of the gorge ahead. It feels slightly like a wild west one-horse town! Tal is about five hours from Syange and offers first-class camping and several bhattis. The waterfall behind the village is stunning.

There is an interesting side trip to the Temung Meadows that is worthwhile both for acclimatisation and if the weather is good for spectacular views of the Manaslu, Himalchuli and Peak 29. It adds another day to the walk-in. Follow the main trail up the valley which climbs spectacularly after passing another fine waterfall. The path passes an old-style suspension bridge of steel and bamboo cables; don't cross it but continue to a new bridge and cross to Dharapani (1,943m/6,375ft). Permits might be checked here. Continue upstream on the west bank without crossing to Thonje where the Dudh Kila joins the main stream. Instead go westwards and ascend on a trail south of the Marsyangdi that leaves the main trail at Dhanagyu. Ascend through forest and meadows for about one hour and then climb steeply up towards the Namum Bhanjyang to the Temung Meadows, fine grazing pastures and a good camp. In all about seven hours from Tal. You rejoin the main trail near Koto.

Day 7: Tal to Chame

Those wanting to get on, without the side trip, should follow the same trail to Dharapani, continue on the west bank of the river but, instead of climbing to Temung Meadows, follow the main trail taking the lower fork. The trail follows the Marsyangdi's meander

Beautiful, fine-sprayed waterfalls are a feature of the Marsyangdi Valley. This one is above Tal.

to Bargarchap (2,164m/7,100ft), which is an interesting town since it marks a change in architecture to flat roofed, stone built houses much more in the Tibetian style. Mani-walls and wheels divide the streets, and lodges with enticing names like 'Pearly Gates' invite you to enjoy their 'heavenly fooding and sleeping'. Spend time having a look at the gompa before continuing through the forest which has now changed to conifers and has a much more alpine feel.

At the village beyond Bargarchap, marked

159

on some maps as Temung, there is a hot spring on the far bank of the river that feels like heaven as you alternate between the hot spring and the cold river. Do use the river to rinse off in, rather than leaving a scum on the hot pool! A lot more trekkers these days use biodegradable soap when they are in the mountains, and this is to be encouraged.

Stay on the south side of the river, crossing several bridges until you finally reach a clearing and the small settlement of Koto (2,629m/ 8,625ft), where there is a check post. Continue on to Chame (2,713m/8,900ft), the district administrative centre for Manang which is surprisingly active, with a police post, a bank, a gompa and some interesting architecture. A lot of weaving on traditional backstrap looms was going on when I passed through. Continue through the town over the small bridge before crossing the Marsyangdi to the north side, passing mani-walls. There is a hot spring on this side slightly downstream. For those wanting to make camp near here Kyupar might be better, in which case you will need to back-track. In all this will take about seven hours from Tal.

North of Chame the deep gorge of the Nar Khola enters the Marsyangdi. A route exists, leading north towards Tibet via the settlement of Nargaon, that would give access to the northern side of the Manang Himal. It is, unfortunately, closed to western travellers. However, in the autumn of 1988 a small group were given permission to visit Nar and approach the Chulus from the Nar Khola valley. This, hopefully, will result in an easing of access and the opening of this approach.

Day 8: Chame to Pisang or Ongre

The main valley swings north-east and the trail follows, passing through pine forest to the village of Taleku, no more than a few houses and a small lodge run by a friendly family with lots of kids that you are expected to amuse whilst dhalbhat is being prepared. The trail descends close to the river where once again there are some spectacular waterfalls and huge boulders. Cross the interesting bridge to the old Khampa settlement of Bhratang (2,919m/ 9,575ft) which has an apple farm and more interesting buildings and should take a little under three hours to reach from Chame.

Cross to the north bank of the Marsyangdi and after a while regain the south bank by either of the two bridges. Continue to climb through fine fir forest to some lovely meadows and clearings with spectacular views back down the valley to glacier-polished rock slabs, over 1,000 metres high forming an enormous amphitheatre. Just as my wife and I were rest-ing near a mani-wall at the edge of a clearing, two wild-eyed, pig-tailed Tibetian characters stampeded along the trail, rearing their horses to a halt before the steep descent to the river. Their animals, short, sure footed creatures, had colourful saddle blankets and their manes and tails were braided with red cloth ribbons. For a brief moment we felt we were being attacked by Khampas!

From Bhatang it is a short hike to Pisang, which, not surprisingly, is base for those attempting Pisang Peak. To get to lower Pisang you can either stay on the south bank or cross by the cantilever bridge to the north bank.

For those going to Chulu East and Chulu Far East, Ongre is the marshalling point for your expedition. This small settlement has a superb mani-wall, an airstrip and a Sherpa Climbing School and Himalayan Rescue Association Aid Post as well as the usual lodges. There is a high route from Pisang that can be taken, in which case Ngawal across the river may make a good centre.

For those that want to gain a little altitude before going on to the mountain I would recommend some hiking on the south side of the valley up the subsidiary valley a little north-west of Ongre that runs toward Annapurna III. There are some good ridges giving superb

Rene Ghilini climbing steep ice on the north side of the *West Ridge* of Hiunchuli.
(Photo: John Porter)

Machhaupuchhare overpowering the view of Mardi Himal which can be seen in front and to the left of the 'fish tail' peak's South-West Ridge, seen on the approach to the Sanctuary.

The simple interior of a tea shop, where milky-sweet tea and glucose biscuits or a bowl of dalbhat head the menu.

Crossing the Nare Glacier on the west side of the Mingbo La beneath the fluted Mingbo Peaks during the descent to Pangboche.

On the summit of Yala Peak in the Langtang looking east to peaks along the border with Tibet including Langshisa Ri, Longpo Gang, Gurkarpo Ri and Dorje Lhakpa.

At the start of the Tower Ridge-like buttress on the *West Face* of Singu Chuli.
(Photo: John Porter)

Mark Twight on the second ascent of the East Face couloir on Lobuje. Everest is
in the distance. (Photo: Alison Jane Hargreaves)

Approaching the Mingbo La from the Hongu Nup Glacier, with the South-East Face of Ama Dablam dominating the view through the col.

Sherpas young and old. The son of Pemba Tharkay practises reading learnt at the Hillary School, whilst his grandparent looks on.

Alex McIntyre at the col on the ridge between Annapurna South and Hiunchuli. Beyond is the West Ridge of Hiunchuli leading with great difficulty to the summit. (Photo: John Porter)

Climbing the steep slope leading to Tilman's Ridge from Paldor Glacier East.

Nick Pretzlick and Mike Tillett approaching the summit of Imja Tse after climbing the South Ridge. On the left is Ama Dablam and in the distance the Lumding Himal.

*Chulu Far East viewed from above Ongre rises above the arid, wind eroded
landscape typical of Manang.*

views of both the Chulus and the Annapurnas.
In the autumn months I have found a variety of
alpine flowers including two different gentians.

For the routes described on both Chulu
East and Chulu Far East a base camp is best
established in the valley that runs up toward
the col between the East and Far East Peaks at
4,700 metres (15,420 feet). The path goes from
Ngawal on the east bank of the Chegaji Khola.
A high camp can be established below the col
in moraines at 5,300 metres (17,500ft), although
several people have had to camp on snow
here. This high camp forms a launching site
for both the South-West Ridge of Far East and
for the East Ridge of East Peak.

Day 9: Ongre to Manang

From Ongre follow the main trail along the
Marsyangdi. The valley floor is quite flat and the

moraines with their arid greyness are sculp-
tured into organ pipe structures and dotted
with colourful bushes of tamarind and berberis.
What woodland there is consists of birch,
juniper, pine and scrubby rhododendron.

To the south the valley is walled in with the
impressive bulk of Annapurna II, Annapurna
III, Annapurna IV and Gangapurna. In one
hour the path leads across the Marsyangdi and
the village of Mungji. There are good campsites
near Sabji Khola. In another half hour the
village of Braga (3,505m/11,500ft) can be seen
terracing the dusty hillside to the right. Once
again there is good camping below the village.
This is one of the most interesting settlements
in the Nyesyang region, the name given to this
part of the Manang. Apart from the houses
which layer the hillside very much in the
Tibetian style there is an ancient gompa which
is over 500 years old. It has some magnificent

A Manangba woman carrying a traditional salt tea maker (Dongmu) through the steep paths of Braga.

art inside its dimly lit rooms, including 108 terracotta statues representing Buddha and various Buddhist saints. An old rogue, the guardian of the gompa, with a massive bunch of keys that unlocked an equally massive iron lock, went on to tell us that the gompa was built over two million years ago, that it contained much that was Buddha's, and that the cost of upkeep was very high. All of this came from a mouth containing blackened relics that were once teeth, on a rakshi-laden breath that would guarantee immortality to whoever it touched.

The town of Manang is less than an hour up the trail and you are welcomed by a pagoda-style entrance arch and stupa carrying a 'Welcome to Manang' sign and a billboard advertising

a local lodge. The town is a dusty place of stone built houses with flat roofs giving way to another house or room above. There are plenty of back alleys to wander along and arches with mani wheels to pass through and from time to time as you round a corner or look through an arch there are superb glimpses of toppling glaciers and massive moraines on the flanks of Gangapurna and the glacial moraine lake on the far side of the river. To the east of Manang you can see Bodzo gompa, which is well worth taking the time to visit. It is an active gompa that has noted wall paintings. The town has plenty of lodges along with more general provision stores, although the prices are relatively high. There are also plenty of traders selling 'original Tibetian antiques'.

Day 10: Manang to Chakadunga

Follow the path through sunless winding alleys and archways between stone built houses. Cross the stream with its prayer flags and mani stones and climb through terraced fields out of town. The view back down the Marsyangdi is most impressive, with the river snaking its way along the flat-floored glaciated trough. The flat-roofed terraced houses, each with its fluttering prayer flag stands in stark and dusty contrast to the tumbling, glistening glaciers across the valley.

As the trail climbs you turn the corner in the village of Tengi (3,642m/11,950ft) and are greeted with stunning views towards Tilicho and the Grand Barrier. Tengi is the last permanent settlement before the Thorong La. You look down on the confluence of the Khangsar Khola, flowing from Tilicho Lake and the Jargheng Khola whose headwaters are the melting snows of the Thorong La; they now join to form the Marsyangdi at this point.

Continue climbing on the trail to the herders' huts at Gunsang from where there is a striking view of the South Face of Chulu Central and West Peak. To date there are no recorded

The impressive South Face of Chulu West and Central seen from the Thorong La trail above Manang. From left to right the skyline ridge runs Chulu West, Chulu Central and Chulu East.

ascents of this impressive flank of the mountain. It does have considerable scope and some impressive lines, although if the rock is as poor as is recorded elsewhere on the mountain the ice lines may present the best options.

Chakadunga is the final yak herders' hut before you reach Thorong Phedi. Follow the yak pastures up a grassy ridge which in turn leads into a hidden valley, which provides a good site for base camp beneath the South-West Face of the mountain (4,400m/14,436ft). Behind camp is the West Ridge of Chulu West. To the south the views of the Annapurnas are superb.

RETURN TREK

There are several options:

1   Pre-book and fly out from Ongre if flights are available. Your agent or RNAC in Kathmandu will be able to tell you if it is possible.
2   Return back down the Marsyangdi or over the Namun Pass.
3   Continue over the Thorong La and around Annapurna.
4   Cross to Tilicho Lake and the Mesokanto La to Jomosom.

Around Annapurna

For those interested in completing the circuit 'Around Annapurna' the route over the Thor-

The Tibetian fortress-like village of Jharkot near Muktinath above the valley of
the Kali Gandaki and the Dhaulagiri Himal beyond.

ong La to the sacred site of Muktinath and
down the Kali Gandaki is described below
giving typical day stages for this well-travelled
walk. From Muktinath back to Pokhara the
route is as well served with lodges catering for
the trekker as anywhere in Nepal, but don't be
put off by this, because the scenery is striking
with a new mountain group, the Dhaulagiri
Himal, dominating the view all the way to
Poon Hill. Traditionally this is the trade route to
Mustang and the Tibetian influence is strong in
both the structure and scenery above Jomosom
as well as the faces and dress of many people
you meet along the way.

Chakadunga to Thorong Phedi

Continue along the main trail, crossing to the
true right bank of the Jargeng Khola in an
increasingly austere landscape to a fairly squalid
lodge before the start of the steep climb to the
Thorong La; this is Phedi. There are campsites
below the lodge (4,404m/14,450ft).

Phedi to Muktinath

If you are taking porters, this crossing shouldn't
be attempted in poor conditions or after heavy
snowfall. Unless you are well-acclimatised it is
a hard day to Muktinath.

From behind the lodge climb steeply up
scree to the west, which leads through a nar-

164

rowing to a notch. The path, if it is now under snow, then ascends along moraines to the crest of the Thorong La (5,380m/17,650ft), which is well marked with prayer flags and mani-stones. The views are spectacular and on either side of the pass are two splendid little peaks, often climbed, that were used as training areas for the Sherpa Climbing School that ran in Ongre. There are good views of the North-West Flank of the Chulu group from the pass.

Descend more steeply on the far side towards Muktinath. The going is straightforward, with a panorama of Dhaulagiri and Tukuche Himal. From the pass it will take about four hours to reach the temples at Muktinath (3,802m/12,475ft). In all, the crossing can take around ten hours. There are places to camp on the descent and you may find a hut selling food and offering shelter, but these should not be relied upon. Below the temples, which are a major site of pilgrimage, there are plenty of campsites and lodges.

From Muktinath the trail into the Kali Gandaki is obvious, but alas provides no official trekking peaks, which is a great pity.

Maintaining a leisurely pace, the following overnight stops are worthwhile.

Muktinath to Jomosom

This is a short day but it will give you a chance to go fossil hunting and enjoy the grandeur of the Kali.

Jomosom to Kalopani

The trail is straightforward and may be busy, but mainly with locals, especially strings of heavily laden pack ponies, colourful and noisy, making their way between Mustang and Pokhara.

Marpha is a town that I always find attractive and like to overnight in, but you may not have time. It's quite different from the other places along this trail.

Kalopani to Tatopani

You might want to do a side trip to the Dhaulagiri icefall before enjoying the murky pleasures of the hot (tato) springs (pani means water) at Tatopani.

Tatopani to Ghorapani

A long, hard climb takes you out of the Kali Gandaki to the pass at Ghorapani. There are, alas, more and more lodges being built at the pass and even on Poon Hill, the splendid look-out west of the pass which is ritually ascended by trekkers at dawn and sunset for one of the most spectacular of Himalayan views – scanning from the Dhaulagiris across the profound gorge of the Kali to the Nilgiris and Annapurnas.

From Ghorapani there are, as ever, options. Either descend on the far side and continue to Birethante, which is roughly a day stage from where you can reach Pokhara in a further day, or climb east from the pass and follow a splendid ridge crest to Deorali above Ghandrung and take a further two days via the Modi Khola and Sarankot to reach Pokhara. This is also the route taken if you want to visit the Annapurna Sanctuary.

If you have the time the latter route going east is the best. There is also a magnificent route out following the long ridge crest south from Poon Hill, but there are no lodges, little water, and in places the path is indistinct When I used it in 1988 it was obvious that very few trekkers had ever passed that way.

17 Pisang Peak (6,091m/19,983ft) and the Chulus

PISANG PEAK

Seen from Pisang the peak rises from yak pastures above the village in a uniform slope to the final summit pyramid which is an undistinguished snow and ice slope. Looked at from above Ongre the peak is a little more interesting and can be seen as a curved ridge, with the face above Pisang being the truncated southern end of the mountain. This is made up of steeply tilted rock, the dip slope of which faces the valley and is well seen in this peak and the great rock slabs further down the valley.

The peak obviously has a lot of scope for exploration and pioneering. The whole of the western flank, which is guarded by a hanging glacier, would appear to offer a considerable challenge, whilst a traverse of the whole summit ridge which connects to a more northern summit before curving back west looks a superb possibility. Access to the western end of the ridge, however, looks problematical as the ridge is guarded by huge rock slabs, a feature on this side of the valley.

THE CLIMB

South-West Face and Ridge

The first ascent was made solo by J. Wellenkamp in 1955 during a German expedition to Annapurna. This same expedition also made an ascent of Chulu East.

From upper Pisang Village ascend a path through sparse wood and pastures to a kharka at 4,380 metres (14,370 feet). This provides a good site for base camp.

A faint trail continues on open hillside, following a ridge and climbing to a shoulder on the South-West Ridge (5,400m/17,716ft), which provides a suitable site for high camp. Under some conditions this may be under snow.

Above, a well-defined ridge leads to the final snow slope which leads quite steeply although without difficulty to the summit. Graded Alpine PD. Descent is made by the same route.

THE CHULUS

These peaks form part of the Manang Himal, which are quite rightly included in the larger Damodar Himal, the eastern limit of which runs south from Chako and Peak 6,687 in a north-to-south direction along the Hunlung Khola, Nar Khola and Phu Khola. To the south it is bounded by the Marsyangdi Khola and the Mesokanta La. To the west its limit is the Kali Gandaki and to the north the Parchekya La (5,447m/17,870ft).

There exists considerable confusion with regard to the name and location of the Chulu peaks and what summit actually constitutes Chulu West and Chulu East, since it soon becomes apparent to anyone that has climbed in the range that several other summits close by, which are actually part of the Chulu massif, are not indicated on present maps of the area.

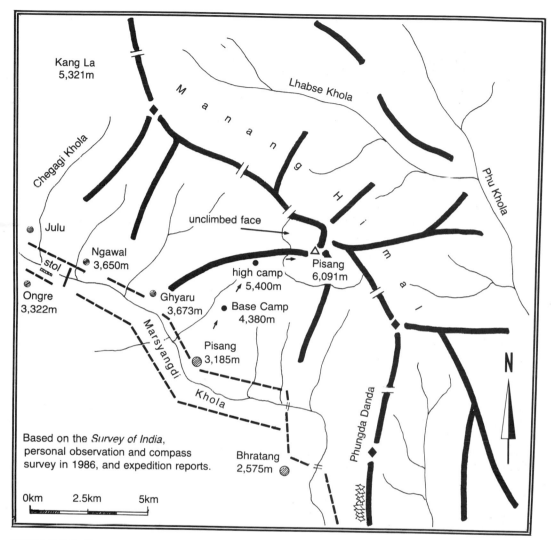

Kang La
5,321m

Lhabse Khola

Chegagi Khola

M a n a n g

Julu

Ngawal
3,650m

unclimbed face

H i

Phu Khola

stol

Ongre
3,322m

Ghyaru
3,673m

high camp
5,400m

Base Camp
4,380m

Pisang
6,091m

m a l

Marsyangdi

Pisang
3,185m

Phungda Danda

N

Based on the *Survey of India*,
personal observation and compass
survey in 1986, and expedition reports.

Bhratang
2,575m

0km   2.5km   5km

PISANG PEAK

For the sake of clarification, four summits can
be included in the Chulu group, two of which
are possible on the permit for Chulu West and
two on the Chulu East permit. What is apparent
is that the available trekking map is highly
misleading.

The highest of these peaks, marked Chulu
West (6,630m/21,752ft) on the trekking maps,
has a recorded altitude from at least two exped-

itions of nearer 6,400m (20,997ft); this might
more accurately be called Chulu Central. The
NMA gives this an official altitude of 6,429
metres (21,060 feet).

South-east of this highest summit is a lower
peak that can rightly be termed Chulu East.
Most of the trekking maps give this an altitude
of 6,200 metres (20,341 feet), although the
official height is 6,584 metres (21,601 feet).

Pisang Peak, West and South Faces, viewed from above Braga Village. The route of ascent climbs the right-hand ice face by its left edge.

Chulu East seen from the south-east at about 4,500 metres. The North-East Ridge is the far right-hand skyline; a major ice ridge must be crossed to reach it.

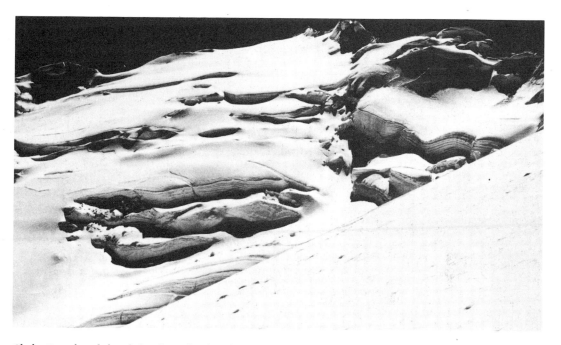

Chulu Central, and the Chulu Glacier bay by which it was first climbed, seen from the North-West Ridge of Chulu West. The route traverses beneath the seracs on the right to gain the central snowfields which are followed without difficulty to the summit pinnacle.

However, continuing two miles east along the ridge is another peak, well seen from the airstrip at Ongre and separated from the East Peak by a col which is 5,608 metres (18,400 feet). This summit has an altitude nearer 6,059 metres (19,880 feet) and should really be termed Chulu Far East. It is often climbed in mistake for Chulu East and many trekking agencies picture it in their brochures, mistakenly, as Chulu East. It would appear that both of these peaks are climbable on the same permit.

To confuse matters more, north-west of what is marked on the trekking maps as Chulu West and what I have called Central is another summit on the same ridge that should be called Chulu West (6,220m/20,407ft). This is marked on some maps as Gungdang (6,630m/21,751ft), although the latter actually exists to the north-west. Both peaks, what I call West and Central, can be climbed from the same

base camp and appear permissible on the same permit. All of the given altitudes appear to be exaggerations when compared with corrected altimetre readings taken on the summits. Hopefully the map of the Chulus on page 170 will help make matters clear.

With regard to first ascents things are less clear. However the following would appear to be correct. Chulu West was first climbed by a Japanese Expedition in 1952 by the South Ridge. The team included M. Takagi, K. Hayashi, S. Nakao, S. Takebushi and a Sherpa. No details are available of their route. The first ascent of the North-West Ridge was made by a Canadian Expedition in November 1979, led by Dr Larry Zaroff with Peter Lev and Sirdar Ang Jangbo (Mountain Travel Nepal).

The first ascent of the central, and highest, peak appears to have been made by Rudolph Schietl, Kevin O'Connell, Sonam Gyao Sherpa

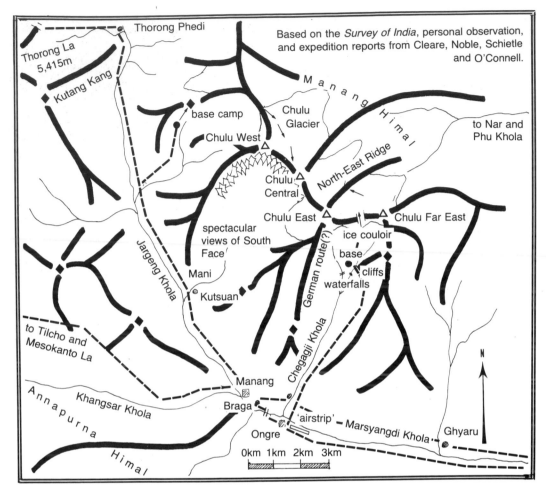

Based on the *Survey of India*, personal observation, and expedition reports from Cleare, Noble, Schietle and O'Connell.

Thorong Phedi

Thorong La 5,415m

Kutang Kang

Manang Himal

base camp

Chulu Glacier

to Nar and Phu Khola

Chulu West

North-East Ridge

Chulu Central

Chulu East

Chulu Far East

spectacular views of South Face

German route(?)

ice couloir

base

Jargeng Khola

Mani

cliffs

waterfalls

Kutsuan

Chegagji Khola

to Tilcho and Mesokanto La

Manang

Annapurna Himal

Khangsar Khola

Braga

'airstrip'

Marsyangdi Khola

Ghyaru

Ongre

0km 1km 2km 3km

N

CHULU PEAKS

and Sonam Chottar Sherpa on 16 October 1981.

Chulu East was claimed by a German Expedition in 1955 that included J. Wellenkamp, H. Biller and F. Lobbichler. There is some confusion as to whether this was in fact an ascent of the Far East Peak, as they made a rapid ascent of the south flank and this seems to fit Far East better. In 1979 Dick Isherwood and John Noble led a party of clients to the summits of both Chulu East and Chulu Far East. Their ascent of the East Peak by its North-East Ridge was a first.

THE CLIMBS

Chulu East (6,200m/20,341)

First ascent of the North-East Ridge was by Dick Isherwood and John Noble, leading a Mountain Travel Climbing Group in May 1979. From high camp established in moraines at 5,334 metres (17,500 feet) climb towards the head of the Chegaji Khola below a col on the ridge separating Chulu East and the Far East summits.

Climb to the col (5,608m/18,400ft) and

Chulu East seen from the south-east, from about 3,870 metres. The cliffs over which the frozen waterfall plunges must be bypassed by a long detour to reach the base of the mountain.

descend, crossing the glacier basin that descends from Chulu East toward the Nar Khola. On the far side of the glacier ascend steep scree slopes to the North-East Ridge at 5,791 metres (19,000 feet). On the first ascent a high camp was established here.

The route continues up the snow ridge ahead to the summit which is exposed at first but is climbed without much difficulty. Alpine PD+. On the first ascent the party descended to high camp for a second night. A smaller, faster group would probably make it back to the camp below the col.

Other Routes

Although I have no route description of it, the long South-East Ridge that runs to the summit from the col appears to offer no great problems although the final slopes appear steep.

Chulu Far East (6,059m/19,880ft)

South-West Ridge

From a camp in the moraines at 5,334 metres (17,500 feet) below the col separating the East and Far East Peaks of Chulu, gain the col (5,608m/18,400ft). From the col follow the South-West Ridge on snow and ice throughout to the summit.

There are several short sections of steep snow or ice (45 degrees) and bulges produced by the glacier. Grade Alpine PD. For those that want to shorten the summit day a high camp can be put on or near to the col.

High camp on the North-East Ridge of Chulu East with the South-East Ridge beyond. The ridge is crossed at a col at the head of the Chegagji Khola.

Descending the impressive North-East Ridge of Chulu East to high camp on the first ascent.

Chulu Far East seen from the approach to high camp. The ascent route climbs to a col on the left and follows the left-hand skyline ridge.

Other Routes

None have been recorded although the South Face of Far East Peak would appear to offer several ridge lines to the left and right of the main serac barrier that would give classic alpine-style climbing in a very fine position. Time will tell.

Chulu West

Ascents of Chulu West and Chulu Central are best made from a base camp in a small valley north of Manang situated off the main trail to the Thorong La. Indeed some of the best views of these peaks can be had from that pass.

North-West Ridge

First ascent was on 4 November 1978 by Dr Larry Zaroff, Peter Lev, Ang Jambo Sherpa (the Mountain Travel sirdar) and Lhakpa Nuru Sherpa.

Peter Lev suggests that the key to finding base camp is to walk above Manang to a yak herder's hut from where you view the South Face of Chulu Central. Go beyond the hut following the yak pastures and walk up a ridge which leads into a hidden valley where it is possible to find a good site for base.

From this camp, ascend steep scree slopes to a col (4,900m/16,076ft), on a subsidary ridge that leads down from the main ridge. To the north of the col ascend snow slopes for 200

Hamish Nichol's party on the 'mauvais pas' of the South-West Ridge of Chulu Far East.

metres (650 feet) to the base of a band of rock at an altitude of 5,100 metres (16,732 feet) and the site for a possible high camp.

Climb the rock band with some difficulty to the north-west shoulder of Chulu West (5,450m/17,880ft), where another camp can be established or alternatively a camp can be placed on a snow plateau above (5,530m/18,143ft). On the first ascent and several subsequent ascents rope was fixed on the rock band. From the plateau continue up the progressively narrowing ridge to the summit (6,250m/20,505ft). Descend by the same route. Alpine AD.

Chulu Central

North-West Face

First ascent was on 16 October 1981 by Rudoph Schietl, Kevin O'Connell, Sonam Gyao Sherpa and Sonam Chottar Sherpa.

The North-West Flank of Chulu West seen from high on the Thorong La. The rocky pinnacle of Central can be seen to the right of the snowy summit of Chulu West.

174

Chulu Central seen from the flank of the North-West Ridge of Chulu West. The route avoids the seracs on the right and gains the snow slopes on the left which are followed without difficulty to the final summit pyramid and pinnacle.

From the same base camp ascend to the col (4,900m/16,076ft). Climb snow slopes to the north of the col to the base of a rock band (5,100m/16,732ft), where a camp is possible. Climb the rock band with some difficulty, continuing to the snow plateau on the ridge beyond (5,530m/18,143ft) and place a high camp. This far the route has been the same as the North-West Ridge of Chulu West.

From this camp, traverse on to the Chulu Glacier basin to the east of the ridge and ascend the broad glacier slopes, avoiding serac obstacles. There is very little in the way of technical difficulty on this section, although in soft snow progress would be very difficult and although the slopes are not steep they may be prone to avalanche in certain conditions.

Continue to the Central Summit which is now well seen, crowned by a definite pinnacle. Continue towards this slope on steepening snow until it is possible to gain the crest of the summit ridge, which may be corniced. This in turn leads directly to a small saddle, beyond which is the final fifteen metre pinnacle. Descend by the same route. Alpine AD.

Other Possibilities

The most obvious is the impressive South Face seen as you follow the trail from Manang to Thorong Phedi. This will undoubtedly, one day, yield routes of considerable difficulty and interest.

175

II ADVICE ON TREKKING PEAK EXPEDITIONS

18 Organising a Lightweight Expedition

Climbing in Nepal, despite the rules and regulations, is relatively straightforward and many people have no trouble fitting an expedition into a four week holiday, although for certain mountains and routes this would be cutting it a little too fine. The rules governing such an expedition are not particularly irksome and although they involve the inevitable dose of bureaucracy, for those wishing to do all of their own organisation, it's simply a matter of procedure and patience. The Nepal Mountaineering Association have produced a small booklet containing the regulations governing the ascent of trekking peaks which I have reproduced in full in Appendix 1.

Those wishing to go on a lightweight Himalayan expedition without the headache of organisation should look to commercial trekking companies working through 'outfitters' in Nepal who offer expeditions to the more straightforward trekking peaks, or to the leading agencies. They can competently outfit and organise lightweight expeditions to any of the listed peaks providing a full range of services to get you to the base of the mountain; the rest is up to you.

Thus the style you choose to adopt in organising and outfitting an expedition will be controlled by many factors, not the least of which are time and money. Briefly outlined below are some of the options.

Commercial Trekking Peak Expeditions

Without doubt this is the simplest method of climbing a peak in Nepal. Many of the leading agencies offer expeditions usually four to six weeks long to the more popular summits such as Island Peak, Tent Peak, Mera and Pisang. On these expeditions clients are normally asked to supply a resumé of their walking/climbing background and a deposit. Once accepted you need only fill out the visa and trek permit forms and the agency does the rest.

They see to it that the peak and trekking permits are gained and all of the necessary bookings for hotels, internal flights and transport are done. They also provide the Sherpa team, which consists of a sirdar (head man) and Sherpa assistants who help organise the porters, make and break camp and invariably carry and climb on the mountain. Most agencies provide a trained cook who can cater to western tastes and a kitchen boy who fetches, carries and does all of the messy chores around the kitchen. They seem to be the first up, bringing the early morning tea, and the last to bed, having finished washing up or preparing things for the next day; truly the Gunga Dins on the mountaineering front.

On commercial expeditions the agencies also provide the shared group equipment, which includes not only tents, the kitchen and mess tent but also technical equipment such

On the summit of Island Peak.

as ropes, snow stakes and ice screws, although this tends to be minimal, in keeping with the technical difficulty of most of the mountains chosen. Many of the agencies also provide sleeping bags and foam pads.

The best companies also provide experienced Himalayan climbers as leaders who have a knowledge of Nepali culture and may speak the language. They teach the skills of high altitude climbing and lead the climb, making the decisions over route finding and safety.

With this kind of 'trip' the client need only furnish his or her personal equipment, according to a list provided by the agency, pay them money and turn up at the airport. Some of the companies also run pre-expedition weekends where members can get together, in Wales or the Lake District, for instance, to find out more about the expedition and each other.

Once in Nepal the members can involve

themselves in the day-to-day running of the expedition as they wish, although in my experience most are quite happy to forgo the chores of cooking, washing up and the daily putting up and taking down of tents in favour of visiting villages, taking photographs, talking with others, and generally enjoying a relaxed holiday, allowing the trip leader and sirdar to deal with problems and organise the daily programme in a style that has been common to mountaineering expeditions for decades. A well-established regime tends to be superimposed on the day, one that most expeditions, on the walk-in and out, tend to adopt.

A typical day on the walk-in begins at dawn with the kitchen boy bringing 'bed tea' to the tent; a hot, sweet brew so beloved by Sherpas. Tea means time to get up and pack for the day. On a 'pukka' trip you might also get a small bowl of washing water!

Kit bags are packed and rucksacks loaded

Men, gods and demons mingle in the streets of Kathmandu.

have this near a village or perhaps by a stream where washing can be done. During the early stages of the trek, when things can be quite hot, it's sensible to sit down out of the heat of the day rather than bash on. Remember you can only go as far as the porters can carry and day stages tend to be quite well established and known to porters.

After lunch there is usually another three or four hours' walking by which time you arrive at camp. Afternoon tea, usually a hot drink and Nepali glucose biscuits, is then the order of the day. This isn't simply a pandering to Imperial nostalgia and a return to Empire but a very practical and civilised way to get down enough fluid to stay hydrated and so help acclimatisation. It's vital to do everything possible during the walk-in to stay fit and healthy so that by the time you arrive at base camp you are capable of going higher.

Once again one would do well to learn from the best-run treks. Providing a bowl of water for washing hands before meals as well as leaving one outside a well-dug latrine could make the difference between summit success or being debilitated after a bout of 'Kathmandu quickstep' and so not be strong enough to go above base.

Dinner is usually ready by six, after which most people sit around camp or hibernate in their tents. A large communal tent which the agencies provide for dining in is a good idea, as people tend to slope off very early to their sleeping bags.

During the day the porters light their own fires and cook their own simple food. The Sherpas also tend to eat separately, something which they prefer; they need a break from their all-too-demanding employers. After dinner is often a good time to get together. Porters and Sherpas tend to sit around fires drinking locally brewed chang and generally entertaining themselves. Having said that, lighting fires is now frowned upon, although it is difficult to enforce this amongst people

with what you need for the day's hike. Whilst members are eating breakfast the camp is taken down and porters' loads organised, a job done by the sirdar and Sherpas. Once packed, the whole bhandabhast gets under way, wandering along the trail towards the next camp. The sirdar and Sherpas manage the porters along the way, making sure there are 'no problems' (a common cry from the modern Sherpa) and that loads arrive at camp, thus freeing members to enjoy the hike, visit villages, tea shops and generally do their own thing.

Lunch is taken, usually a kind of brunch after three or four hours' walking. I like to who are used to sitting around fires and for whom western ideas of conservation, during a cold night, is of little relevance.

Obviously this routine doesn't apply to groups using local bhattis (lodges) during the walk-in. On the other hand in some areas, the Khumbu for instance, I tend to favour a mixture of camps and local lodges.

Once at base camp and perhaps above the snowline the Sherpas, who are better equipped, tend to do the load carrying to higher camps. Not all agencies like their Sherpas to go above base, in which case all carrying and route finding is done by team members. On the other hand the better agencies charge a premium for climbing Sherpas which in part pays for their insurance and in part goes to the Sherpas.

On the commercial trips the Sherpas of the leading agencies tend to have amazing mountaineering credentials. I think of past expeditions with sirdars and Sherpas such as Lakpa Dorje, Ang Jambo, Dawa Tenzing and Pemba Tarkay; men of the highest calibre with expeditions and a tally of summits between them second to none, who provide a depth of experience from which we could all learn. On the other hand many of the Sherpas seem to depend for their climbing on high levels of fitness and minimal technical skill, which is undoubtedly the reason why so many have come to grief on major expeditions.

On the organised expedition most things apart from visas, airport taxes and some meals are included in the price, although you are normally required to take out your own insurance cover.

WORKING THROUGH AN AGENCY

Quite distinct to a commercial expedition is a lightweight expedition made up of a group of friends who none the less operate through a trekking agency, allowing the agency to deal with the paperwork at the Kathmandu end.

The agency may also provide a full trekking service, looking after all the arrangements to get the climbing team to and from base camp, providing the same organisation as for a commercial trek with regard to staff and food.

The major difference is that the group will know each other and have decided on the objective and the duration of the expedition and the style and difficulty of the ascent they wish to make. In this respect they are much the same as a normal expedition to any of the major peaks in Nepal, which differs usually only in scale and cost.

On the other hand most of the agencies are very flexible in the kind of arrangements they allow, given that they then charge you for the services, provided it is simply a matter of agreeing beforehand about what services you want and what the agency is charging for.

Thus it is possible for a group of climbers to have their trek and peak permits arranged and perhaps the provision of a reliable Sherpa crew including a cook and kitchen. They, 'the team' are then responsible for purchasing food, hiring porters, arranging transport and making payments as they occur. Thus an expedition can be arranged to suit individual needs and bank balance.

DOING IT YOURSELF

Many climbers with the time and energy enjoy doing the whole thing themselves. Given that there are certain requirements governing trekking peaks, such as the need for a registered sirdar and for a recognised agency to get your peak permit, many of the agencies in Kathmandu are willing, for a 'service charge', to supply their agency name and a Sherpa sirdar recognised by the NMA and provide little else by way of facilities.

A strong Sherpa team on the Far East Summit of Lobuje East. The true summit is behind rising beyond the obvious and difficult gap.

Trek and Peak Permits

You will need to complete the Climbing Permit application form (*see* Appendix I Rules and Regulations) and return it to the Nepal Mountaineering Association on Ram Shar Path which is north of the Singha Durbar in Kathmandu.

As well as the peak permit you will also require a trekking permit. Unfortunately you will need to go to another office for this since they are issued by the Central Immigration Office of the Home and Panchyat Ministry at Maiti Devi near Dilli Bazaar in Kathmandu.

As with all permits you will need to supply at least two passport photographs. At the same time as getting the trek permit you might want to get a visa extension. Trekking permits can take up to two days to process and the office may be busy so you are advised to arrive early and to check that there are no religious holidays, of which there are many, when all offices close, sometimes for several days.

These permits should be carried with you on the trek and will be checked at numerous police posts along the way. Should you leave you passport in Kathmandu for safe keeping, permits can be used as an official document to change money.

After that everything else is up to you. Along with the Sherpa you arrange the transport, hire what porters you need and organise the expedition in the style you wish. For many this may mean using the lodges where available on the walk-in, or indeed you may wish to enjoy a very traditional style expedition or trek to the mountain.

Obviously there are plenty of options with regard to how you organise your expedition. Having someone do most of the work is going to cost more; on the other hand 'doing it yourself' takes a lot more time and energy. For those without a group of like-minded friends wanting to climb a Himalayan peak, a ready-made expedition, booked through an adventure travel company, may be the only way to go. Organising your own expedition right down to the permits and porters is fascinating but it can also be hard on the nerves and patience (although of course slicing a way through the problems has its own rewards).

Before leaving home – in a perfect world – you would have planned the whole thing in intricate detail, be medically fit and innoculated according to current recommendations, have all your equipment and know exactly what you want to do. On the other hand you may have done few or none of these things in which case a proper expedition to any of these peaks can still be organised according to Tilman's dictum, 'on-the-back-of-an-envelope'. To which one might add, 'as long as you know what you're doing'.

Having arrived in Kathmandu without a normal 30 day tourist visa the accommodating Nepalese immigration officials allow you to buy an on-the-spot seven-day visa which can then be extended at no extra cost. Having cleared customs most climbers take a taxi to the Thamel district of town, no doubt because it has the cheapest and best-known tourist hotels and guest houses alongside the widest selection of safe places to eat. All this crammed into an area thick with second-hand equipment, curio, book and clothing shops. Definitely the hub for the active in Kathmandu, whereas the lodges close to 'Freak Street' off the Durbar Square still tends to attract the hippies; aged and otherwise. A selected list of one to five star hotels can be found in Useful Addresses (page 219).

For those intending to 'do their own thing' the following tips might be useful in finding a way around the fascinating maze that is Kathmandu. To begin with get yourself a street plan of Kathmandu which is available from most bookshops and hotels.

Trekking Agencies

If you haven't done the ideal thing and contacted an agency before leaving home to find out what they have to offer and at what cost it's time to do so. My advice would be to opt for the best agency you can afford, particularly if the trip you intend is in any way out of the ordinary, prolonged or difficult logistically. On the other hand if you simply want their name on the permit and little more, it doesn't matter. A selected list of agencies in Kathmandu can be found in Useful Addresses.

Sherpa Sirdars

If you don't intend hiring a sirdar from an agency, which is the usual thing to do, there are plenty of Sherpas looking for work in and around Thamel; some may be recognised by the NMA as sirdars and are good men, others are blatantly not, but will nevertheless promise the earth! In the final analysis it becomes a matter of questioning and judgment, and hiring a reliable Sherpa from an agency I feel is the best answer unless you have been given a contact through a trusted friend.

Climbing and Trekking Equipment

Should you have left home without something, or lost baggage in transit, all is not lost since most things are available in Kathmandu. Do look around not only in the shops but also on the notice boards in the lodges and cafes in Thamel where penniless climbers try to sell off their gear before they do a deal with the hard-nosed shop keepers. Just about everything you need for an expedition is available, but don't expect to get it for nothing. Those days are over and the shop keepers specialising in climbing and trekking gear are quite likely to pull out a manufacturer's brochure to emphasise just how much a piece of equipment is worth and what a real bargain you're getting! On the other hand be prepared to barter – the asking price is rarely the final price.

Food

Good food for the trek and climb is readily available in Kathmandu, not just surplus expedition food that has been sold off, but locally processed foods produced to fill a need in the trekking market. These include soups, noodles, muesli, dried fruit and nuts, all specially packed in smaller quantities in plastic bags. As well as these, locally made biscuits, honey, teas and jams are all available along with tinned goods imported from India. Although there are lots of stores selling these goods there is an area off the New Road called Pako where the best selection seems to be available and I can recommend the Fresh House amongst the many small 'supermarkets' in that area. However, if you have got particular needs and wants the best advice is to take it with you from home. You don't need to buy everything in Kathmandu and on some of the treks re-supply of things like lentils, rice, meat and fresh vegetables can be done along the way, a task that is best handed over to your sirdar. On the other hand you would do well to organise the high-altitude rations before leaving Kathmandu.

Sherpa-Style Kitchen

If you are not using an agency and are a large enough group to need a cook you will need to supply a kitchen, which in Nepal means all manner of aluminium pots and pans, chopping boards and ladles. Once again, this is where a good sirdar is indispensible and will be able to tell you just what you need. In the area around Asan Tole there are stores specializing in just such objects; the prices are fixed and aluminium pots are sold according to weight. A pressure cooker is a great item on expedition.

Large paraffin stoves are also available. A good sirdar may have a regular partner that acts as cook, in which case he may have a kitchen you can hire. A full kitchen doesn't come cheap. In 1987 it cost me around NR (Nepali Roupees) 5,000/–, but this also included a paraffin pressure lamp. Kitchen equipment may be available for rent from some of the stores and from Sherpas in Namche Bazaar.

Porters

By and large, porters tend to be available just about everywhere, although those involved in trekking may seem scarce during the main trekking seasons. With larger groups, hiring of porters is definitely a job for the sirdar, who will know exactly where to find them, what to pay them and what they are to carry. For treks in remote areas be prepared to pay them something in advance so that they can buy food. You should also be prepared to supply porters with warm clothing, including trousers, a jacket, hat, socks and gloves, as well as dark glasses for walking in snow and some kind of boots. The normal issue footwear are Chinese basketball boots! Remember to get a large size, as porter feet tend to be as broad as they are long, and unused to being cramped into a narrow shoe. Locally knitted socks and gloves are available in Thamel. Failure to look after your porters can obviously lead to trouble not only in the form of strikes but also in the unforgivable form of exposure. Although the sirdar looks after the porters you are ultimately responsible for their well-being and must make sure that their stoicism doesn't result in injury.

For camps in remote areas where porters are unable to get local lodging you may also have to provide them with shelter. Once again this is where a large mess tent is useful, since a surprising number of porters can cram together in one, which also helps them keep warm.

It should also be remembered that porters

are made up of many different ethnic groups; they are not all Sherpas even though Sherpa has become the generic name for anyone who carries a load. By and large the Sherpas tend not to do day-to-day portering jobs unless you are in the Khumbu, but rather they have the more responsible roles of sirdar and cook, although recently I have seen more Gurungs and Tamangs getting these responsible jobs. In the Khumbu your sirdar is likely to hire yaks instead of porters for load carrying and they usually carry twice as much as a porter for about two-thirds the rate, although this is always negotiable. If you do use yaks or Dzo (yak/cow cross) remember they cannot cross high snowy passes and certain types of terrain, so make sure your sirdar knows your intended route exactly. I have heard of groups that wanted to cross the Tso La, for instance, but were foiled because they didn't have porters.

Buses

There are several ways of getting to the start of your expedition, be it Trisuli, Pokhara or Jiri. Local buses are certainly the cheapest method of travel and are in themselves an adventure. Crowded, noisy and dangerous they have an unforgettable aroma that is animal, vegetable and mineral in one. There are minibuses that ply the same routes that are a little more comfortable and a little more expensive.

On the other hand, a larger group may need to hire a private vehicle. Taxis are an obvious choice and several may be the answer for a journey to say Sundarijel or Trisuli. On the other hand minibuses can also be hired from most travel agents in town.

Most of the buses leave from the main bus station which is on the east side of the Tundhikhel parade ground, although the Trisuli bus leaves from Pakanajol, west of Thamel, and the Pokhara bus from outside the main post office.

Internal Flying

As well as the buses, Nepalese Airlines (RNAC) who have their office in the New Road, have an extensive network of internal flights. By and large they are very reliable given the vagaries of mountain weather. Flying into certain areas always seems to be easier than flying out, as most people tend to prefer to fly out. It is always worthwhile booking ahead and this is best done through an agent. Card-carrying students should also note that they are favoured with a 25 per cent discount on flights.

Money

Before leaving Kathmandu you should carry enough Nepali currency for most of your needs, although there are obviously banks along the way. Changing money on the black market, although giving a better rate, is illegal. Ideally you should try to carry small denomination, clean, untorn notes for your day-to-day dealings, although as time goes by fewer and fewer people raise an eyebrow when you give tham a 100 rupee note for tea and biscuits in a bhaati. Having said that, tens and twenties in large numbers are more convenient.

EXPEDITION CHECK-LIST

Before leaving:
Establish team members
Research peak
Set dates
Contact agency for services/prices/outline
    programme
Book international flight
Obtain visas
Obtain insurance
Get the correct innoculations
Return peak and trek forms to agent
Make hotel bookings
Book internal flights

Gather equipment
Buy food

In Kathmandu:
Contact agency/insurance/emergencies
Check bookings for internal flights/transport
Collect and check permits

Meet sirdar
Check items of equipment supplied by agency
Buy provisions
Change expedition money
Check hotel reservations
Make return flight confirmations

19 Equipment

Making a list of equipment for mountaineers about to embark upon a Himalayan expedition seems a bit like trying to teach your grandmother to suck eggs. On the other hand, many climbers going to Nepal for the first time may be a little bemused about what to take and what not to take. There are no hard and fast rules about gear and climbers contemplating a new or difficult route will already know the equipment they like to use. Obviously difficulty and style will very much dictate the type and amount of technical equipment carried.

At one end of the continuum, commercial climbing groups going to, say, Mera Peak or Pisang take little in the way of technical equipment outside of stout boots, an ice axe and perhaps a down jacket, relying on a good day and an easy plod to the summit. Even for high camp they need little more than standard mountain tents as the bulk of the equipment is carried. This is the case on traditional expeditions by climbing Sherpas who invariably do the cooking and in many cases the trail blazing, leaving the 'climber' with his barely acclimatised body to haul him/her self to the top in the few days allotted, in a tight schedule, for the climb.

At the other end of this continuum is the lightweight climbing team aiming at a difficult multi-day ascent involving several bivouacs and a climb in fine style, during which they carry all their own equipment, cook and generally fend for themselves and are willing to wait for the weather and have time to properly acclimatise for their project.

At the end of this chapter I have included an equipment check-list. It is not intended that you take all and everything mentioned, but rather that you use it as a kind of *aide memoire* before you go.

ON TREK

For most of us the trek is a real holiday and light, loose clothing is the order of the day. Cotton trousers, track suit bottoms and T-shirts are normal. A lot of people wear shorts during the day on trek, that includes porters and Sherpas, but you should be aware that some Nepalis would find this offensive especially in their homes. Women in particular would do well to carry along a light cotton skirt for trekking in or visiting homes.

Many people like to wear running shoes for trekking, whilst others prefer lightweight walking boots; both are ideal and it is really a matter of preference, although the latter are obviously more suitable for muddy, wet or snow-bound trails.

Unless you're walking in at the end of the monsoon your chances of experiencing rain on trek are slight. For this purpose an umbrella is ideal, providing both shade from the sun and protection from any rain. The small, folding umbrellas that fit easily into a rucksack are cheap and plentiful in Kathmandu.

Remember that each day you will have to carry all the things you think you will need during the day because once porter loads are packed and on the move it's often impossible to get into them until evening.

Standard ridge tents used at high-camp on Mera Peak. Beyond, the striking South-East Face of Peak 43 at the head on the Hinku Valley.

Kit Bags

By far the best way to pack equipment for porters to carry is in large kit bags or holdalls. The tough zippered holdall is certainly a lot easier to use for personal kit where you want access to it every day rather than the military style kit bag which opens at one end. Many expeditions use large plastic drums which form a single porter load and certainly provide good protection for food and awkward climbing gear. Fitting a padlock to zips and openings is also a good idea and helps to prevent petty pilfering. If you are carrying a lot of equipment in similar containers it's worth labelling and listing their contents.

Tents

Tents on expedition need to serve many purposes. They need to be roomy and comfortable since you spend a lot of time in them whilst at the same time they need to be light enough to carry to high altitudes, and still be capable of withstanding severe mountain weather. To this end it seems to me that the modern geodesic dome tents are ideal, giving as they do more living space for a given floor area. Free standing domes are also more easily pitched in difficult places where anchorage might be a problem. If you find putting them up in Wales at the weekend difficult, on the mountain at 19,000 feet it will be an even greater test of your mental acuity. Little things like colour coding poles and sleeves might just help. A pole repair kit is worthwhile. I would mention here that a snow shovel is very useful for building platforms, digging out buried tents and making snow holes, both an alternative and a necessity on some routes. If you have never had to do it, it is hard to imagine how difficult it is to dig out a buried tent with just your hands or an ice axe. A small tent brush for sweeping out snow as well as brushing snow off clothing is also useful.

Stoves

Cooking on the trek is not a problem; the cook tends to do it very efficiently using three or more stones to make a hearth, and some firewood, or if they are not available a large paraffin primus which roars away endlessly. On the commercial trips these same stoves are carried to high camp by the Sherpas and used accordingly. Personally I don't like them for it seems to me that no matter how careful you are the paraffin pervades everything, so like a Monty Python skit you end up having a menu that includes paraffin with everything: chapatti and paraffin, chips and paraffin, dhal bhat and paraffin, so that in the end even the cups absorb the paraffin and your hands are perpetualy coated in soot and oil. In part of course this has something to do with the quality of Nepali paraffin, which at best is poor and needs to be carefully filtered. However, it remains the cheapest form of fuel available when wood is not used for cooking.

My own choice of fuel on the mountain is gas. The now traditional Bluet Gaz stove using a butane/propane gas mix (the cylinders with red lettering) are simple and efficient, and not affected by cold temperatures. Used in conjunction with a tower stove they are the lightest and most efficient cooking system available for mountain use. A limited supply of these cylinders are always available in Kathmandu and Namche Bazaar and it is not a great problem shipping some out as long as you inform the airline. It's useful to carry a few spare washers for the inlet valve of the stove and a few pricking needles for cleaning the jets. I would also suggest a spot of superglue to keep the washer in place. A few gas lighters in with the high altitude cooking kit is also a good idea. A washing-up sponge or cloth in the cooking kit is great for mopping up condensation in the tent during cooking, which in turn means less frozen rime at night and less tent-rain during the day.

Boots

Boots for Himalayan climbing have really undergone a revolution in a very short time. Heavy leather double boots are a thing of the past and I can think of few climbers that have hung on to them, other than for nostalgic reasons or outright meanness! Have a look around the 'gear' shops of Thamel in Kathmandu and see the monster footwear that was *de rigueur* when men were men and mountains were kicked into submission. The modern, lightweight plastic double and in some cases single boots are ideal footwear and most mountaineers contemplating a Himalayan expedition probably have them. For many climbs an alpine mountaineering boot with a Yeti-style gaiter is also suitable but more prone to freezing overnight at high camp. The more serious and prolonged the project, the more important it becomes to have the best high altitude boot. The usual criteria regarding a good fit applies also to Himalayan climbing, to which I would add a little extra room is no bad thing.

Crampons

Everyone has their own style of crampons for the kind of ice climbing they are into. What surprises me is the number of people on their first Nepal trip who invest in a new pair of double boots and don't re-fit their crampons, and find that the straps are too short to fit around the larger boot and a gaiter once they are at base camp. For most Himalayan climbing you tend to need longer spikes than for Scottish ice and, if you have a choice, modern quick release bindings save a lot of effort and tend to be lighter; a definite plus at altitude.

Sleeping Bags

Sleeping bags can sometimes be a bit of a problem. On the mountain and high up we

Even on a clear day cold winds and altitude make windproof shell clothing and down jackets essential; approaching the Central Summit of Mera Peak.

all like to sleep warm and a bag suitable for the freezing conditions on the mountain is unlikely to be the right answer for the walk-in through, say, the subtropical conditions north of Pokhara. A zipped sleeping bag is a simple solution and more and more manufacturers have gone over to this. My own preference is for two sleeping bags, neither heavyweight, but when combined they provide superior warmth and are ideal on the walk-in when used alone. One of my bags also has a Gore-tex outer which makes it great for bivouacs and for inside the tent where the rime frost that forms at night tends to drip on everything once the sun gets on the tent, making down sleeping bags damp and inefficient. Of course a lightweight synthetic outer bag would also do the trick.

Shell Clothing

Outer wear tends to be a very personal thing. My own choice is for a combination Gore-tex salopette and a jacket rather than a one-piece suit, which seems much more suitable for winter Himalayan use. I also find the combination more versatile on hot days, when over trousers or a jacket may not be needed, and basic bodily functions also are much easier to perform. What is essential is that your outer-wear, whoever it is made by, must be windproof. This is far more important than being waterproof, especially high up, where if it is raining it probably means you have chosen the wrong season and are climbing during the monsoon, so you shouldn't be there anyway!

Layering System

It seems to me that the principles of a 'layering system' really come into their own in the Himalaya where day and night temperatures alternate between extremes and clothing needs to be functional and readily adapted to suit the prevailing conditions. I much prefer having several light, warm layers that can be swapped around rather than bulky sweaters or fleece jackets. By and large I think fleece clothing in the form of salopettes and sweaters are great, being both light and warm, but my preference is for wool long johns and vest rather than synthetic LIFA style garments which I don't find as comfortable, and just about everyone complains that they 'stink' after a couple of days' wear. Being able to ventilate without having to strip off seems very important, when even at moderate altitudes the effort seems so much more.

Having equipment that is comfortable in use, not too restricting or too loose but at the same time making sure that there are no niggling cold gaps is vital.

Head Gear

A good sun hat, both for the walk-in and on the mountain has always been a must for me, despite spending a lot of my time in the mountains. I can think of nothing more enervating and likely to produce a sickly headache than a day at altitude in brilliant snow with your brain baking inside a hatless head. I've seen everything from Y-fronts to knotted handkerchiefs on the heads of mad dog mountaineers, used in vain attempts to keep off the sun, much to the amusement of the Sherpas. A companion on an expedition once likened complaining sunburnt climbers to haemorrhoids; in that they were hanging around in clusters going bright red and were a pain in the backside!

A balaclava-style helmet or hat with ear flaps is essential, especially in windy conditions.

Gloves

Gloves are always a problem. Dachstein-style mitts seem to be a favourite amongst British mountaineers, although my own preference is for an insulated ski glove with a Gore-tex and Thinsulate construction. I also use lightweight thermal liners, which are great for photography or cooking.

Repair Kit

Repair kits have, in my experience, tended to be what other people in the party carry. Every well-organised group should have one to repair the lifetime guaranteed items and replace the essential but breakable bits and pieces. A good sewing kit, some ripstop repair material for tents, an aluminium sleeve for tent poles and crampon replacement pieces are all useful. I've also found a tube of superglue pretty important for repairing Yeti gaiters and broken sunglasses, and just about everything else that simply comes apart in your hands! Cooker spares are vital.

Ice Screws and Stakes

Ice screws are just about standard and quantity will very much depend on what you intend doing or how many you think you might drop. Kathmandu and Namche Bazaar seem to have an unlimited supply of 'Russian' titanium ice screws which weigh nothing and cost less and certainly cut down the excess baggage problem. Snow pickets, something most of us never use in Europe, are available in and around Kathmandu. Ex-expedition stock, they come in all manner of shapes and sizes, are very useful and are probably used more on the average trekking peak climb than ice screws. They are certainly useful for fixing handlines.

Harness

One thing you should check is the fit of your harness over the kind of clothing you might be wearing on the mountain. I've seen numerous climbers failing to fit their usual one over all the extra gear they were wearing.

Rucksack

Most modern rucksacks carry well, although many, it seems to me, are becoming too complicated and too heavy. The main criteria for an expedition pack is that it is large enough, if you are doing your own carrying, to hold what you want on the inside, rather than having to strap all manner of things on the outside and so looking and sounding like a tinker's cart! This becomes even more important where trying to carry down from a high camp a mass of hurriedly packed gear and part frozen tents that seem to have expanded to fit the infinite space of the mountain rather than the stuff sacks in which they came.

Water Bottles

Large water bottles are a must on Himalayan expeditions where most people find problems getting enough liquid. I normally carry two one-litre Nalgene bottles which I have found to be the best. Filled with hot water last thing at night it can even act as a hot water bottle for the first hour or so!

The 'pee's de resistance' is the wide-necked plastic bottle, a must for any bona-fide Himalayan mountaineer, where a mixture of high liquid intake and perhaps a few diamox make getting up at night inevitable, and the anticipated misery enough to keep you awake in the first place. My experience is that both men and women can become equally adept at this skill. For those that forgo the bottle, the great outdoors awaits you with memories of star-filled skies, moonlit mountains and frozen nether regions!

The most successful Himalayan mountaineers I've climbed with seem to be well organised and quickly get into a routine with their equipment, wasting little time and energy in getting ready, and have the system worked out so that they adapt to changing conditions easily and seem to stay relatively comfortable. This becomes increasingly important the longer you spend on the mountain.

High Altitude

If you are going to make up high altitude rations it is worth remembering that most people experience a loss of appetite high up, and the biggest single need is for liquid. My advice and preference on the mountain is for liquid food and lots of choice rather than, say, a single bulk item of dried food.

A daily ration would consist of lots of packet drinks: tea, fruit drinks, ovaltine and instant soups. I include sugar for the drinks as well as lots of individual bars of chocolate and well-wrapped cheese, biscuits and sausage, or a tin of paté. The aim is to give lots of fluid and tasty items that can be eaten easily, giving plenty of calories but taking little preparation. For the few days one is above base my own feeling is that there is no need for a balanced or healthy diet. Rather, an unbalanced high liquid, high energy intake is what's needed.

EQUIPMENT CHECK-LIST

This list doesn't represent what you must take but is simply a guide, an *aide memoire* to help you tick off the things you might need and have to pack.

Boots and shoes:
Comfortable shoes for travelling and for Kathmandu
Trekking boots or running shoes
Down boots for camp/thongs
Double boots

Climbing gear (personal):
Harness
Crampons
Ice axes
Crash hat
Head torch/batteries/bulbs
Ascenders
Descender

Gloves:
Lightweight thermal
Dachstein mitts or insulated ski glove
Overmitts
Silk liner

Headwear:
Sun hat
Balaclava or ski hat

Socks:
Light cotton athletic socks
Wool climbing socks

Gaiters:
Yeti style
Neoprene overboot

Shirts:
Long sleeved cotton
Long sleeved wool
T-shirts

Underwear:
Regular everyday use
Wool long underwear
LIFA style

Trousers:
Shorts
Long cotton hiking
Warm/climbing trousers/breeches
Tracksuit/fleece

Sweaters:
Lightweight fleece/wool for travel
Fleece/wool for climbing

Sleeping bag:
Down high altitude bag
Lightweight down or synthetic
Cotton liner
Gore-tex bivvi bag or cover
Sleeping pad (Karrimat) or Thermarest

Rucksack and kit bags:
Large capacity rucksack for climbing and carrying
Day bag for trek/shopping
Kit bag/holdall for porter load
Duffle for leaving things in Kathmandu

Waterproofs/shell clothing:
Climbing jacket
Salopette trousers, preferably full zip legs
One-piece wind suit

Insulated clothing:
Down jacket
Down trousers
Down vest

Bits and pieces:
Towel
Washing kit
Personal first-aid kit
Repair kit
Sunglasses
Climbing sunglasses or goggles
Sun screen and glacier cream
Lip salve
Plastic bags
Altimeter
Compass
Maps
Notebook/pens/pencil
Camera gear/batteries/film
Toilet paper
Swimsuit
Reading material
Penknife
Wide-necked bottle
Marker pen
Stuff sacks
Wet wipes
Walkman and tapes

Eating utensils:
Cup – large capacity/strong plastic
Knife/fork/spoon
Plate
Bowl
Two 1-litre plastic water bottles

Group equipment:
Tents
Ropes
Tapes/slings
Karabiners
Ice screws
Snow bars
Deadmen
Rock pegs
Rack/nut/friends

Cookers
Tower stove
Cooking pots
Medical box
Porter clothing (?)
Dining tent/tarp
Sherpa kitchen
Pressure cooker
Water containers
Plastic containers for butter/oil/sugar/fuel
Plastic bags for locally bought food
Paraffin lamps
Repair kit
High altitude rations
Camp chairs/tables
Toilet tent (!)

20 Maps

For trekking purposes all of the major areas of Nepal are well covered by large scale maps that are perfectly fine for finding you way, since to a great extent the major ridge lines, the rivers and most of the villages are plotted quite accurately. For mountaineering use, however, the maps to some areas are poor to the extent of being misleading, and appear to have been drawn from memory by an aged mystic.

We should not complain, however, since this only heightens the adventure, and a good sirdar, in any case, will get you to the foot of the mountain. Just try to imagine Tilman, Hagen and Roberts roaming the valleys, passes and glaciers trying to make sense of Nepal's complicated geography. If this doesn't satisfy you, think of the French in 1950 on Annapurna not simply trying to find a route but also trying to find the mountain.

My own feeling about the maps of Nepal is that they are best used in conjunction with good photographs, and to this end looking at as many books, journals and reports of your chosen area as possible and studying the photographs with map in hand will give you a feel both for the area and for the cartographer's artistic limitations.

Despite the fact that the US Army Map Service (AMS) U502 Series exist to a scale of 1:250,000 they are difficult to get in the UK. The Alpine Club and Royal Geographical Society libraries have copies but Stanford's do not.

Most of the trekking maps are based on the original Survey of India to a scale of 1:63,360 and to that extent are accurate. The original survey was carried out between 1924 and 1927, with a further aeriel survey completed in the 1960s.

Without doubt the best maps available for mountaineers in Nepal are what are called Schneider Maps, after Erwin Schneider, a cartographer who supervised the field work. These maps, printed in Vienna by Kartographische Anstalt Freytag-Bernt unt Artaria, to the scale of 1:50,000 with 40 metre contour intervals, are first class. However, do not expect the kind of accuracy one finds in the Alps or Britain. Alas, not all of the areas covered by this book are covered by these maps, the most notable exception being the Annapurna Region

The Rimpoche Lama of Thyangboche Gompa at the puja, during Mani Rimdu.

which, as far as maps are concerned, is a mountaineer's nightmare and must be regarded as the mysterious west! The Schneider Maps are generally available from good map suppliers and in Kathmandu.

For those areas outside the Schneider coverage, the most useful maps are the popular and widely available Mandala Trekking Maps, which are single colour photocopied maps to a scale of 1:250,000, although this does vary for some areas. These are next to useless for mountaineering purposes but they help you to know what peaks you are looking at – most of the time. Unfortunately, one version doesn't always correspond to another, even of the same area, and one has a definite feeling that the cartographer is an admirer of Picasso, or even at times of Dali.

With regard to availability the following are the best maps for the areas involving trekking peaks.

If the Mahalangur Himal sheet is not available, the same peaks are covered by the more generally available Schneider Khumbu Himal sheet, 1:50,000. This map also covers the northern flank of Kwangde and the Ngozumpa Valley, as well as the upper Hongu Basin. The Mandala: Helambu/Gosainkund/Langtang/Ganja La map is useful, for both Paldor and Naya Kanga, and covers all of the trekking routes mentioned in the text.

As well as the Schneider maps there are Mandala Sheets that cover all of the areas and treks mentioned in this book and are ideal at 1:125,000, both for route planning and for getting a feel for the overall geography.

In 1977 an atlas of maps entitled *Himalaya* was published by Gakushunkenkusha Ltd as part of the *Mountaineering Maps of the World* series, edited by Ichiro Yoshizawa. It provides some excellent detail to fill between the gaps in existing maps of Nepal.

Peak	Map
Mera	Schneider: Shorong/Hinku 1:50,000
Kusum Kanguru	Schneider: Shorong/Hinku 1:50,000
Kwangde	Schneider: Shorong/Hinku 1:50,000
Lobuje Peak	Schneider: Mahalangur Himal 1:25,000
Mera Peak	Schneider: Mahalangur Himal 1:25,000
Pokalde	Schneider: Mahalangur Himal 1:25,000
Imja Tse	Schneider: Mahalangur Himal 1:25,000
Parchamo	Schneider: Rolwaling Himal 1:50,000
	Schneider: Khumbu Himal 1:50,000
Ramdung	Schneider: Rolwaling Himal 1:50,000
Naya Kanga	Schneider: Helambu/Langtang 1:100,000
	(Although this is a recent map (1987), the information is often inaccurate.)
Paldor	Mandala: Helambu/Gosainkund/Langtang/Ganja La 1:125,000
Mardi Himal	Mandala: Pokhara/Jomosom/Manang 1:125,000
Hiunchuli	Mandala: Pokhara/Jomosom/Manang 1:125,000
Tharpu Chuli	Mandala: Pokhara/Jomosom/Manang 1:125,000
Singu Chuli	Mandala: Pokhara/Jomosom/Manang 1:125,000
Pisang	Mandala: Pokhara/Jomosom/Manang 1:125,000
Chulus	Mandala: Pokhara/Jomosom/Manang 1:125,000

The best maps available for the areas involved in trekking peaks.

Everywhere you look in the Kathmandu Valley,
even the most modest buildings of a certain age
have wonderful Newari carved woodwork. But only
the locals can stomach the ice-lollies!

Readers should be aware that nearly all of
the maps use different spellings at various
times for the same peaks and villages. The
Mandala maps in particular can be confusing
in that from one edition to another names can
change, as can the position of villages! You
might also find that local villagers use quite a
different name altogether from the map and
your sirdar and Sherpas yet another! The
Schneider maps also run into problems here,
especially in the Khumbu where Tibetian
rather than Sherpa names appear to have been
used for places and peaks. (See Useful Addresses, page 219, for map suppliers.)

21 Staying Healthy

Just about everyone who visits Nepal sooner or later suffers from some kind of stomach problem; Kathmandu Quickstep, as it's affectionately know, doesn't in most cases cause any more distress than a couple of days' inconvenience.

On the other hand, the possible medical dangers of travel in the Third World from hepatitis, cholera and dysentery through meningitis to malaria are beyond the scope of this book. Likewise first aid is covered elsewhere. Anyone interested in finding out more could do no better than to have a look at James Wilkerson's book *Medicine for Mountaineers*.

Another important source of information is the UIAA (International Union of Alpine Associations) Mountain Medicine Data Centre in London, which is run by consultant neurologist and mountaineer Dr Charles Clark. The Data Centre can provide a reference list of articles and specific publications dealing with all aspects of mountain medicine.

However, a few tips from a fellow traveller will at least forewarn you as to the problems you are likely to encounter. One of the most important things to do before you leave home is to speak with your doctor and ask for advice about inoculations, recommended and required. He is also most likely to be able to prescribe some of the items you may need, such as antibiotics and pain killers for your medical kit which cannot be bought over the counter. Failing this, the small pharmacists around the backstreets of Kathmandu sell just about everything as long as you know the generic name rather than the brand name of the drug you need (for instance, Acetazolamilde rather than Diamox).

You should also make sure that your teeth are in good order and that your fillings are all in place. There's nothing quite like thin, cold air and altitude along with a mug of hot, sweet Sherpa tea for searching out cavities.

Kathmandu Quickstep and Delhi Belly

On arrival in Kathmandu, take care of your health. Personal hygiene is critical; be extra vigilant about washing your hands. Water is undoubtedly the most common cause of stomach upset, so make sure that all the water you use is boiled and filtered, or has iodine in it. Even in the best hotels the water will get you, so be careful when cleaning your teeth and taking a shower not to swallow the water from the tap. Many of the hotels put jugs of water on the bedside; make sure this has gone through a ceramic filter and the maid hasn't filled it straight from the tap; better still use iodine tablets. On the trail, maintain your vigilance. Most of the water purifying tablets available which don't contain iodine don't seem to work. If you are unable to get iodine tablets you can buy ready-made iodine solution in Kathmandu. A couple of drops added to the water does the trick, including killing giardia cists, which are not removed by boiling.

Many of the cafés and restaurants around Kathmandu look very western, and serve good food, but even in the best of them you need to be on your guard. Lots of the things look irresistible and are eaten with delight, to be followed (at best) by a night sitting on the loo with your head in the sink. Find out about the best places, and by that I mean safe places, and use them. Be careful of raw food and some salads, even the ones washed in iodine. Avoid the wayside stalls selling to locals which often look good and are certainly very cheap. It does take a while to get used to the changes that go on with your gut flora and fauna. If you must go native, stick to dhalbhat. On the other hand, once on the trail, the bhattis provide good food and may cause you little problem. It does of course vary, with some people able to eat heartily at any bhatti without upset, whilst others get sick at the sight of food. Tea and bottled soft drinks seem fairly reliable, although the squeamish would do well not to look at the way cups and glasses are washed and dried, or to look for dead things in the bottom of the bottle.

Many people find they have their biggest problems at the beginning or the end of a trip in Kathmandu rather than on the trail. After that, it's good luck and bon appétit. If your luck runs out, do remember to stay hydrated, and a few sachets of rehydration powder, literally a pinch of salt and sugar, added to pure water, can work wonders along with the right antibiotics to cope with the various gastro-intestinal problems that crop up, of which Giadia Lamblia seems the most common (Bactrim seems to provide a cure). It's worth carrying a range of antibiotics that cover a spectrum of problems, plus a diagnostic chart that the medical books have to help you diagnose the problem and so provide the cure.

Altitude Problems

Altitude-related problems, including acute mountain sickness (AMS), pulmonary oedema and cerebral oedema are the most obvious causes for concern especially amongst those that are going to new altitudes and have no idea how they are going to respond. Even old hands at altitude are likely to have problems, but experience tends to make you more aware of the danger. Once again, there are endless volumes written on altitude-related problems. The best advice is to go high slowly and give your body time to acclimatise. Stay hydrated and don't push yourself too soon. Work high and sleep low, especially during the early days on the mountain, and if you are feeling bad, descend. Acetazolamide (Diamox) seems to help for most people and despite the inconvenience of being a diuretic and producing tingling in the face and fingers, it is worth considering for those on a tight schedule and unlikely to acclimatise well. My own experience is that it makes breathing more regular, especially at night, which definitely improves my sleep pattern so that at high camps I'm less likely to wake up hypoxic. The best preventative, however, is sensible acclimatisation and a schedule that gives you time to adjust to the rigours of altitude. This is realistic, since the trekking peaks are not too high and most fit people can acclimatise satisfactorily at a suitably rapid pace. Even then, what Tilman recognised as 'mountaineer's foot' (the inability to put one in front of the other), remains quite common – there is no cure.

Eye Problems

Dirt, dust and bright sunlight reflecting off snow are obvious dangers. Most of the time it is a matter of personal hygiene and remembering to wear a good pair of sun glasses. The smoky environment of the lodges can also cause problems. Precaution and cleanliness seem the best solution.

Sunburn

This is a common and painful problem and it is not unusual, after one day on the snow, for people to develop large sun blisters on their cheeks, nose and lips that can make life miserable as well as spoiling all the 'hero shots' for the folks back home. The answer is to use the very best sun screen and lip salve, and protect yourself wherever possible, especially if you know you're sun sensitive.

Climber's Cough

Sore throats and a hacking cough seem to be par for the course on expeditions. Initiated in the dry, dust laden atmosphere of Kathmandu where everyone seems to be coughing and spitting, by the time you carry a few loads in the rarer air of altitude the base camp dawn chorus can sound like a nineteenth century T.B. ward. If you get a chest infection or upper respiratory infection, which is usually marked by the production of green phlegm and difficult breathing, it is time to hit the antibiotics. Otherwise, boiled sweets or normal cough drops usually help a sore, dry throat.

Cold Injury

In Himalayan mountaineering, extreme cold and blood viscosity combine, providing a high risk environment for cold injury. Being aware of the problem, good equipment, hydration and personal care will go a long way to preventing injury. After that you have to accept it as a risk and know how best to treat it until you can get medical help. Once again the medical text books mentioned in Further Reading (page 216) cover this more thoroughly than I have the space to.

Haemorrhoids

This seems to be a common problem amongst mountaineers, undoubtedly the result of physical effort and load carrying; a bit like giving birth! Once again, hygiene is vital, a box of wet wipes carried in toilet kit will help, so will a packet of suppositories in the medical box.

Medical Box/First-Aid Kit

Whether you carry an extensive medical box capable of dealing with all manner of things or whether you opt for a simple first-aid kit very much depends on your expertise. If you have trouble covering a cut with a plaster or bandaging a sprained ankle, stick to basics or make an effort to find out more. Those with a more extensive repertoire will have no problem whatsoever in filling a box with all the things you think you might need from antibiotics and pain killers through splints, sutures and bandages to rehydration mix, flea powder and worming pills.

The major hospital in Kathmandu, and outlying hospitals and dispensaries, are listed under Useful Addresses (page 219).

22 Emergencies and Rescue

Perhaps one of the major differences between Alpine and Himalayan mountaineering is the sense of commitment that comes from being in a remote place beyond the help of others, so that one is influenced by factors beyond those of say, technical difficulty and objective danger. In Europe, the knowledge that rapid rescue and evacuation are on call, followed, if required, by outstanding medical services, undoubtedly gives some climbers the confidence to attempt routes they would otherwise stay off.

In Nepal things are different. Even on the easiest of peaks, unless there are other parties about, you are on your own and groups climbing in the Himalaya have to be willing and able to handle their own rescue and evacuation. This sense of being on your own is obviously a big factor in success in the Himalaya and many mountaineers, when faced with the cold reality of this, find the odds unacceptable and don't achieve what they and others expected.

Even in the more popular trekking areas such as the Khumbu and Annapurnas there are no rescue facilities as such, although the Himalayan Rescue Association, which offers medical help and runs small field hospitals, does a good job in helping trekkers and climbers that call on them.

Nepal does have helicopters, flown by RNAC and the army, that do respond to emergency call outs, but since rescue missions are not their normal operational role you might find that even if you can contact them they might be a long time coming.

Outside of Kathmandu and Pokhara you will find little in the way of hospitals and qualified medical help. The HRA hospitals and the Hillary hospital at Kunde usually have resident doctors, but don't expect them to be there. Outside of that the small village dispensaries and what might be called, by locals, hospitals are usually of little help. It's worth remembering that many commercial trekking groups include doctors as a normal part of the group, who may then help in an emergency; however, some do not. In the past I've been annoyed by trekkers who were doing things on the cheap, and then expected a free handout of antibiotics and basic first-aid items from better organised groups and individuals. True to the 'spirit of the hills' we have a responsibility to each other, but we also have a duty to look after ourselves in the first place.

The net result of all this is that any expedition, no matter how big or small, takes on the responsibility for its own health and rescue, should the need arise, and that includes the health of porters and Sherpas alike. Trekking and climbing in Nepal does throw up its own medical problems, beyond those of high altitude, that one doesn't usually encounter in the Alps and these could, in the context of an expedition, be life-threatening.

Should an emergency occur on the mountain, expedition members, as I have said, will have to effect their own rescue and to this end would be wise to learn a few techniques of self-rescue, including ways of lowering, lifting and carrying, before they are needed. There are no special techniques for Nepal, and numerous books covering these techniques are on the market. .

On the other hand, at various stages of an expedition there are normally plenty of people around quite used to carrying and should you

*A sick climber getting medical help from the expedition doctor on the Hongu
Nup glacier below the Mingbo La, a serious situation for illness or injury.*

need to portage or stretcher someone, man-power is not a problem. In the Khumbu region yaks can also be used to good effect for carrying someone, should their injuries allow it, and in the Annapurna region horses are also available.

In the event of a team member becoming sick or injured and needing to be evacuated you have the following options:

1 Carry them out by man or beast to the nearest road head or STOL airstrip, having sent ahead and organised a vehicle for transport back to Kathmandu.

2 Should the situation be very serious, needing immediate hospitalisation, a helicopter can be called for. Calling for a helicopter when there are other options available jeopardises future helicopter rescue in real emergencies and as an option it should be considered carefully before being taken up.

Even when calling out a helicopter it is worth bearing in mind several factors with regard to rescue. Firstly, it could take several days for a runner, even doing several day stages in one day, to get help. Secondly you must decide whether or not the terrain is suitable for a helicopter pick-up. In the European Alps one has got used to 'choppers' lifting people from the ice-fields of the Eiger and Matterhorn. In Nepal the machines are too precious for that kind of thing even if they could do it, and altitude is also a problem with 5,000 metres, or thereabouts, being the ceiling for helicopter rescue. Helicopters tend only to land in the valleys, and certainly not above the snow line.

Having opted for a helicopter evacuation it is best to follow a standard procedure so that, with everyone singing from the same hymn book, the right result is achieved. Before leaving Kathmandu it is wise to discuss with your agent what their normal procedure is in the case of an emergency, should you call out a helicopter. Make sure you have someone at the agency to send a radio message to and that they are willing to act on your behalf. Ideally, you should have them return the radio message, letting you know what actions they have taken and if and when the helicopter is coming. I would also suggest that you send an identical report to your embassy or consulate, RNAC and the Himalayan Rescue Association in Kathmandu in the hope that something will happen. You should have insurance to cover a rescue; on the other hand your agent may expect you to put up a bond, since helicopters don't come cheap. As Robin Marston of Mountain Travel Nepal says to clients when briefing them about rescue, 'No matter how sick you are, try to get a window seat and enjoy the view – it's an expensive one'.

Having sent a request for a helicopter, it is not wise to assume that one will be forthcoming and the soundest advice would seem to be that if a patient can be moved, do so, and make it clear in the message that this is what you intend to do and that you will remain in each camp until 11 am before moving on.

Camp should be made where there is enough space for the helicopter to land. It will need a relatively flat space 40 metres by 40 metres, the centre of which should be marked with a large 'X'. Ideally there should be no large trees or rock faces. Finally, a smokey fire should be built to help indicate wind speed and direction at ground level, preferably set to one side or downwind in order not to obscure the landing zone.

Should the helicopter eventually get to you and you are almost at the road head you will still be charged for air time, or alternatively there may be a cancellation fee to pay.

You should also be aware that RNAC does not transport dead bodies and it's unlikely that you will get porters to carry one out. The usual practice tends to be burial above the snowline or cremation below. Once again there is a procedure to follow:

1 A message notifying name, cause and time of death should be despatched to a reliable contact, if you have one, so that relatives can be told before the press releases the information.
2 All valuables where possible should be removed from the body, listed and retained by the group leader.
3 The body should be cremated and the ashes collected. The cremation should be witnessed by a local policeman, or village headman, or, if possible, some person not associated with the trek and their names and addresses recorded. Another member of the group should also act as a witness.

When making a request for a helicopter, the message should be clear and accurate saying exactly what you require without listing the things you do not. For instance, do not state 'stretcher not required'.

The message you send should be made out in the following order:

1 State name of pick-up place and region. You should also give the altitude if it's above 3,000 metres.
2 'Most immediate' should be stated if there is a genuine possibility of death within twenty-four hours without hospitalisation. Otherwise, 'As soon as possible' (ASAP) is all that is required.
3 State type of sickness or injury.
4 State whether a stretcher or backboard is required.
5 State if oxygen is required.
6 State if doctor is attending patient.
7 State number of people to be evacuated.
8 State name of casualty.
9 State group leader's name.

Descending the moraines of the Imja Valley towards Chhuckung after climbing Island Peak. Beyond the clouds are the peaks of Taweche (left) and Cholatse (right).

Having made these pessimistic comments about helicopters not showing up you might just be lucky and within an hour or so of receiving your message one could be on its way.

Keeping a list of the location of airstrips, radio transmitters and medical centres will be of value to any expedition visiting an area for the first time. These are given in Useful Addresses (*see* page 219).

23 When and Weather to Climb

Most people think of Nepal as having two climbing seasons related to climate. The first is the pre-monsoon, or spring period and the second is the post-monsoon or autumn period. However, my experience is that climbing on the trekking peaks is possible any time between October and May, even into early June; indeed the first ascent of Singu Chuli was made in June.

Often the weather is fine, and indeed for most trekking purposes may appear perfect, but on the more remote and difficult approaches conditions may make climbing impossible. This should be borne in mind when attempting crossings of high passes in the early spring or after the monsoon.

The monsoon period lasts from June until the end of September, when you can expect rain almost every day, making conditions difficult for trekking. Leeches are also a big problem along the trail at this time. Many expeditions choose to walk in during late September to maximise the amount of time they have on their peak.

During October and November, the high season for climbing and trekking, the conditions are usually ideal with clear skies and stable weather, although you might experience the unconsolidated remains of heavy snowfall, left over from the monsoon. The early mornings and nights become increasingly cold during October and my experience is that short, sharp storms can put down a considerable amount of snow that doesn't melt, making the going difficult on some routes.

December and January make up the winter season and they are the clearest and coldest months, with frosty nights and spectacular daytime views. The reliable weather with little snowfall makes this an attractive climbing time for those who can put up with the colder conditions. It's worth remembering that as both the days and nights get colder, fresh snowfall is unlikely to melt and indeed may remain as unconsolidated depth hoare, conditions that can make for strenuous and dangerous climbing. By and large the high winds of the winter jet streams don't have a great effect at the altitude of the trekking peaks.

During the early months of the year, February and March, the days and nights become warmer and the stable weather of winter gives way to less reliable conditions, with storms, increased snowfall and daily cloud build-up.

By April and May things have warmed up considerably, so that for treks beginning low down, at Pokhara for instance, conditions can be very hot indeed with temperatures in excess of 38°C (100°F) not uncommon. The days become increasingly hazy with the gradual build up of clouds, so that by late morning or early afternoon the peaks are obscured. From time to time a huge convectional storm will clear the air, but on the mountains afternoon snowfall is not uncommon, the only saving grace being that things are getting warmer and not colder as the spring passes into summer, so that several inches of overnight snow often burns off before midday. The other feature of the spring months, is the abundance of flowers.

APPENDICES

I Rules and Regulations

The Nepal Mountaineering Association has produced a four-page booklet of rules and regulations with regard to 'Trekking Peaks' which have been in effect since August 1981. These climbing rules are laid out below in full. Copies of this booklet are available from the NMA at: Ram Shah Path, Kathmandu, Nepal.

CLIMBING RULES

1   In exercise of the powers conferred by His Majesty's Government, the NMA has made the following rules to be observed for the climbing of the peaks of the Nepal Himalaya listed in Appendix 1.

2   These rules come into force at once.

3   Definition: Where applicable definitions for these rules will be the same as those for His Majesty's Government Mountaineering Expedition Regulations 1979 and its first amendment, 1984.

4   Permission:

(i) Any person or mountaineering team desirous of climbing a peak listed in Appendix 1 must receive permission from the NMA. Application to climb the peak must be made in the form prescribed in Appendix 2.

(ii) Permission to climb the peaks will be granted for one month only.

(iii) Permission may be extended if necessary for another period of two weeks.

(iv) The period of time granted relates to time spent climbing above base camp. The trek to and from the base camp is not included.

(v) Application for a climbing permit may be made at any time by the mountaineering team concerned. The permit will be granted on the first come first served basis.

(vi) Each climbing party will be given a permit as prescribed in Appendix 3. The right to give permission to another party for climbing the same peak during the same period is reserved by the NMA.

(vii) NMA will recommend to the Immigration Office of His Majesty's Government for obtaining a trekking permit of the area to the team members.

5   Payment of Fee: A climbing fee of US $300 will be charged for peaks mentioned under Group A and US $150 for peaks mentioned under Group B in Appendix 1. The permission issued will be for a period of one month for a group up to ten persons. An additional amount US $7.50 per person will be charged if the group exceeds more than ten persons.

For extending the permission, an additional 25 per cent charge of the total amount of the initial fee will be made for each extra week.

The leader or the climbing member of the team must collect the permit in person from the NMA.

6   Refund: In the event of cancellation of the permission by the NMA or the failure of the expedition to materialise due to some other reason the fees already paid will not be refunded.

7   Every individual or party granted a climbing permit shall be accompanied by a Sirdar/Guide, who must be registered with the NMA. Functions and Duties of the Sirdar/Guide:

(a)   To assist the climbing party with recruitment of porters and other staff, control of porters, local purchase of food, etc., and to solve any problem that may arise to the best of his ability.

(b)   To report to the NMA in case the party spends more than the prescribed time limit in the mountain.

(c)   To ensure that the climbers comply with the terms of their permit.

(d)   To ensure that the climbers/trekkers follow the specified route.

(e)   To ensure proper disposal of waste materials.

(f)   To report to the NMA any infringement of the climbing rules.

(g)   To report any serious incidents to the nearest police post.

The Sirdar/Guide shall be employed from the day the climbing party begins the trek until the trek is finished. The Sirdar/Guide will be provided with the following facilities:

(a) Minimum daily allowance to be paid as per the rules of His Majesty's Government, Ministry of Tourism.
(b) Food and tent accommodation.
(c) Climbing equipment and necessary clothing if required to go above base-camp.
8. Insurance: All employees going above base camp must be insured for personal accident to the value of NR 75,000/-.
9   Nomination of Representative in Kathmandu: Each party granted a climbing permit will nominate a representative in Kathmandu to act in liaison between the NMA and the climbing party. The representative may be an individual or an organisation registered with the NMA. The nominated representative will be responsible for making necessary arrangements for the climbing party in case of accidents or any other unforseen circumstances.
10   Submission of Report: On conclusion of the climb and on return to Kathmandu the party will submit a report to the NMA in the form prescribed in Appendix 4.
11   Power to Cancel the Permit: The NMA may cancel or withdraw the climbing permit at any time with or without showing any particular reason.
12   Non-Compliance of the Regulations: Where any trekking party acts in contravention to the climbing permit or indulges in acts of unsocial or outrageous behaviour contrary to the customs and culture of the people of Nepal, the NMA may recommend to HMG to take necessary measures in accordance with the Article 37 of Mountaineering Regulation 1979.
13   Protection of the Environment: Base camp and other camps will be left perfectly clean at the conclusion of the climb. No foreign materials such as fixed ropes, pitons, etc., shall be left on the mountain. All rubbish and waste material must be burnt or otherwise disposed of.
14   Revision of Regulations: Any article of this regulation may be revised or amended by the NMA with prior permission of HMG of Nepal.

APPENDIX 1

Group A

Name of Peak	Height	Region
1 Hiunchuli	6,441m	Annapurna Himal Gandaki
2 Singu Chuli	6,501m	Annapurna Himal Gandaki
3 Mera Peak	6,654m	Khumbu Himal Sagamartha
4 Kusum Kanguru	6,367m	Khumbu Himal Sagamartha
5 Kwangde	6,011m	Khumbu Himal Sagamartha
6 Chulu West	6,419m	Manang District Gandaki
7 Chulu East	6,584m	Manang District Gandaki
8 Imja Tse	6,160m	Khumbu Himal Sagamartha
9 Parchamo	6,187m	Rolwaling Himal Janakpur
10 Lobuje	6,119m	Khumbu Himal Sagamartha
11 Ramdung	5,925m	Rolwaling Himal Janakpur
12 Pisang	6,091m	Manang District Gandaki

Group B

Name of Peak	Height	Region
1 Tharpu Chuli	5,663m	Annapurna Himal Gandaki
2 Kongma Tse	5,849m	Khumbu Himal Sagamartha
3 Naya Kanga	5,844m	Langtang Himal Bagmati
4 Pokalde	5,806m	Khumbu Himal Sagamartha
5 Mardi Himal	5,587m	Annapurna Himal Gandaki
6 Paldor Peak	5,896m	Ganesh Himal

APPENDIX 2

APPLICATION FOR CLIMBING PERMIT

To:
The General Secretary
Nepal Mountaineering Association
Post Box No 1435
Kathmandu

1   Name of peak .... Height ....
2   Period for which permit is desired: ....
3   Trekking route: ....
4   Climbing route: ....
5   Name, nationality and address of leader of team:
     Full name: ....
     Nationality: ....
     Passport number: ....
     Home address: ....
     Local address in Kathmandu: ....
6   Name, nationality and passport number of members in team:
     Name: ....Nationality: ....Passport no: ....
     Name: ....Nationality: ....Passport no: ....
                                         (list may be attached)
7   Appointed representative in Kathmandu: ....
     ....
8   Name and organisation or address of Sirdar/Guide to be employed:
     Name: .... Book No.: ....
     Address: ....
     Organisation: ....
9   Fee: Climbing permit fee of US $ .... is attached.
     Number of persons: ....

RULES AND REGULATIONS

Dear Sir

I understand the rules of Nepal Mountaineering Association and agree to comply with the rules. Nepal Mountaineering Association will not be responsible for any loss of life, accident or damage to the members of the team during the course of the expedition. I have the necessary Trekking Permit issued by the immigration department for this trip.

Date: .... Signature of group leader: ....

APPENDIX 3

NEPAL MOUNTAINEERING ASSOCIATION

Permit No: .... Date: ....

CLIMBING PERMIT FOR TREKKING PEAKS

1 Name of peak: .... Height: ....
2 Climbing period: From: .... To: ....
3 Trekking route: ....
4 Climbing route: ....
5 Name, nationality and passport number of the leader of the team granted permit:
   Name: ....
   Nationality: .... Passport number: ....
6 Name, nationality and passport numbers of team members: .... (list may be attached)
   Name: .... Nationality: .... Passport no: ....
   Name: .... Nationality: .... Passport no: ....
7 Name of representative in Kathmandu: ....
8 Name of Sirdar or Guide: .... ID Card no: ....
9 Office of the Sirdar or Guide: ....
10 Permission granted for .... persons.

Signed: ....

Secretary, Nepal Mountaineering Association

Note: Please take your trekking permit from Central Immigration Office for this expedition.

APPENDIX 4

NEPAL MOUTAINEERING ASSOCIATION
CLIMBING PERMIT REPORT

To:
The Secretary
Nepal Mountaineering Association
P.O. Box 1435
Kathmandu

Dear Sir

In accordance with the terms of my climbing permit no. ....
Dated .... I submit the following report:
Peak climbed: ....
Duration of climbing period: ....
Result: .... (If not successful, why?)
....
Accident or any unusual occurence: ....
....
Brief report on the service of the Sirdar/Guide: ....

Suggestions: ....
....
....
Description of the trek route or trail (100 words): ....
....
....
....
Name and address: ....
Yours sincerely,

....

II Accommodation and Agencies

Accommodation

Nepal offers a complete spectrum of places to stay, from five star hotels to simple flea-bitten doss houses. It must be said that the best hotels are to be found in Kathmandu, although Pokhara has some good hotels, and the Tiger Tops Jungle Lodge in the Terai is an exotic form of luxury for those on safari.

Apart from the leading hotels such as the Soaltee Oberoi, Yak and Yeti and the Annapurna there are a wide range of smaller hotels and guest houses in Kathmandu that offer clean and comfortable accommodation for the budget-conscious traveller. If you are working through an agency they will be able to pre-book accommodation for you, and bookings can obviously also be made by post. However, many people simply turn up on the day and find a room, which for small groups seems to work, although at the height of the trekking season rooms in the more popular hotels are at a premium.

On the trail, simple accommodation can be had in small lodges (bhattis), the simplest form of which provide a space for a foam pad and a place near the fire where you share food with a family, usually a meal of rice and lentils (dhalbhat). In the more popular trekking areas the lodges are much more sophisticated and may provide small private rooms and dormitories with foam mattresses. They may even have hot showers, many of which burn an unjustifiable amount of precious wood for what really is an indulgence. In some of the national parks a few of the lodges have installed solar panels and more efficient water-heating systems. As they become more sophisticated many of the lodges offer extensive menus, catering for cosmopolitan western tastes. Both the food and accommodation are cheap and it seems to me to have little to do with sound economics, so that it always grates to hear a trekker argue about the price of a glass of tea or packet of biscuits which may be one rupee more than he paid the night before further down the trail.

A small selection of hotels in Kathmandu and Pokhara, covering a wide spectrum in price and quality, can be found in Useful Addresses (page 219). At the cheaper end of the market there are scores of places to choose from.

Trekking Agencies in Nepal

Things have gone a long way since Jimmy Roberts founded Mountain Travel, Nepal's first trekking company, in 1965 when the kingdom had a total of forty tourists (if you also include expeditions). Today there seem to be dozens of agencies offering trekking services in Kathmandu. Most come and go, as is the nature of business; on the other hand there are a few companies that have gone from strength to strength, maintaining the highest standards, providing the best Sherpa crews and equipment and have the organisation to service expeditions and deal with the many and various administrative hassles at various government offices.

Not all of the agencies have experience with

climbing groups and their mostly part-time staff may have little or no expedition experience. Mostly they deal with groups of tourists happy to do the standard and well-known treks. If you intend using their full services you would do well to find out what experience they have of expeditions, both trekking and major peak climbs. On the other hand, companies like Mountain Travel Nepal, Himalayan Journeys and Sherpa Co-operative have a known track record and in the case of Mountain Travel have been at the forefront of trekking peak exploration.

Prices vary a great deal but, as you would expect, so do the services. Shop carefully, ask questions and find out what they can and are prepared to do and what back-up they offer once you are in the field. Finally, 'you pays your money and takes your choice'. Trekking agencies are listed in Useful Addresses (page 219).

Further Reading

Any attempt to produce a full bibliography of works on Nepal and its mountaineering and trekking would simply result in an endless gazette with as many pages as this book itself. Rather than that, I have selected what I feel is the best book available on a given topic, and the most useful and readable should you be marooned in an airport waiting for a flight or in a high camp waiting for the weather!

As well as the books mentioned, anyone seriously considering a Himalayan expedition and wanting to research the exploration of a particular region further should become acquainted with the *Himalayan Journal* and the journals of the major Alpine Clubs, as well as the leading international magazines such as *Mountain Magazine, Iwa To Yuki, Alpinismus, La Montagne* and *Revista della Montagna*.

Medical

Hackett, Peter, *Mountain Sickness: Prevention, Recognition and Treatment* (American Alpine Club, New York).
(Perhaps the best little book available on the subject, written by one of the most knowledgeable specialists in high altitude medicine.)

Houston, Charles, *Going High* (American Alpine Club).
(The story of man at altitude for those with an interest in the medical and sometimes morbid.)

Steele, Peter, *Medical Care for Mountain Climbers* (Heinemann, London).
(A very useful book, but not as comprehensive as Wilkerson.)

Wilkerson, James A., *Medicine for Mountaineering* (Seattle: The Mountaineers).
(A comprehensive and practical book useful for doctors and laymen alike.)

For an up-to-date bibliography on all published articles and specific publications on mountain medicine, contact the UIAA Mountain Medicine Data Centre, c/o Dr Charles Clarke, St Barthlomew's Hospital, London.

Trekking

Armington, Stan, *Trekking in the Nepal Himalaya* (Lonely Planet).
(A good little guide book to trekking routes in Nepal with useful chapters on preparation for trekking, written by a man with a deep love of Nepal who runs both the best bar in town – the Rum Doddle Restaurant in Thamel – and one of the leading trekking agencies, Himalayan Journeys.)

Bezruchka, Stephen, *Trekking in Nepal* (Sahayogi Press, Kathmandu).
(The most comprehensive trekker's guide, with useful chapters on the country and its people.)

Van Gruisen, Lisa, *Nepal: An Insight Guide* (APA Productions, Hong Kong).
(This is a beautifully illustrated and fully comprehensive general guide to Nepal, with stacks of information about Kathmandu, customs and culture, but it does not really cover trekking in any detail.)

Natural History

Fleming, Fleming and Bangdel, *Birds of Nepal* (Avalok, Kathmandu).
(The most comprehensive and lavishly illustrated field guide to the country's birds.)

Polunin and Stanton, *Flowers of the Himalaya* (Oxford University Press, London).

Schaller, George B., *Stones of Silence* (Viking Press, New York).
(An interesting account of this noted naturalist's travels in search of elusive wildlife in Dolpo. This is the other half of the Mattheson's Snow Leopard story.)

Stainton, J.D.A., *Forests of Nepal* (Murray, London).
(A standard work on Nepal's flora.)

Storrs, Adrianne and Jimmie, *Discovering Trees in Nepal* (Sahayogi Press, Kathmandu).

Culture and General

Berstein, Jeremy, *The Wildest Dreams of Kew* (Simon and Schuster, New York).
(A personal and amusing profile of Nepal.)

Bista, Dor Bahandur, *People of Nepal* (Ratna Pustak Bhandur, Kathmandu).
(A useful look at the diverse ethnic groups found within Nepal, and the book I have found the most useful in helping me understand its people.)

Fantini, Mario, *Mani Rimdu* (Toppan Co., Singapore).
(A good picture book that unfolds some of the mystery of Mani Rimdu, although it's difficult to know how accurate an interpretation it is of the dance drama.)

Fleming, Robert and Linda, *Kathmandu Valley* (Kodansha International, Tokyo).

Furer-Haimendorf, Christoph, *Himalayan Traders* (John Murray, London).
(An academic but readable book on the highland traders of Nepal.)

Hagen, Toni, *The Kingdom of Nepal* (Kummerley and Frey, Berne).
(A well-illustrated primer to Nepal.)

Shirahata, Shiro, *Nepal Himalaya* (Heian International).
(A coffee table picture book giving some magnificent images.)

The Story of the Mount Everest National Park (Cobb/ Horwood Publications, New Zealand).
(A lavishly illustrated book about the Khumbu and the Mount Everest Park written and edited by members of the park service. Full of good, accurate information.)

Mountaineering

This list could be vast, so here are just a few names to wet the appetite.

Bonington, Chris, *Annapurna South Face* (Cassell, London).
(A must for climbers visiting the Sanctuary.)

Bowman, W.E., *The Ascent of Rum Doodle* (Dark Peak, Sheffield).
(If after reading endless expedition accounts all written to the same formula you can take no more, read about the world's highest mountain to exactly the same formula but in the vein of Monty Python. Good rainy day reading.)

Cleare, John, *World Guide to Mountains* (Mayflower Books, London).
(Some good chapters packed with information regarding peaks, passes and glaciers in the various areas of Nepal.)

Herzog, Maurice, *Annapurna*
(Epic account of the French ascent of Annapurna, the first 8,000 metre peak to be climbed.)

Hillary, E., *East of Everest* (Dutton, New York).
(The story of the New Zealand Expedition to the Barun.)

Hunt, John, *The Ascent of Everest* (Hodder and Stoughton, London).
(A mountaineering classic that includes a lot of material about early ascents of Khumbu trekking peaks.)

Mason, Kenneth, *Abode of Snow*
(A classic now republished, covering early exploration and mountaineering.)

Murray, W.H., *The Scottish Himalayan Expedition* (J.M. Dent, London).

Noyce, Wilfrid, *The Fish's Tail*
(Account of the 1957 Machhapuchhare Expedition with some good material on the Annapurna Sanctuary.)

Noyce, Wilfrid, *South Col* (Heinemann, London).
(A personal account of the 1953 Everest Expedition by one of the finest writers of that generation.)

Rowell, Galen, *Many People Come, Looking, Looking* (The Mountaineers, Seattle).
(A beautifully illustrated book covering several expeditions to Nepal and other Himalayan countries.)

Shipton, Eric, *The Untravelled World* (Hodder and Stoughton, London).

Tilman, H.W., *Nepal Himalaya* (Cambridge University Press, London).
(A good book from a famous mountaineer with a lot of interesting material on Langtang, Ganesh and Manang. This has now been reprinted as the collected works of Tilman by Cordee.)

Weir, Tom *East of Kathmandu*
(An account of the Scottish Himalayan Expedition to Rolwaling.)

Many of the classic mountaineering accounts are no longer in print. Fortunately some are being reprinted and are generally available in the best bookshops and equipment stores. Surprisingly, Kathmandu has some of the best book shops I know, where a wealth of recent titles, old books and modern reprints are available. For the serious book collector they are definitely worth a visit and the excess baggage.

Useful Addresses

Radio Stations in Trekking Areas

Everest Trek and Khumbu
Jiri, Namche Bazaar, Salleri (south of main trail near Junbesi), Charikot (South of Rolwaling), Lamobagar, Lukhla.

Langtang
Rasua, Garhl, Dhunche.

Ganesh
Lari Mine, Samathang.

Annapurna Region
Pokhara, Gorkha, Kusma, Baglung, Beni, Jomosom, Ongre, Chame, Chomrong.

Hospitals and Dispensaries

Major Hospitals in Kathmandu

Bir Hospital
Kingsway
Kathmandu
Tel: 11119

This is located in front of the Tundhikhel Parade Ground.

Shanta Bhawan United Mission Hospital
Patan
Kathmandu
Tel: 21034/21048/21634

This hospital has foreign staff.

Everest Trek and Khumbu
Jiri (dispensary and small hospital)
Kunde (hospital; doctor in residence)
Phaplu (dispensary and small hospital)
Pheriche (HRA hospital; doctor often in residence)

Langtang
Kathmandu is the nearest hospital, although there are some medical facilities at the hydro-electricity works in Trisuli Bazaar.

Annapurna Region
Pokhara (hospital; foreign missionary staff)
Baglung (government hospital; Nepalese staff)
Sikha (dispensary with nurse)
Ampipal (north of Gorkha airport; hospital/dispensary with foreign staff)
Ongre (HRA trekkers' aid post; doctor often in residence)

STOL Airstrips

Everest Trek and Khumbu
Jiri (schedule flights; radio)
Lukhla (daily RNAC flights – usually!; radio)
Syangboche (charter flights only October/May; radio)
Phaplu (frequent schedule flights; one day south of regular trail)
Lamidanda (south of Aisyalukharka; regular flights; three days south of regular trail)

Langtang
Kyangjin (marginal strip used in extreme emergencies)
Thangjet (just north of Syabrubensi, in Bhote Khosi)

Annapurna Region
Balewa (near Baglung; regular flights; radio)
Jomsom (regular flights, often cancelled due
to high winds; radio)
Ongre (pilatus only; radio)
Gorkha (regular STOL service)

Hotels

Kathmandu
Soaltee Oberoi
Tahachal
PO Box 97
Kathmandu
Tel: 11211

L'Annapurna
Durbar Marg
Kathmandu
Tel: 11711

Yak and Yeti
Lal Durbar
PO Box 1016
Kathmandu
Tel: 13318

Crystal
594 Shukra Path
PO Box 29
Kathmandu
Tel: 12630

Yellow Pagoda
Kantipath
PO Box 373
Kathmandu
Tel: 15337

Shangrila
Lazimpat
PO Box 655
Kathmandu
Tel: 12354

Nook
Kantipath
PO Box 594
Tel: 13627

Shakti
Thamel
Kathmandu
Tel: 16121

Sidharta
Kantipath
PO Box 1280
Kathmandu

Kathmandu Guest House
Thamel
Kathmandu
Tel: 13628

Blue Diamond
Jyatha Thamel
Kathmandu
Tel: 13392

Narayani
Pulchowk Lalitpur
PO Box 1357
Kathmandu

Star
Thamel
Kathmandu
Tel: 12803

Summit
Kupondole Height
PO Box 1406
Kathmandu

Dwarika's
Battisputali
PO Box 459
Tel: 13770

Eden
5/261 Om Bahal
Kathmandu
Tel: 13863

Pokhara
Fish Tail Lodge
Phewatal
Pokhara
Tel: 71

Annapurna
Airport
Pokhara
Tel: 27/37

New Crystal
Airport
Pokhara
Tel: 35/36

New Snowview
Airport
Pokhara
Tel: 25

Trekking Agencies

This is a small selection of the many agencies
that exist, comprising agencies which I have
either had personal contact with, or know
people who use them.

Mountain Travel Nepal
PO Box 170
Kathmandu
Tel: 12808

Himalayan Journeys
PO Box 989
Kathmandu
Tel: 15855

Sherpa Co-op Trekking
PO Box 1338
Kathmandu
Tel: 15887

Ama Dablam Trekking
PO Box 3035
Kathmandu
Tel: 16211

Annapurna Trekking
PO Box 795
Kathmandu
Tel: 12736

Himal Treks
PO Box 2541
Kathmandu
Tel: 15561

Lama Excursion
PO Box 2485
Kathmandu
Tel: 11786

Nepal Trekking
PO Box 368
Kathmandu
Tel: 14681

Map Suppliers

UK
Stanford's
12-14 Longacre
London WC2E 9LP

USA
Library of Congress
Geography and Map Division
Washington D.C. 20540

Index

Note: Bold numbers denote page numbers of illustrations.